FINANCE AND WORLD POLITICS

STUDIES IN INTERNATIONAL POLITICAL ECONOMY

General Editor: Philip G. Cerny
Senior Lecturer in Politics, University of York, UK

In the modern world, international and cross-national economic relations have formed increasingly dense webs of power, constraining and shaping the activities of people and governments. As we approach the 21st century, 'security' is less military and more economic in character. Economies themselves are less 'national' and more global. And the politics of states are caught up in increasingly autonomous patterns of trade, international capital flows, global markets and transnational institutions, both public and private. Against this background, international political economy focuses on problems and debates which are not only central to political decision-making in the real world, but also crucial to academic analysis and theory-building in contemporary world politics and economics.

The Studies in International Political Economy series is aimed at a thoughtful readership concerned about wide-ranging issues relevant to the contemporary world. The authors represent a new generation of scholars in the field, and the issues and debates which they address will help define the intellectual agenda for the 1990s and the 21st century.

Finance and World Politics

Markets, Regimes and States in the Post-hegemonic Era

Edited by

Philip G. Cerny

Senior Lecturer in Politics
University of York
United Kingdom

Edward Elgar

Published by
Edward Elgar Publishing Limited
Gower House
Croft Road
Aldershot
Hants GU11 3HR
England

Edward Elgar Publishing Company
Old Post Road
Brookfield
Vermont 05036
USA

British Library Cataloguing in Publication Data

Finance and World Politics: Markets,
Regimes and States in the Post-hegemonic
Era. – (Studies in International
Political Economy)
  I. Cerny, Philip G. II. Series
332

ISBN 1 85278 883 6

Printed in Great Britain at the University Press, Cambridge

Contents

Contributors

PHILIP G. CERNY is Senior Lecturer in Politics at the University of York, UK. Born in New York City, he holds degrees from Kenyon College (BA), the *Institut d'Études Politiques* (Paris) (*Certificat d'Études Politiques*) and the University of Manchester (PhD). During the past decade he has also been a Visiting Associate Professor of Government at Dartmouth College, Visiting Professor of Politics at New York University and the American University of Paris, and Guest Scholar at Harvard University, the *Fondation Nationale des Sciences Politiques* and the Brookings Institution. He is the author of *The Politics of Grandeur: Ideological Aspects of de Gaulle's Foreign Policy* (1980), *The Changing Architecture of Politics: Structure, Agency, and the Future of the State* (1990), and 'Plurilateralism: Structural Differentiation and Functional Conflict in the Post-Cold War World Order' (*Millennium: Journal of International Studies*, April 1993). He is also editor of *The Politics of Transnational Regulation: Deregulation or Reregulation?* (special issue of the *European Journal of Political Research*, March/April 1991). He is currently writing *Global Finance and the Competition State*.

STEPHEN GILL is Professor of Political Science at York University, Toronto, Canada. Born in Yorkshire, England, he holds degrees from the Universities of London (BA), Essex (MA) and Birmingham (PhD). He has also taught or been a visitor at the Universities of Wolverhampton, Warwick and Oxford, Virginia Commonwealth University and the University of California at Los Angeles. During 1990–91, he was Hallsworth Senior Research Fellow in Political Economy in the Department of Government, University of Manchester. In 1990 and 1992 he was a Visiting Scholar in the Faculty of Law, University of Tokyo. He is the author of *The Global Political Economy: Perspectives, Problems and Policies* (with David Law) (1988), *American Hegemony and the Trilateral Commission* (1990), and *Restructuring Global Politics* (in Japanese) (1992). He is also editor of *Atlantic Relations: Beyond the Reagan Era* (1989) and *Gramsci, Historical Materialism and International Relations* (1993). He is currently writing *The Emerging World Order*.

ERIC HELLEINER is Assistant Professor of Political Studies at Trent University, Peterborough, Ontario, Canada. Born in New Haven, Connecticut, he holds degrees from the University of Toronto (BA) and the London School of Economics and Political Science (MSc and PhD). He was previously Lecturer in International Relations at the LSE and was also the guest lecturer at York University, Toronto, for their Summer School on Global Finance and the Emerging World Order in 1990. He is Associate Editor of *Policy Sciences* and a member of the governing board of the International Political Economy Section of the International Studies Association. He is the author of *The Emergence of Global Finance: States and the Globalisation of Financial Markets in the Postwar Period* (1993), 'States and the Future of Global Finance' (*Review of International Studies*, January 1992), and 'Money and Influence: Japanese Power in the International Monetary and Financial System' (*Millennium: Journal of International Studies*, Winter 1989/90).

GEOFFREY R.D. UNDERHILL is Lecturer in Politics and International Studies at the University of Warwick, Coventry, UK. Born in Vancouver, Canada, he holds a BA from Queen's University, Kingston, Ontario, and a DPhil from Oxford University (St. Antony's College). He has previously taught at the University of Stirling, Scotland, and McMaster University, Hamilton, Ontario. He is the author of 'Industrial Crisis and International Regimes: France, the EEC and Trade in Textiles' (*Millennium: Journal of International Studies*, Summer 1990) and 'Markets Beyond Politics? The State and the Internationalisation of Financial Markets' (*European Journal of Political Research*, March/April 1991). He is also co-editor (with Richard Stubbs) of a new textbook, *Political Economy and the Changing Global Order* (forthcoming 1994). He is currently writing *Industrial Crisis and the Open Economy*.

PETER A. VIPOND is Principal Lecturer in the Department of Financial Services, Faculty of Business, London Guildhall University, UK; he previously taught in the Department of Politics and Government in the same institution. Born in Leeds, England, he holds degrees from the Universities of Leeds (BA), Essex (MA) and Oxford (MLitt). He has also been a visiting lecturer at the *Institut de Management Européen des Affaires*, Besançon, France, and is Secretary of the University Association for Contemporary European Studies (UACES). He is the author of 'Financial Services and the Internal Market', in L. Hurwitz and C. Lequesne, eds, *The State of the European Community* (1991) and 'The Liberalisation of Capital Movements and Financial Services in the European Single Market: A Case Study in Regulation' (*European Journal of Political Research*, March/April 1991). He is currently writing *The Political Economy of the European Financial Area*.

Preface and acknowledgements

Money and finance have always been at the heart of International Relations, both in the form of nation-states seeking to gain and store up wealth and in the guise of financial markets and banks seeking to expand and integrate their activities across borders. After the heyday of international 'high finance' (*haute finance*) in the late 19th century, the ills of the Gold Standard from the First World War through the 1920s and the Great Crash of 1929 prompted national governments in the 1930s and 1940s to seek to control the destabilizing and speculative tendencies which they saw in international finance. They approached this task through a combination of tighter domestic regulation and international monetary cooperation. In the United States, in particular, New Deal financial regulation strengthened the dollar at home and abroad, while postwar monetary dominance was the cornerstone of American hegemony in the international political economy. This in turn was a key factor in generating the Long Boom, which lasted from the late 1940s to the early 1970s. The breakdown of that postwar system, however, has opened the way for a revival of international 'high finance' – this time based on floating exchange rates, financial market deregulation and the information technology which can shift money and financial instruments around the world with the tap of a key.

In this book, the authors analyse the political and economic reasons why financial markets have so rapidly become 'transnational', increasingly binding government policymakers – foreign and domestic – into new webs of power. They look at the breakdown of the old system, but focus chiefly on the problems of the new. Since the late 1960s, states have had to cope with major new constraints produced by the international financial system. Governments have experimented with a wide range of responses, including deregulation and re-regulation, cooperation between governments in the Group of Seven (G7), and adding financial services to the General Agreement on Tariffs and Trade (GATT) in the Uruguay Round. Furthermore, different states and regions – especially the United States, the European Community and Japan – have followed different paths with varying levels of success in attempting to control this 'second financial revolution'.

It is because of the new transnationalization of finance, the authors argue, that American hegemony is dead. Indeed the possibility of any nation-state or states exercising 'hegemony' in the future is negligible too. At the same time, domestic economic policy in the United States as elsewhere has been condemned to 'embedded financial orthodoxy' – long-term austerity punctuated by financial bubbles and panics. If the national state can no longer control international money, then who will?

Most of the established literature on international political economy has focused predominantly on production and trade – not money and finance. We argue that money and finance are of central and primary significance for a genuinely theoretical and analytical understanding of both international relations in general and international political economy in particular.

This book is intended to fill two gaps in the field. In the first place, we hope that it will be widely used in Britain, North America and elsewhere as a teaching book for upper-level undergraduate courses *and* for MA and PhD courses in international relations and political science. The political economy of international finance as a field of study is rapidly growing at both undergraduate and postgraduate levels on both sides of the Atlantic – and of the Pacific too. This book is also suitable for use in economics, finance, management and business school courses. Finally, sociology and social policy courses often also deal with issues of class, power and money; they too will find this book useful.

In the second place, however, this book is also aimed at a wider market concerned with issues of national and global relevance. It explores a vital issue-area of fundamental significance to policy debates in contemporary advanced industrial societies among both public and private sector groups. The analyses and arguments examined here cut to the heart of the kind of wide-ranging policy reappraisal currently being undertaken in and around not only the Clinton Administration but other governments in the developed world too. The book provides perspectives which are often insufficiently addressed in the policy-oriented and economic literature. Virtually all of the mid-range material which focuses specifically on financial deregulation and 'globalization' has been written by economists, financial journalists and other financial analysts. They generally take for granted that a 'freeing up' of financial markets will lead to the more efficient allocation of capital in general, and they often assume that the globalization of markets will ultimately lead to some sort of spontaneous transnational cooperation to smooth out market failures.

The authors in this volume, in contrast, focus instead on the *real* political processes at work at both domestic and international levels – and, in particular, on the cross-cutting linkages between these levels. They identify the conflicts and the contradictions, the compromises and the unintended consequences, between coalitions of interests, politicians, public and private bureaucracies, international organizations, transnational market actors and the like, that have led to today's predicament. The chapters form an unusually broad and yet analytically coherent and surprisingly integrated range of empirical topics and levels of analysis, as the sub-title indicates. In the first place, these topics cover such critical aspects as financial *markets* and institutions, international *regimes* and transnational political mechanisms, and different *states* and regions. In addition, however, the authors at another level all focus on the same key analytical issues and arguments. They all concur, in particular, on the weakness of the dominant paradigm in the international relations field: hegemonic stability theory. And each is aware of the crucial importance of the 'structural power' of international finance in shaping wider processes of power and decision-making in international relations – and in the domestic political economy too. They all address the same set of theoretical questions, and come up with comparable – although not identical – conclusions.

The authors in this book represent a significant new generation of scholars in the field, writers who will continue to develop their arguments for some years to come. We are a genuinely 'transatlantic' group: one US citizen, educated in America, France and Britain, working in the UK [the editor]; one Canadian, educated in Canada and Britain, also working in the UK; one UK citizen now working in Canada; one Canadian citizen, born in the US and educated in Canada and the UK, now back working in Canada; and one UK citizen working in the UK. We all have international teaching as well as research experience, ranging from Tokyo to Paris. We all address intellectual debates which are current not just in Britain and North America, but in international political economy, international relations and political science in general. And we all hope that our contributions will be of use for informing wider public debates on economic policy and the role of the state in the 1990s and the 21st century.

We would like to thank the professional associations which provided conference forums where the authors have been able to come together to share their ideas, and where the book was born and took shape: Paris, in April 1989 (European Consortium for Political Research); Washington, DC, in April 1990 (Council for European Studies); Vancouver, British Columbia, in April 1991, and Atlanta, Georgia, in March 1992 (International Studies Association); the University of Warwick, Coventry, in December 1991 (British International Studies Association); and Heidelberg, in September 1992 (Standing Group in International Relations, European Consortium for Political Research). We would like very much to thank the other participants in these meetings.

A major influence on all of us, however – both at some of these meetings and in other settings and circumstances over the years – has been the work and the encouragement of Professor Susan Strange, now retired from the London School of Economics and Political Science and the European University Institute in Florence, but continuing to contribute her ideas and expertise at the University of Warwick. She has, both through her own intellectual efforts and through her support for others, played a leading part in saving the concept of transnationalism itself from both its early oversimplifiers and its more dogmatic neorealist critics. She has in particular been extremely influential in developing a sophisticated framework for analysing the structural power of states, non-state actors, markets, economic sectors, institutions and the like – one which will influence analysts long into the future.

Philip G. Cerny
York, England

PART I

THE PROBLEM OF FINANCE IN INTERNATIONAL POLITICAL ECONOMY

1 The political economy of international finance

Philip G. Cerny

Human relationships are principally made up of three elements. The first consists of relationships of power or force, of systematic patterns of conflict, domination and submission. The second consists of relationships of exchange, of 'truck and barter', as Adam Smith put it, which enable groups of people to accomplish things together through a division of labour which they could not do as solitary individuals. The third consists of relationships of affect, identity and culture, of social bonds with a special group of others who share kinship, common values, or mere close acquaintance – relationships of 'justice' and 'friendship', as Aristotle described them. Politics – sometimes seen as a fourth element – is the particular amalgam or compound of these different kinds of relationships, a conscious human construction which builds into an overarching, ongoing pattern of control of the process of mixing the other three elements. Institutionalized political systems are those patterns which reproduce themselves over time. The institutionalized political systems which we call 'states' are the complex structures which have evolved or have been established in the modern era in order to systematize and manage the blending of these three kinds of relationships.

In the course of modern history – over the past 500 years or so which have seen the emergence, consolidation and spread of the nation-state as the dominant organizational unit of world politics – feelings of affect, identity and citizenship have for the most part been appropriated by the nation-state through the development (and often the proactive inculcation) of national cultures. Despite the spread of such 20th century ideologies as Western capitalism and Soviet communism, nationalism has been the main cultural legacy of this period, as we have seen even more clearly since the fall of the Berlin Wall in 1989 as well as in the politics of the Third World. Institutionalized political systems, too, have increasingly taken the form of nation-states; international law and international regimes are the products of the politics of states and depend upon the continuing consent of governments.

The international system, by contrast, has primarily been the arena of the politics of military power, on the one hand, and of political economy, on the other. The first of these, the politics of military power (or 'security'), has been mainly characterized by the projection of the resources and goals of domestically organized nation-states into the international arena. 'Collective security' at the international level is by definition fragile at best in a Hobbesian world of independent, self-regarding nation-states, and stabilization usually requires the presence of a balance of power among states seen as unitary agents.

Political economy is only contained with difficulty within the national cage, and is only controlled with difficulty by a hierarchical state. Truck and barter between and across national boundaries existed long before nation-states emerged; they have constrained the way that states have developed; and they have been less and less amenable to state control, especially since the Second World War and the growth of a more open international economy. At the same time, markets have bypassed national regulations, command economies have collapsed and governments have seen Keynesian fine-tuning and the national welfare state undermined by import penetration and financial flows. Recently these changes have led state actors (bureaucrats and politicians) to try to transform political institutions and policy-making processes themselves into agents of internationalization, mainly in order to promote competitiveness.

In this context, international political economists have for the most part tended to focus on trade politics and the politics of production (the 'real economy') in explaining the dynamics of the international political economy – taking the American emphasis on free trade in the postwar period as the touchstone of its developing structure. In contrast, the authors in this book look to the political economy of international finance. We believe that there are certain characteristics of money and finance, and of the markets and other structures through which they flow, which give finance a critical role in shaping world politics. This is especially true of the late 20th century, when the main conflicts between powerful nation-states, conflicts rooted in the Cold War, have quite suddenly dissolved. But it has also been true of critical eras in the past.

I   Money and world order

Money and finance today constitute an increasingly abstract representation of the process of exchange of goods and of values between human beings. Money has always represented an attempt to assess the *relative* value of things and ideas exchanged between people and groups of people, but until recently it also had an alternative life as a commodity itself – from simple coinage to its most advanced commodity form, the gold standard, by which the economic life of the 19th century in particular was organized and measured. Even then, however, lines in a bookkeeper's ledger were more important for a general understanding of the social, political and economic role of money than physical gold. At the end of the 20th century, money consists primarily of electronic impulses stored in computer memories and transmitted instantaneously world-wide 24 hours a day – from the ubiquitous credit or debit cards of the ordinary consumer to massive minute-by-minute transfers in the international currency markets.[1] Money is not merely an economic phenomenon; like ideology, it is also a cultural phenomenon. Finance thus constitutes an intellectual challenge different in kind from most other structural issue areas in international relations.

The modest aim of this book is to provide an introduction to some of the problems and consequences which derive from the changing role of money in the world, and the way that that role interacts with other dimensions of society, politics and economics. A major theme of the book, taken up in different ways by all of the authors, is the way that developments in international and transnational finance – given that finance within countries is increasingly inseparable from finance between and cutting across countries – interact with changing relationships and structures of power in the international arena, in particular the question of *hegemony*. We live in a 'post-hegemonic' era, a period when it is no longer possible for any one hegemonic state (such as Britain in the late 19th century or the United States in the mid-20th) to provide the 'public goods' of political and economic stability to the world capitalist order (and to do so because it thinks it to be in its own interests). This situation has come about to a great extent because of the way that nation-states themselves, and therefore hegemony itself, are inextricably intertwined with the structure of international finance. Therefore we are not dealing just with money. Money 'dematerializes' other relationships, creating a 'structured field of action' within which they are linked together. Just as financial issues were at the core of the phenomenon (and also the theory) of hegemony, so they are also at the core of the problematic of 'post-hegemony' – what a post-hegemonic world order will be like.

In setting out the issues and perspectives represented in this volume, our approach is quite straightforward. In Part I, Chapters 1 and 2, we look at some of the background necessary for understanding, first, the academic and intellectual significance of finance in the wider arena of international relations (and political science) and, second, the problems and tensions built into the preceding epoch of international financial relations, the post-Second World War international financial system which was established at the Bretton Woods Conference in New Hampshire in 1944. In Part II, Chapters 3, 4 and 5, we examine some of the structural changes to international finance itself over a more recent period, the late 1980s and early 1990s. These changes all represent ongoing issues: the way that the internationalization of finance is intertwined with changes in systems and practices of financial regulation (deregulation and re-regulation) across different countries; the development of international cooperation between the main financial powers (the Group of Seven, or G7); and the most significant attempt to establish a set of international rules for more open 'trade' in financial services which forms part of the Uruguay Round of the General Agreement on Tariffs and Trade (still unfinished at the time of writing). In Part III, Chapters 6, 7 and 8, the focus shifts to the main declining and rising financial powers themselves, the United States, Europe and Japan, looking both at the way their domestic financial systems interact with international finance and at what their changing fortunes may mean for the emerging global financial order – and for the international system in general.

The main theme shared by all of the authors is that the *control* of the way that finance flows around, through and between countries is at the core of the structure of the international system itself. So long as this systemic control – not so much power over particular market outcomes, but what Peter Vipond in Chapter 7 calls the capacity of the state to 'design' the structure of financial markets and systems – is in the hands of a particular state, especially a hegemonic state, then the government of that state has an unrivalled capacity to provide *stability* to the world economy. However, when that capacity is not only spread across several states, but also cross-cut and challenged by more autonomous transnational financial markets and linked financial structures, both hegemony and stabilization raise new questions and problems, concerns which are at the core of the issues addressed in this book.

Stability is probably the most important of all public goods for an international order without a supranational government. Of course military supremacy is an important part of the international stability equation, but it ultimately depends upon the threat of the direct application of force by the hegemonic state or by a group of states. Design control over the international financial system, however, as with other markets, simply establishes a set of rules for the interaction of myriad individuals, and day-to-day decision-making is decentralized to a wide range of market actors. Therefore while military force is clearly a 'top down' form of power, part of what Marx called the 'superstructure' of society, stable markets are inherently the sinews of the 'base' (or 'substructure' or 'infrastructure'), holding society together through myriad individual exchanges which feed back into the system itself and reinforce it.

There is thus a subtle relationship between the 'design capacity' of the state, which is undoubtedly part of the superstructure, and the stability of the base. On the one hand, design capacity needs to be exercised in a way which is stabilizing and not destabilizing; that is, it must be compatible with the development and intensification of decentralized market decision-making while maintaining allocative efficiency. But on the other hand, if market decision-making is in turn to be efficient and self-sustaining, it must itself be stable and not undermined, for example, by corrupt, market-distorting or monopolistic practices which feed back in destablizing ways into the system. Furthermore designing an international financial system is inherently problematic in the absence of an international 'state'. Although international 'regimes' such as the Bretton Woods system can develop a certain amount of legitimacy and authority, their autonomy can be fragile under systematic pressure.

II   Political economy, finance and international relations

Several features of this problematic relationship between finance and world order are addressed by the authors in this volume. The first is the relationship of the abstract financial economy to the economy of material production, 'making things', often called the 'real economy'. Economists and economic historians are divided over this issue. Some see a 'free' and open financial system as the ultimate guarantee of allocative efficiency throughout the economic system, as money will spontaneously flow into its most productive and profitable uses. Others see such an open financial economy as a potential drag on the productive economy, because money can be made so easily from the trading of money; thus a 'free' financial market system may crowd a significant amount of money out of less profitable but more productive uses (meeting real demands and needs in society) and into what is called *rentier* capital. The frequent charges of 'short-termism' levelled against open financial markets, as well as the accusation of 'churning', where brokers keep buying and selling the same financial instruments and take a profit each time, are characteristic of the latter view. If financial capital is indeed parasitic in this way, then the design capacity of the system must be highly interventionist in such a way as to channel money into more materially productive uses.

But the issue of the 'financial economy' versus the 'real economy' goes much further, indeed to the heart of the world order. For it leads into the fundamental question of how power and order are established and maintained in the first place, and how they decay. As we have already mentioned, it is commonplace nowadays to agree that international relations are played out on two analytically distinct and structurally contrasting kinds of arenas, 'playing fields' or 'structured fields of action'. The first is that constituted by military power and political *Realpolitik*; the second comprises the international political economy.[2] In the first arena, the currency of control – power, influence and system stability – is physical force. Of course the amount, usability and effectiveness of physical force derive from a more complex set of factors, including size, geopolitical location, economic resources, a cultural sense of the 'national interest' and the autonomous political will of 'state actors' (bureaucrats and politicians). But the fundamental organizing unit is the nation-state. The international system is one of Hobbesian 'anarchy', although based on anarchy among states rather than anarchy among individuals. This has several behavioural consequences.[3]

This world of force and power, usually referred to in academic international relations as the question of 'security', therefore most clearly reflects the division of the planet into nation-states. Without an overarching state-like structure of collective security at supranational level to hold an *international* 'monopoly of legitimate violence', the preeminent unitary actor has indeed been the most institutionalized form of political system, the nation-state. Defending the national territory is usually seen as the primary and indeed overriding duty, responsibility or function of the state itself, that is, of the institutions of the state and of the various office holders ('state actors') who occupy positions of authority within those institutions. The concept of the 'national interest' is the overriding criterion for decision-making in this sphere. Furthermore, given that domestically the state claims the 'monopoly of legitimate violence' within the territory (to use Max Weber's famous term), this means that structures of force established by the domestic state – essentially the armed forces – are organized in a very hierarchical fashion. Indeed the military is normally by far the most hierarchical bureaucratic structure within the state.

Therefore the structure of international security is predominantly one of conflict and cooperation between states, states which are first and foremost self-interested and self-regarding. In this context, security relationships have a high potential for instability. Alliances are by definition conditional (even if they can in some circumstances lead to more complex and long-term bonds); in effect, 'the enemy of my enemy is my friend'. Ensuring national security often seems to require an increase in armaments and military preparedness, but this can actually reduce national security if other nation-states do it too. In such a case it may lead either to destabilization or to outright conflict. This is what is called the 'security dilemma', and is characterized by arms racing. Different manifestations of the security dilemma are often seen, for example, as the main cause of the First World War and at the core of the politics of nuclear weapons in the Cold War.

The structure of international security itself is usually seen to derive from the interaction of two dimensions of power: hierarchy and polarity. The first of these, the hierarchy of international power – the pecking order of nation-states in the security arena – is based primarily on the possession of military and related strategic resources. The better endowed states will usually have disproportionate influence over outcomes in the system, although the elements of national interest (with its part of domestic input) and of national will (with its national culture component) are also significant features. Where the more powerful states can effectively impose their will on the less powerful, a certain stabilization will occur. However a sufficient disparity in resources to establish effective dominance in and of itself is unlikely to occur, given the existence of a multiplicity of states with different levels of power resources. Alliances, technological developments and changes in the conception of the national interest can also occur which may upset any precarious stability based solely on the hierarchy of military power.

Within the resource givens of this hierarchy, however, the second dimension of power and security comes into play. Certain configurations of powerful states can crystallize into relatively stable 'balances of power', in effect system equilibria. The way that a *bipolar* balance of power works – its dynamics – will be familiar not only from the recent Cold War but also from Thucydides's classical treatment of the Peloponnesian Wars between Athens and Sparta. The dynamics of multipolar balances of power (for there are several variations) are most familiar from the period from the end of the Napoleonic Wars until the First World War, when relative stability gradually deteriorated into general war, and from the period between the two world wars, when a more extreme form of multipolarity undermined all attempts to balance the system.

Ultimately, then, the stabilization of power relations in a system based on independent nation-states depends upon the emergence of a configuration of power in which the dimensions of hierarchy and polarity fuse into a working balance of power. When that balance decays, or when the actors reach a point when dynamics inherent in the balance itself lead to destabilization – as with the outbreak of the First World War, or with a perceived need in a crisis to end a cycle of arms racing by actually using the weapons previously acquired – then military conflict is the ultimate sanction. Military conflict itself is also a balancing mechanism, of course; wars are often seen as the main historical cauldrons in which new systemic balances can emerge. Despite the tendency to conflict inherent in a system of independent nation-states, however, states themselves desire first and foremost to survive. Therefore, although they may wish to abandon a particular balance of power when circumstances suggest that a certain configuration is (or has become) inimical to the national interest, in fact they will usually be constrained by the danger of self-destruction from going too far.

III Structural dynamics of international finance

The structural dynamics of the international political economy are usually seen to be quite different from those of the security order. But the question is, how different? As we will see later in the book, some analysts borrow quite heavily from security-based conceptions of world politics, and argue that the international political economy is also primarily organized around the need for cooperative or equilibrium outcomes among states, states which are primarily self-regarding in economic terms in a way that is analogous to their behaviour in the security arena. Others, including those in this book, argue that international economic relations are increasingly difficult to shoe-horn into the nation-state mould – that they are neither domestically hierarchical nor capable of being insulated from the outside world, and that they in fact increasingly cut across and even ignore national boundaries. Although modern capitalism is the product of the emergence of the nation-state, as competing national elites (starting in Europe and spreading throughout the world) sought to increase their wealth as well as their military power, dramatic increases in transnational economic interpenetration and interdependence, especially in the 19th century and again after the hiatus of the Great Depression and the Second World War, have led to a vast expansion of international markets, multinational corporations, foreign direct investment, continually growing trade, and an international financial system of unrivalled scope and complexity.[4]

In this context, the authors in this volume are fundamentally in agreement that the most international, the most transnationalized and the most constraining structure in the international political economy is international finance. Finance is the 'infrastructure of the infrastructure', the most integrated 'playing field' in the world order. This is not to say that finance is wholly international or cosmopolitan. It is merely to say that it is the *most* integrated aspect, relatively speaking, of the international system. Two interrelated problematics, then, arise from this unique position of finance for our understanding the relationship between finance and the world order: in the first place, there is an ongoing tug-of-war between national governments and transnationalized markets for control of the design of the international financial system (and therefore of the domestic systems which are inextricably intertwined with it); and in the second place, the relationship outlined earlier between the financial economy and the real economy is a long way from being resolved.

The authors in this book, to a greater or lesser extent and with some differences of emphasis, argue that the transnationalization of finance has not only become an *autonomous* process – in Margaret Thatcher's words, that 'You can't buck the markets' – but also that in a range of highly significant ways it is actually *in the ascendancy over the real economy*. In this sense, then, the development of the transnational financial structure is setting growing constraints on both state and private actors, increasingly subordinating both government intervention and industrial decision-making to specifically financial criteria and norms. Indeed some authors here go so far as to suggest that the transnationalization of finance is at the heart of the booms, slumps and austerity policies of the 1980s and 1990s.

These changes in the salience and impact of international finance lead to the issue of whether (and how) financial systems are actually constituted at the international level. Given that there is no broadly supranational state at the global level, about the only way to set up, maintain and adapt such systems might seem to be through the interaction of the most powerful nation-states, however episodic or incomplete. The classical answers of 'realist' and 'neo-realist' international relations theorists would involve some form of cooperation between a concert of leading states with common interests in the economic expansion of the international capitalist system and the enforced acquiescence of the rest. However history and the application of a form of collective action theory derived from the seminal work of Mancur Olson[5] have suggested that this form of collective action is difficult to maintain and enforce because of the unwillingness of at least some of the actors involved to pay their share of the costs of cooperation.[6]

Instead several prominent writers (following Olson) have argued that the most likely way that cooperation could be sustained would be in cases where one actor was both (a) disproportionately endowed with resources so as to be *able* to pay the costs by itself and (b) *willing* to provide the requisite 'public goods' by itself alone because it judges the benefits to itself to sufficiently outweigh the costs. This, in terms of international relations theory, is what is meant by neo-realist writers when they speak of 'hegemony'. As we shall see later in the book, 'hegemonic stability theory' (HST), also called the 'theory of hegemonic stability' (THS), has been adopted by many analysts in recent years as a seemingly powerful tool in attempting to explain how the international financial system has been designed and maintained during key periods of modern history.

IV   The critique of hegemonic stability and the transnationalization of finance

The writers in this book, however, are broadly critical of hegemonic stability theory. They adduce a number of arguments for this stance. In the first place, they suggest that, although British hegemony in the 19th century and American hegemony in the 20th were real and significant phenomena, they represented not the automatic translation of material power resources into financial control, but rather a specific conjunction of social, economic and political forces during particular historical epochs. These social forces comprised not only state actors and domestic interests but also international markets and other transnational economic structures.

Indeed, the economic historian Karl Polanyi, writing in his seminal work, *The Great Transformation*, in 1944 (cited in different ways by several of the writers in this volume), argued that in the late 19th century, the period often labelled as one of 'British hegemony' was actually controlled not by Britain or by the British state *per se*, but by a market-like network or structure of powerful financial market actors which may have been centred in London but which stretched around the financial world. Britain of course played a key role in making the system work, but this wider network, which Polanyi called *haute finance*, was essentially a transnational one, cutting across British, French and other financial systems and tying them into a set of international norms and practices, underpinned by the gold standard. In this book, too, Eric Helleiner (Chapter 2) shows how such a more complex analysis provides a much fuller and more accurate picture of the period which saw the emergence of 'American hegemony' after the Second World War. Thus the wider international 'power' of Britain and America respectively, while a significant part of the equation, was certainly not the whole of the picture and was in many ways as much effect as cause.

In the second place, they argue that system change over the past 25 years or so has resulted not from a decline of America or American hegemony *per se*; rather the equation of cause and effect has been the other way around. American decline has been the consequence of changes in the transnational market structure. Of course these changes have themselves resulted from the very success of the sorts of policies pursued by the United States during the postwar period, when the United States was by far the predominant economic and financial power in the world, and therefore American hegemony (it is agreed) did broadly exist in the international economic and financial system. In these circumstances, the 'economic war aims' and postwar goals of the United States were permeated with three sorts of belief about the role of economics and finance in the world order. There was first a consciousness which came to the fore through the group which called themselves 'internationalists' within the Roosevelt Administration in the 1930s that a successful and peaceful international order had to be based on an open international trading system which would permit capitalism to expand and would avoid the closing of economic borders characteristic of the Great Depression, of fascism and of Stalinism.[7] Furthermore there was a belief that such a system needed to be *institutionalized at an international level*, that is, that it was not sufficient for a hegemonic power like 19th-century Britain to provide informal guarantees, because mercantilist rivals would be too powerful (as shown by the experience of the First World War and the interwar period). Finally there was an elite awareness that the United States had to use its disproportionate economic and political power in the aftermath of the Second World War to establish and to guarantee such a system, at least until it was up and running by itself.

American hegemony, therefore, along with the new hegemony within the United States of anti-isolationists or internationalists in both of the major American political parties (bipartisanship) as well as within the Administration, was indeed essential for the establishment and guaranteeing of the new international economic system. At the same time, however, that system itself was supposed to work at arm's length. As it increasingly did so, with the recovery of Europe and Japan and a boom in world trade, the United States became more and more ambivalent about some of the consequences of the system it had set up. The key to the structure was the system of fixed exchange rates, based on the United States' willingness to guarantee the value of the dollar in gold. But as the dollar itself came under increasing pressure from other countries in the late 1960s to be devalued – for reasons dealt with in more detail by the authors in this volume – the United States unilaterally abrogated the Bretton Woods system.[8]

The subsequent move, after 1971, to a system of floating exchange rates, which had the support of the newly fashionable monetarist economists in the early 1970s, essentially created a totally new situation for the international economic and financial systems. Although in the short run, in the 1970s, it led to an outbreak of 'neo-mercantilism' and attempts to impose new forms of protectionism, its most important consequence was the freeing of *financial* exchanges from the disciplines of the fixed exchange rate system. The shift to floating exchange rates thus led to an explosion of financial flows, the deregulation of domestic financial systems, experiments in international financial crisis management and a variety of attempts to develop new partial and global regimes (for example, the European Monetary System and the General Agreement on Trade in Services, respectively) for the regulation of international finance.

The key to change, therefore, was not the decline in US hegemony as such, but the crystallization and consolidation of genuinely *transnational* and increasingly autonomous financial markets. These came to be more and more important with regard to financial transactions in general, both in terms of volume of transactions and in terms of the structure of the financial marketplace itself. These changes were not so much the results of decisions by states, but rather, as Susan Strange has argued, the consequence of a series of *non-decisions*; the real agent of change was the transnationalization of markets themselves.[9] Furthermore, interstate cooperation in the changing of market structures was a marginal factor; the failure in 1971–3 to agree on a workable system of managed exchange rates to replace the Bretton Woods arrangements undermined serious cooperation in these matters for nearly 15 years (and, as Stephen Gill shows in Chapter 4, such cooperation is still highly circumscribed and fragile).

The neo-realist logic of collective action was thus turned on its head in the financial arena, and unilateral deregulatory decisions led to a widening circle of deregulation across countries, regions and the globe. In this structural sense, then, the authors in this volume argue that the very concept of hegemony must be reassessed. To say that American hegemony was (and perhaps could only be) of the 'arms-length' variety in the postwar period is not to deny that the American role in setting up and guaranteeing the Bretton Woods system was perhaps the key *conjunctural* factor in its early success, but merely to argue that the key *structural* factor in its success was rather different. This structural durability lay in the way that the system was capable of being transformed over time into, and ultimately replaced by, a more and more transnationalized financial system based on an increasingly autonomous international financial market-place.

V   The transnationalization of finance and the power of the state
The final criticism of hegemonic stability theory in the book is much simpler, and derives from the first two. This is the view that in future the hegemony, not merely of any one nation-state, but of any nation-states *per se*, is increasingly unlikely. Any future national control would be limited, indirect and constrained to conform to the imperatives of the transnational financial markets. Within this context, the United States, despite its market power and the role of its deficit financing in setting the pace for certain markets, is too internally fragmented in terms of its political institutions, regulatory system and interest group structure to exercise much influence on the transnational financial structure. The European Community, similarly, despite the coming of the European Financial Area and the Single Market, certainly seems to lack hegemonic potential, as Peter Vipond shows. The EC not only suffers in terms of political authority from continuing divisions between the member states and Brussels, but has also found that the goal of monetary union has so far been both a bone of contention (with Britain's 'opt-out' enshrined in the Maastricht Agreement, now itself in doubt) and a fragile reed (with the withdrawal of sterling from the Exchange Rate Mechanism). Japan may still be gaining in financial power relatively speaking, as Eric Helleiner argues in Chapter 8, but its future influence is problematic and is likely to be exercised in such a way as to reinforce, rather than undermine or alter, the wider international financial structure.

At the same time that the influence of particular states is waning, furthermore, processes of transnationalization are proceeding apace. These processes are not, however, developing primarily through the establishment of international regimes to coordinate cooperation. Although a General Agreement on Trade in Services, as Geoffrey Underhill argues, would ratify changes already in progress and further level the playing field somewhat, it would not represent a qualitative leap forward. The G7, as Stephen Gill shows, may develop an increasing role in crisis management, but is not coherent enough to be the focus for a new round of international cooperation which would lead to the emergence of an effective regime in the financial field. However he does think that the influence of transnational financial capital is growing, and may increasingly affect G7 through both private and public elite networks in the future. Finally, of course, such existing groups as the Bank for International Settlements (BIS), despite the relative success of the 1988 Basle international capital adequacy standards for banks, and the International Organization of Securities Commissions (IOSCO) lack the autonomous political authority to act effectively.

Indeed, the main motor force of change, as the present writer argues in Chapter 3, is the increasing transnational integration and competitive deregulation/re-regulation of financial markets themselves. As currency and securities are more and more traded internationally, as multinational firms seek increasingly to speculate and hedge their financial resources, as foreign direct investment continues to expand, and as banking systems diversify and banks have to compete on an ever-widening international scale, the cycle of deregulation – reluctantly supported and sometimes even promoted by the state – will continue to widen. Governments, international regimes and regulatory authorities within governments will increasingly come to be 'whipsawed' between different sectors and firms in the financial services industry seeking the most amenable regulators and the most permissive rules – what is called 'regulatory arbitrage' or 'competition in laxity'. Governments will be internally split and different 'state actors' linked into different policy communities will increasingly operate within *transnational networks*, with securities regulators establishing networks with securities regulators abroad as well as with (often multinational) securities firms, competing with similar networks among banking regulators or insurance regulators and their pressure group constituencies and so on.[10] In addition deregulation may complicate these networks further as markets are further decompartmentalized. And even where the state does try to make authoritative economic policy (under the pressure of growing democratic demands) that policy will be circumscribed by ever-tighter financial considerations in the quest to boost international financial competitiveness – anti-inflationary policies, tax cuts and incentives, spending cuts and generally trying to 'get more out of less'.

Polanyi argued that markets are created by states in order to promote the general creation of wealth; that the self-regulating markets which states have attempted to design are liable to distortions, failures and widespread social injustices; and that states, in turn, must always attempt to find new ways to control markets to limit those distortions, failures and injustices. In effect, the Keynesian welfare state which grew out of the experiences of the 1930s and 1940s was the product of governments' attempts to do just that in order to counteract the potential dangers of a new world slump. But in a world of transnationalized finance, a world in which 'competition states' have lost the power to use a range of financial controls and policy instruments to shape and promote economic development, who is to counteract the failures of the new *haute finance*?

VI   Financial transnationalization and the future of government policy

There are somewhat different stances on this vital question taken by the authors of this book, although all agree that it looks like a labour of Sisyphus. Broadly speaking, some authors are more optimistic, some more pessimistic. Among them, Stephen Gill is broadly pessimistic, but even so suggests that perhaps the elites of the new transnational financial structure will in the end influence governments to cooperate in a strengthened G7. Eric Helleiner suggests that Japan, although not a fully-fledged hegemon in the neo-realist sense, will increasingly exert a stabilizing influence on the system. Geoffrey Underhill and Peter Vipond are fairly agnostic, seeing an ongoing politics of negotiation both within and across borders. The present writer sees states themselves as increasingly fragmented and constrained by the imperatives of international financial competition.

What is interesting in this environment is the way that politicians, bureaucrats and policy analysts are beginning to look for approaches which will enable them to cope more effectively with the new financial constraints. Probably the most interesting aspect of the campaign and economic ideas of President Bill Clinton in the United States is his focus on reducing and streamlining the size and operation of government bureaucracies while actually *strengthening* processes of 'governance' or 'steering' through recurrent contracting and systematic monitoring of the performance of highly flexible bureaucracies.[11] This is the result of an attempt by a range of policy analysts to assimilate into policy-making and policy implementation theory the lessons of 'flexible manufacturing systems' in industry.[12] At the same time, following the approach outlined by his advisor Robert Reich, Clinton is suggesting that government policy should also focus on state promotion of 'immobile factors of capital' – essentially infrastructure and 'human capital' such as education and training (especially those oriented towards the high value-added end of the Third Industrial Revolution) – rather than trying directly to influence more mobile factors such as the direct promotion of finance and industry.[13] In other countries, however, attempts to cope with the new financial constraints have either been seen as part of the wider free-market approach of Reaganomics and Thatcherism characteristic of the 1980s, or have been grafted onto neo-corporatist structures, as in Scandinavia. At the international level, too, we are beginning to hear growing calls from politicians, bureaucrats, journalists and academics for the creation and/or strengthening of international regulatory regimes, including the BIS.

But whether or not any of these approaches is successful in dealing with the transnational financial structure remains to be seen. In the shorter term, government policy is likely to consist at best of various forms of muddling through, partial experimentation and reactive rather than proactive attempts to deal with the new constraints in practice. Unlike the 1920s, however, and in spite of a strong belief to the contrary in the 1980s embodied in the views of Ronald Reagan and Margaret Thatcher, there seems to be a widespread recognition today of the importance of the state's role in the design of markets and the maintenance of stability. In contrast to the early 1930s, too, there is a widespread awareness that neo-mercantilism and protectionism are increasingly counterproductive. What is most different from the Keynesian welfare state pattern, however, is a sense that the state itself is not somehow set apart from the market, that there is not a rigid distinction between 'market' and 'hierarchy', but rather a range of mixes between the two which includes the state itself.[14] The private sector is not always characterized by efficient competitive behaviour (indeed it is often the vehicle of greed and monopoly) and the state is not merely a vehicle for protective cartels and special interests. Indeed, in recent years, probably the most significant trend is the 'commodification' or 'marketization' of the state apparatus itself in the pursuit of international competitiveness – what has elsewhere been called the 'competition state'.[15] This means that the state has become an agent of its own transformation. But it is perhaps in the arena of finance that the state has been most fully 'marketized': in its regulatory systems, in its economic policy and in its very organizational structure.

VII   Conclusions: finance and world politics

Finance, we argue in this book, constitutes the 'infrastructure of the infra-structure' – the structural bottom line or most significant common denominator (although certainly not the lowest) within the international political economy. The control of finance has always been one of the major functions of national state apparatuses, and the transnationalization of finance has led – in the mid-to-late 19th century, in the 1920s and today – to severe problems for the maintenance of political stability and economic growth. In the 19th century, these problems were for a time solved by a system which was partially held together through British hegemony, but the growth of more mercantilist forms of competition and the beginnings of Britain's long economic decline led to the failure of the system in the First World War and to futile attempts to reconstruct it afterwards. In the 1920s, these problems were not solved but indeed made worse, as the 1929 Wall Street Crash demonstrated; the 1930s were subsequently characterized by a vicious circle of destabilization and slump, only partly relieved by corporatist and Keynesian experiments prior to the Second World War. In the late 1980s and early

1990s, too, a tenacious recession and the volatility of financial flows have provided a contrast both to the bubble boom of the mid-1980s and to the long boom from the end of the 1940s to the early 1970s.

The transnationalization of finance, however, has taken on a more wide-spread and structurally complex form in the late 20th century. National security considerations have diminished in importance over several decades, and the end of the Cold War has underlined just how far this process has gone. In political economy, governments have promoted the transnationalization of finance, while ongoing processes of deregulatory competition since the collapse of Bretton Woods have expanded international financial markets in myriad directions and circumscribed the scope and power of the state not just in financial regulation but in economic policy more generally. Furthermore economic linkages have been increasingly shaped by financial imperatives, as the financial economy calls the tune for the real economy, whether in terms of short-term financial flows, patterns of investment, the restructuring of industries and markets, or the contours of state economic intervention. Finally, in the international political economy, whether in terms of markets, regimes or states, the transnationalization of finance has developed its own autonomous structural dynamic, a dynamic with regard to which international politics has yet to find a workable consensus on objectives or a feasible method of control. Indeed one might say, echoing Cordell Hull, that the world order follows the financial order.

Notes

1. Susan Strange, 'Finance, Information and Power', *Review of International Studies*, **16**, (3), (July 1990), pp. 259–74.
2. See James N. Rosenau, *Turbulence in World Politics: A Theory of Change and Continuity*, Princeton, NJ: Princeton University Press, 1990.
3. Cf. Hedley Bull, *The Anarchical Society: A Study of Order in World Politics*, London: Macmillan, 1977 and Kenneth Waltz, *Theory of International Politics*, Reading, MA: Addison-Wesley, 1979.
4. For an exploration of this transnationalization process and a development of the concept of 'transnational structures', see Susan Strange, *States and Markets: An Introduction to International Political Economy*, London: Pinter, 1988.
5. Mancur Olson, *The Logic of Collective Action*, Cambridge, MA: Harvard University Press, 1971.
6. For a recent exploration of these issues which argues that the possibilities of collective action in a multipolar system are perhaps greater than other analysts would suggest, see Robert O. Keohane, *After Hegemony: Cooperation and Discord in the World Political Economy*, Princeton, NJ: Princeton University Press, 1984.
7. See Lloyd C. Gardner, *Economic Aspects of New Deal Diplomacy*, Boston, MA: Beacon Press, 1971.
8. See Fred L. Block, *The Origins of International Economic Disorder: A Study of United States Monetary Policy from World War II to the Present*, Berkeley and Los Angeles: University of California Press, 1977.
9. Susan Strange, *Casino Capitalism*, Oxford and New York: Basil Blackwell, 1986.
10. Analogous tendencies have been observed in a range of issue areas, including high technology and the chemicals industry.

11. See David Osborne and Ted Gaebler, *Reinventing Government: How the Entrepreneurial Spirit is Transforming the Public Sector, from Schoolhouse to Statehouse, City Hall to the Pentagon*, Reading, MA: Addison-Wesley, 1992.
12. See Michael J. Piore and Charles F. Sabel, *The Second Industrial Divide: Possibilities for Prosperity*, New York: Basic Books, 1984.
13. See Robert Reich, *The Work of Nations: Preparing Ourselves for 21st-Century Capitalism*, New York: Alfred A. Knopf, 1991.
14. As well as, for example, 'networks'; see Grahame Thompson, Jennifer Frances, Rosalind Levačic and Jeremy Mitchell (eds), *Markets, Hierarchies and Networks: The Coordination of Social Life*, London and Newbury Park, CA: Sage Publications, 1991. I would argue, however, that networks are only one of a wide range of structures which blend and fuse the analytically polar ideal types of 'market' and 'hierarchy'.
15. P.G. Cerny, *The Changing Architecture of Politics: Structure, Agency and the Future of the State*, London and Newbury Park, CA: Sage Publications, 1990, especially Ch. 8.

2 When finance was the servant: international capital movements in the Bretton Woods order

Eric Helleiner

One of the most spectacular developments in the global political economy in recent years has been the emergence of an extremely open and liberal international financial order. Since the 1960s, the volume of private international financial activity has grown very quickly. Moreover, in the last 15 years, states across the advanced industrial world have moved to fully dismantle their capital controls. The USA began this trend in 1974, removing its capital controls programme that had been in place since 1963. More dramatically, in 1979, Britain abolished its 40-year-old capital controls regime. The British move was copied in Australia, New Zealand and Denmark in 1984–5. By 1988, the countries of the European Community had agreed to the complete abolition of their capital controls within two to four years and the Scandinavian countries followed with similar announcements in 1989–90. Finally, throughout the 1980s, Japan also progressively liberalized its extremely rigid capital controls which had been in place since the early 1930s.[1]

It is often assumed that the emergence of an open, liberal international financial order has been a product of the 1944 Bretton Woods Agreement. As the constitution of the postwar liberal international economic order, the Agreement is said to have promoted both a liberal trading order and an open and liberal global financial system. This chapter demonstrates that the Agreement in fact embodied a very restrictive financial order in which capital controls were strongly endorsed. As Richard Gardner puts it, the Bretton Woods authors 'sought to make finance the servant, not the master, of human desires – in the international no less than in the domestic sphere'.[2] The emergence of an open, liberal global financial system in recent years is thus better seen as reflecting the collapse of the Bretton Woods financial order rather than its realization.

There is a second important reason to study the Bretton Woods discussions concerning international capital movements. Despite the dramatic nature of the liberalization process in the 1980s, there has been very little public debate concerning the relative benefits and drawbacks of a liberal international financial order. In Bryant's words: 'Financial activity and its regulation are widely perceived as arcane subjects, especially in the international dimension. Average opinion is thus inattentive, even somnolent.'[3] By contrast, during the Bretton Woods negotiations, there was a very lively discussion on these issues. The authors of the Agreement, in defending their proposals for a restrictive financial order, explained in detail why they preferred a world different from that which we now inhabit. Their opponents responded by outlining clear reasons to favour a liberal international financial order. Despite the obvious contemporary relevance of these discussions, little attention has been given to them by scholars in the field of international political economy.[4]

This chapter is divided into four sections. The first situates the Bretton Woods discussions in the context of the financial history of the interwar period, concentrating on the growing disillusionment with liberal approaches to international financial movements after the international financial crisis of 1931. The second section outlines the initial Bretton Woods proposals composed in 1941–2 by the chief negotiators of the two major allied economic powers: Keynes from Britain and White from the USA. It is shown that, far from disagreeing, the two negotiators saw eye to eye on the need for a restrictive regime for international financial movements in the postwar world. The third section describes how these proposals were modified somewhat in the face of opposition from the New York financial community. The conclusion sums up the importance of these discussions for the contemporary context.

I   The structural break in financial affairs in the 1930s

To understand the Bretton Woods discussions concerning financial movements it is necessary to return briefly to the international financial history of the interwar period. The financial history of this period can be sharply divided in two, with the 1931 international financial crisis marking the divide. The decade of the 1920s was dominated by an initiative by private and central bankers across the industrial world to restore the pre-1914 liberal monetary and financial order in which they had held so prominent a place.[5] Beginning at international monetary conferences such as those at Brussels in 1920 and at Genoa in 1922, they called for a return to balanced budgets, independent central banks, free financial movements and above all the international gold standard. This political initiative to rebuild the pre-1914 world was led by the two most powerful groups of financiers of the postwar world – those in the City of London and New York. By the mid-1920s, the bankers had achieved their goal: the international gold standard had been resurrected and an active circuit of international private lending had been revived.

The bankers' victory was to be short-lived, however. In the 1929–31 period, the confidence of private international lenders rapidly deteriorated because of many factors, including the US stock crash in 1929, the subsequent depression, the continuing reparations and war debt muddles, and the large underlying imbalances in payments patterns. In the face of these problems, bankers across the advanced industrial world tried desperately to preserve the liberal international financial and monetary order through initiatives such as the creation in 1930 of the Bank for International Settlements (BIS), a body which was supposed to facilitate central bank cooperation as well as to depoliticize the debts and reparations issue.[6] They were, however, unable to prevent the complete crisis of confidence which came in 1931. Enormous speculative capital flight and a total collapse of long-term lending forced Germany and Austria to introduce exchange controls in the middle of the year. By September, enormous speculation against sterling forced Britain itself to leave the gold standard. The bankers' vision of restoring the pre-1914 world lay in ruins.

The 1931 international financial crisis was important not just in bringing the collapse of international capital markets and of the international gold standard. Equally significant, it marked the beginning of a kind of socio-ideological 'structural break' in financial affairs. As one German financier noted at the height of the crisis: 'What I have just experienced means the end of a way of life, certainly for Germany and perhaps other countries as well... The common vision of the future has been destroyed.'[7] Largely discredited by the crises, the private and central bankers who had dominated financial politics before the 1930s were increasingly replaced at the levers of financial power by professional economists, industrialists and labour groups working through their respective finance ministries or treasuries. Where the bankers had advocated a laissez-faire approach to domestic financial issues and the following of automatic 'rules of the game' in the international financial sphere, these new groups favoured a more interventionist approach that would make domestic and international finance serve broader political and economic goals. In Hirsch and Oppenheimer's words: 'Monetary standards no longer imposed. Rather, overriding political and economic circumstances determined monetary standards'.[8]

Like the departure from the gold standard, the increasing use of capital controls represented an important part of the structural break from liberal traditions in financial affairs. To be sure, the pre-1931 period had not been completely free of capital controls. The French and Germans, for example, had frequently restrained capital exports in the pre-1914 period by controlling flotations of foreign securities. Even the stalwart liberal financial powers in the 1920s – Britain and the USA – had subtly attempted to regulate the flow of international capital.[9] What was new, however, was the comprehensive nature of the controls. Moreover, whereas controls had generally been used before 1931 in a temporary fashion to achieve foreign policy goals, for example denying to enemy states access to one's own capital markets, capital controls were now introduced as permanent aspects of new economic strategies.

Not surprisingly, the first to use comprehensive capital controls were those countries who departed most quickly and dramatically from liberal financial traditions domestically: Japan and Germany.[10] Although initially introduced for the practical purpose of defending the balance of payments during and after the 1931 crisis, comprehensive capital controls in these countries soon came to be seen as more lasting features of their economic policies. Facing severe domestic economic crises, both Japan and Germany were early experimenters with unorthodox domestic policies such as deficit financing and accommodative monetary policy. Moreover, as the pressures of militarization increased during the 1930s, both states began extensive direct intervention in their domestic financial systems to allocate scarce capital resources. Both macroeconomic management and state-directed financial allocation forced a change in attitudes towards movements of international finance. Macroeconomic management, for example, could easily be disrupted by speculative financial movements or by capital fleeing artificially low interest rates. Similarly government attempts to ration and allocate capital would be disturbed if borrowers and investors had access to international capital markets. Capital controls thus became an integral feature of the new domestic strategies.

The structural shift away from liberal policies with respect to international financial movements in the USA and Britain took place more slowly. It was out of these experiences that the Bretton Woods discussions emerged. In the USA, the economic and financial crises of the early 1930s acted as a catalyst for a dramatic realignment of political coalitions that culminated in Roosevelt's election in 1933. Supported by a coalition of farmers, labour groups and 'progressive' business leaders, the Roosevelt Administration identified the New York financial community, and especially the Morgan financial empire, as responsible for the economic chaos of the time. A series of important initiatives were launched in an effort to bring financial and monetary policy under greater democratic control. Domestically, new financial regulations were introduced to moderate competition, increase investor protection and reduce Morgan's power. Reforms were also instituted to make the Federal Reserve system more politically accountable and a non-New York banker with decidedly non-orthodox views, Marriner Eccles, was appointed its head. Internationally Roosevelt took the USA off the gold standard in April 1933, describing it as one of the 'old fetishes of so-called international bankers'.[11] Moreover, in a move particularly important for understanding the Bretton Woods discussions, control over international monetary policy was shifted from the Federal Reserve Bank of New York to the

Treasury which under the leadership of Henry Morgenthau had become a centre of New Deal radicalism.

Little effort was made initially to interfere with international movements of finance. Although Congress broadened the President's powers to control foreign exchange transactions, and prohibited foreign loans to governments which were in default to the USA, these initiatives were of little practical consequence.[12] Moreover the Exchange Equalization Fund set up in 1934 made little effort initially to sterilize capital flows moving in and out of the USA. By 1936, however, the disruptive effect of increasingly large inflows of capital flight from Europe on the US macroeconomy forced a change in attitude.[13] Whereas such movements had proved helpful in keeping domestic interest rates low when the USA had been in recession, they were increasingly viewed as inflationary by 1936–7. Although many in the Treasury favoured introducing exchange controls to curb these flows, their proposals were strongly opposed by more liberal thinkers in the government, as well as by the New York financial community who were worried that New York's position as an international financial centre would be weakened.[14] In place of exchange controls, the Treasury began to sterilize the monetary effect of the inflows after December 1936. At the same time, and as a direct precursor to the Bretton Woods plans, the Treasury initiated discussion with Britain concerning possible cooperative efforts to control this 'hot money' which might not require the use of exchange controls.[15]

The coming of war and the initiation of planning for the postwar order had the effect of encouraging a decisive shift away from liberal financial traditions in the US government. The war demonstrated the potential effectiveness of exchange controls and indeed of all kinds of domestic financial intervention which had become integral parts of the war effort.[16] The initiation of postwar planning encouraged creative and ambitious thinking. In particular, Morgenthau made it clear that he would use the whole effort of postwar planning to build a 'New Deal in international economics'.[17] The proposals would be part of a broader struggle against the bankers at home and abroad that had dominated the international financial realm in the 1920s. As he put it, the objective would be 'to move the financial center to the world from London and Wall Street to the United States Treasury, and to create a new concept between nations in international finance'.[18] His active support for Norway's proposal at the Bretton Woods conference to abolish the BIS, for example, was 'a matter of international propaganda' and reflected his desire to 'drive the usurious moneylenders from the temple of international finance'.[19] In the words of one American columnist, every effort would be made to prevent a 'financial pact under which Wall Street and the City would be able to dictate international monetary policy and block social and economic reform through their control of foreign lending'.[20] Morgenthau chose Harry Dexter White to oversee the planning, largely because of White's loyalty to the principles of the early New Deal. Indeed, by the late 1930s, White had become a convert to Keynesian economics as well as to the idea that 'centralized control over foreign exchange and trade' might be necessary to protect national planning strategies.[21]

Turning to the British case, the September 1931 exchange crisis which forced Britain off the gold standard also brought important political changes. As in the USA, the Treasury assumed greater influence over monetary affairs, and the Bank of England and private international bankers in the City of London lost much of the power they had held in the 1920s.[22] Important changes in policy also quickly followed. The Treasury insisted on a much more accommodative monetary policy which was oriented towards domestic goals instead of external balance. Internationally an Exchange Equalization Account was set up under the Treasury's jurisdiction to intervene in exchange markets and offset the effects of short-term gold movements on domestic monetary conditions. Moreover, in June 1932, a complete prohibition on public loans to overseas borrowers was introduced in order to protect sterling. While relaxed later that year for Commonwealth and Empire borrowers, a strong surveillance procedure remained on the foreign lending of private City firms and 'foreign issues were permitted only if there was a compelling case that they would benefit British industry'.[23] Despite the dramatic nature of these changes, the British Treasury in fact remained largely wedded to orthodox principles in its outlook.[24] The goal of its low-interest rate policy, for example, was not that of macroeconomic management but rather that of reducing its own debt service costs. In the fiscal realm, the Treasury remained committed to balanced budgets. It was not until the war that attitudes changed considerably. Not only did the war make it necessary to introduce exchange controls, but more importantly it brought an influx of academic economists into the Treasury who were committed to more activist and interventionist economic policies. The most important of these economists was John Maynard Keynes.

In addition to rapidly becoming a dominant figure in the British Treasury during the war, Keynes took on the task of devising the plans for the postwar international economy that would be discussed with the Americans. Like Morgenthau and White, Keynes hoped to devise an order that would consolidate the financial and economic experiments of the 1930s. In particular he articulated more clearly than any other thinker of the time the intellectual case for capital controls. He had already in 1933 said 'let finance be primarily national' on the grounds that the policy autonomy of governments must be defended from financial flows.[25] In 1941–2, Keynes also strongly endorsed the interventionist German proposals for the postwar world and made it clear that, like the Germans, he believed that 'control of capital movements, both inward and outward, should be a permanent feature of the post-war system'. In his words, 'a proposal to return to the blessings of 1920–33 will not have much propaganda value'.[26]

II   Early plans of Keynes and White

The Bretton Woods negotiations are often portrayed as a battle of wills between Keynes and White, who are said to have held different views on the way the postwar international economy should be organized. With respect to their views concerning international movements of private finance, however, this was far from the case. As we have seen, both were strongly supportive of an order that would permit capital controls.

In their respective early drafts, Keynes and White outlined two central reasons why capital controls would be necessary in the postwar world. First, international financial movements could not be allowed to disrupt the policy autonomy of the new interventionist welfare state. Their key concern was protecting the new national macroeconomic planning techniques that had emerged in the 1930s. Drawing on the US experience in the late 1930s, White, for example, noted that capital controls 'would give each government much greater measure of control in carrying out its monetary and tax policies' by preventing 'flights of capital, motivated either by prospect of speculative exchange gain, or desire to avoid inflation, or evade taxes or influence legislation'.[27] In addition to fearing such 'short-term speculative movements or flights of currency', Keynes also worried that 'movements of funds out of debtor countries which lack the means to finance them' would impose an undue balance of payments constraint on domestic macroeconomic objectives.[28]

Keynes noted that it was not just such 'abnormal' financial flows – that is, those motivated by purely speculative considerations – which disrupted national macroeconomic planning, but also 'normal' flows which responded to interest rate differentials between countries.[29] A country with a current account deficit, for example, that attempted to maintain lower interest rates than the prevailing international norm would find itself subject to severe 'disequilibrating' outflows of such movements. Similarly, a country with a current account surplus wanting to raise rates above those existing elsewhere would attract 'disequilibrating' capital inflows of this nature. If interest rates were to be determined by domestic macroeconomic priorities and not by considerations of external balance, such financial movements would need to be controlled in order to avoid external constraints on such policy. As Keynes explained:

> Freedom of capital movements is an essential part of the old laissez-faire system and assumes that it is right and desirable to have an equalisation of interest rates

in all parts of the world...In my view the whole management of the domestic economy depends upon being free to have the appropriate rate of interest without reference to the rates prevailing elsewhere in the world. Capital control is a corollary to this.[30]

Keynes and White noted that the policy autonomy of the new welfare state was threatened by financial movements in two other ways. First, as Japan and Germany had discovered, the new domestic financial regulatory structures which had been created for the purpose of facilitating industrial and macroeconomic planning would be undermined if savers and borrowers had access to external financial markets. As Keynes told the British House of Lords, the endorsement of capital controls in the Bretton Woods Agreement would ensure that 'our right to control the domestic capital market is secured on firmer foundations than ever before'.[31] Second, the welfare state also had to be protected from capital flight induced by 'political reasons' or a desire to evade 'burdens of social legislation'.[32] In Keynes's words: 'Surely in the post-war years there is hardly a country in which we ought not to expect keen political discussion affecting the position of the wealthier classes and the treatment of private property...If so, there will be a number of people constantly taking fright because they think that the degree of leftism in one country looks for the time being likely to be greater than somewhere else.'[33] White concluded that capital flows should not be permitted to 'operate against what the government deemed to be the interests of any country' even if this involved restricting 'the property rights of the 5 or 10 percent of persons in foreign countries who have enough wealth or income to keep or invest some of it abroad'.[34]

In addition to wanting to protect the policy autonomy of the new welfare state, Keynes and White also favoured capital controls in order to preserve a stable international exchange rate system and liberal trading order. With respect to the former, White noted that speculative financial movements were 'one of the chief causes of foreign exchange disturbances'.[35] Such capital flows would need to be controlled if a stable set of exchange rates was to be maintained. With respect to the trading system, Keynes noted that large and volatile movements of finance from countries with a current account deficit to those with a surplus might induce large 'painful and perhaps violent' offsetting adjustments on the less flexible trade account.[36] Such adjustments would likely increase political pressure for protectionist measures. Capital controls would be needed, thus, to prevent international financial movements from 'strangling' international trade, instead of playing 'their proper auxiliary role of facilitating trade'.[37]

Keynes and White's worries about speculative and disequilibrating financial movements disrupting stable exchange rates and liberal trading relations were widely shared after the experience of the interwar years. The difficulty of maintaining stable exchange rates in an open financial order had been demonstrated in the 1931 crisis when enormous speculative financial movements had forced many states off the gold standard. Even the orthodox Gold Delegation of the League of Nations' Financial Committee was led by this experience to recommend in its 1932 report that short-term financial flows be controlled and that only equilibrating financial flows used for 'productive purposes' be permitted.[38] By wartime, there was widespread consensus – well publicized in Nurkse's 1944 League of Nations report – that capital controls were needed to defend a stable exchange rate system.[39] The retreat by Germany and Japan into systems of exchange control in the face of enormous capital flight in 1931 also seemed to point to the incompatibility of a liberal financial and trading order. Similarly the large speculative capital flows in the 1930s were seen by many to have disrupted traditional trading patterns. The US Department of Commerce, for example, concluded in 1943:

> Unless brought under control in the future, capital movements of this [speculative] nature might readily nullify other efforts to attain greater stability in international transactions and would decrease the amount of dollars available to foreigners for purchases of American goods and services.[40]

Keynes and White's advocacy of capital controls did not blind them to the possible virtues of certain types of international capital movements. Although speculative flows were to be controlled, White agreed with the League of Nations' Gold Delegation that international flows of 'productive' capital should be encouraged.[41] Keynes, too, favoured 'legitimate' capital movements that would 'satisfy practical needs' in international commerce and provide 'genuine new investment for developing the world's resources', just as international investment had in the pre-1914 period.[42] Similarly, whereas 'disequilibrating' movements of capital were to be controlled, both Keynes and White noted that capital movements from countries with a surplus on their current account to those with a deficit were to be favoured in that they would 'help to maintain equilibrium' in the international monetary system.[43] Both Keynes and White hoped that the various activities of the Bretton Woods institutions would in fact promote 'productive' and 'equilibrating' flows by reducing exchange rate instability and by restoring confidence in international economic conditions.[44]

Although these flows would be encouraged, both Keynes and White made it clear that the overriding 'norm' in their plans was that of controlling capital. The disruptive nature of 'speculative' and 'disequilibrating' flows of capital was considered so severe that states had to be given the right to use capital controls. The priority given to capital controls reflected the importance they attached to the goal of defending the policy autonomy of the new welfare state. The particularly disruptive nature of financial movements made a liberal financial order less easy to reconcile with desires for policy autonomy than, for example, a liberal trading order. 'Embedded liberalism' – the desire to create a open international economy that would not interfere with the policy autonomy of the new welfare state – was thus pushed in the 'embedded' direction in the financial sector.[45]

The priority given to controlling finance also reflected the 'secondary' status of a liberal financial system in their vision of a liberal international economic order. Faced with the prospect of a liberal financial system disrupting a stable international exchange rate system and liberal trading order, there was consensus at Bretton Woods that the former should be sacrificed in order to preserve the latter. The scepticism towards the benefits of a liberal financial system partly reflected the way in which the international lending of the 1920s had ended in the financial disaster of early 1930s.[46] It was also a product of the fact that 'free finance' had not achieved the same sacred status as 'the gold standard' and 'free trade' in liberal thinking. Indeed, when the virtues of international capital movements had been discussed in the pre-1931 period, it had usually been in terms of their contribution to the gold standard and a liberal trading system. Among those who had initiated academic discussion in the interwar period of the absolute benefits of a liberal international financial system – of whom White was one of the more prominent – there was a widespread feeling that the classical case in favour of free trade was less relevant to the financial sector. As Ohlin had argued in 1936: 'there is a decisive difference between the role of such transfers [capital movements] and the functions of an exchange of commodities. The latter is a prerequisite of prosperity and economic growth, the former is not.'[47]

Keynes and White's proposals concerning capital movements were important not just in outlining so clearly why capital controls were now seen as necessary. Equally important was their discussion concerning how to make such controls effective. Both recognized that states had had great difficulties in the 1930s controlling financial transactions. Thus, in addition to granting states the right to use capital controls, Keynes and White outlined two further provisions designed to make such controls actually work. First, to prevent financial movements taking place in a disguised form as current account payments, they noted that all states would need to have the right to institute systems of exchange controls to screen current account transactions for illegal financial movements. As Keynes explained: 'If control is to be effective, it probably involves the *machinery* of exchange control for *all* transactions, even though a general open licence is given to all remittances in respect of current trade.'[48] The second mechanism was more compatible with an open world economy. Following up discussions held between the USA and Britain in the late 1930s, Keynes and White noted that countries would be able to increase the effectiveness of their capital controls by cooperating in enforcing each other's regulations. As White put it: 'Almost every country, at one time or another, exercises control over the inflow and outflow of investments, but without the cooperation of other countries such control is difficult, expensive and subject to considerable evasion.'[49] Keynes, too, observed that control of capital movements 'will be more difficult to work, especially in the absence of postal censorship, by unilateral action than if movements of capital can be controlled *at both ends'*.[50] Although Keynes strongly recommended cooperation in his plans, White went even further and made such cooperation *obligatory* in his. As he noted in his 1942 plan, governments would be required:

> a) Not to accept or permit deposits or investments from any member country except with the permission of the government of that country, and b) To make available to the government of any member country at its request all property in form of deposits, investments, securities of the nationals of that member country.[51]

III   Opposition from the New York bankers
The early proposals of Keynes and White met strong opposition from the New York financial community, who disliked the way in which countries would be *permitted* to use capital controls on a permanent basis under the plan. Even more distressing for them was the notion that countries might be *forced* to institute such controls under White's cooperative control provisions. At one level, the New York bankers' objections to the capital control provisions reflected a worry that such controls would disrupt their international business. Any obligations the USA undertook to control 'unproductive' flows, for example, would remove what had been a lucrative business in the 1930s of receiving speculative flight capital from Europe. More broadly, a regime permitting other countries to control capital movements might prevent the rebuilding of an open, liberal global financial system from which they, as the world's leading bankers, would derive considerable benefits. In particular, they feared that Britain would use capital controls to prevent them from challenging the City of London's dominant position within the sterling area.[52]

The bankers' objections were not, however, motivated only by considerations of direct self-interest. Equally important seemed to be the task of opposing the 'principles' set forward by Keynes and White. Although they concurred with Keynes and White on the desirability of productive and equilibrating flows of capital, they did not share their concern with the way disequilibrating and unproductive flows would interfere with the policy autonomy of the new welfare state. Particularly offensive was the notion that 'normal' flows (that is, those responding to international interest rate differentials) might be seen as undesirable because of the way they could disrupt domestic macroeconomic planning through their disequilibrating nature. Hostile to the idea of national fiscal and monetary planning, the bankers did not see such disequilibrating flows as undesirable, but merely as a reflection of an inappropriate interest rate policy. If rates were adjusted 'appropriately' – that is, towards the objective of maintaining *external balance* instead of domestic macroeconomic targets – 'equilibrating' movements of short-term finance would be attracted to cover the external imbalance. Indeed such interest rate adjustments had formed the basis for the functioning of the pre-1931 gold standard. Keynes and White's explicit rejection of these orthodox policies – the 'rules of the game' of the gold standard – and their advocacy of capital controls were heresies which would prevent the restoration of what Keynes had called the 'old laissez-faire system'.

The bankers also held a different view from Keynes and White on the question of speculative, or 'abnormal', flows. They were not blind to the damage that such flows had caused in the interwar period to stable exchange rates and liberal trading relations. For the most part, they even agreed with Keynes and White that it would be necessary for many countries to control such flows to prevent damage in these areas.[53] Where they differed, however, was in stating that such controls should only be *temporary*, restricted to a transition period until the 'root' cause of the speculative flows could be eliminated. Although political instability and floating exchange rates were important causes, the principal 'root' cause was perceived to be the 'unorthodox' domestic economic policies introduced in the 1930s. Robert Warren, of the financial house Case Pomeroy and Co., for example, noted that 'hot money' was related to the 'distrust' of currencies. 'These currencies are distrusted', he explained, 'by reason of government deficits.'[54] Whereas Keynes and White sought to preserve and extend the ability of governments to pursue active national macroeconomic planning by controlling speculative flows, the bankers hoped to eliminate the flows through an all-out assault on these very policies.

Some of the bankers were also inclined to applaud the way speculative flows exerted a healthy discipline on governments attempting to pursue such 'unsound' policies. Winthrop Aldrich of Chase National Bank, for example, argued that a dollar free of all capital controls was needed to 'check domestic inflationary pressures' which might result from the government management of the national economy.[55] This positive role which the bankers ascribed to the financial markets of disciplining improper government policy was reflected in their broader opposition to the creation of international *public* institutions such as the International Monetary Fund (IMF) to govern international financial affairs. They were highly doubtful that an institution run by governments could effectively act as substitute for the efficiency and rationality of a market-oriented system. In the words of Benjamin Anderson, 'The more I see of government economic policy, the more I trust the automatic forces of free markets.'[56] The only international institution in which they had faith was the Bank for International Settlements (BIS) because it was run not by government bureaucrats but by 'pragmatic' central bankers.[57]

A final source of the bankers' opposition to capital controls was a concern about their compatibility with a 'free' form of government. Whereas Keynes and White had seen controls on the investment behaviour of a wealthy minority as an essential ingredient for democratic government, the bankers viewed such controls as overly 'coercive' and reminiscent of the 'Hitlerian monetary system'.[58] As Jacob Viner explained, to be effective, capital controls would require 'censorship of communication' and 'crushing penalties for violators' that 'quite frankly, rather frighten me'.[59] Another critic, quoted approvingly by J.H. Riddle of the Bankers' Trust Company of New York, noted: 'A perpetuation and legalization of control over capital movements is not compatible with any notion of a world that supposedly combats violence and dictatorial forms of governments.'[60]

If these were the sources of their disagreement, what practical alternatives did the New York financial community propose? As a final goal, they favoured a system in which there was complete freedom for financial movements.[61] In a transition period before internal and external stability had been achieved, however, they were prepared to accept that capital controls might be helpful in preventing speculative financial flows from disrupting trade and exchange rate stability. To minimize this transition period, they rallied around the 'key currency' plan advocated by John Williams of the Federal Reserve Bank of New York. Williams argued that the quickest way to create a stable world economy would be to rapidly restore convertibility to the world's two most important currencies, the dollar and sterling.[62] This was to be achieved by removing all controls on the dollar and by extending a loan to Britain to encourage the rapid restoration of sterling's convertibility. The scheme provided the New York bankers with an additional reason to oppose White's proposals concerning obligatory cooperative capital controls. If the USA was forced to adopt capital controls, it would be prevented from taking on this type of 'key currency' leadership role. As Winthrop Aldrich of Chase National Bank made clear, if the dollar was to provide 'a sure anchorage for the currencies of other nations', it would need to be freed of all controls 'including [those on] short or long-term capital movements'.[63]

Although White had not consulted the New York banking community in drafting his initial proposals in 1941 and 1942, three developments forced him to take their views more seriously.[64] The first was the success of the

Republican Party in the Congressional elections of autumn 1942. With many of the Republicans more sensitive to the bankers' opinions than their Democratic colleagues, White was forced to listen to the bankers' demands more seriously if any final deal stood a chance of getting through Congress.[65] The second was the outspoken opposition of Winthrop Aldrich. In contrast to other bankers who opposed the proposals, such as W. Randolph Burgess, Leon Fraser and Thomas Lamont, Aldrich had been an active supporter of the New Deal in its early years and he was widely seen by the Roosevelt Administration as one of the most enlightened of the Wall Street community. His statements thus carried considerable weight not only within the Administration but also with the public at large.[66] Third, White was forced after his initial drafts to discuss his plans in interdepartmental committees which included members of the Federal Reserve System and State Department who were generally more sympathetic to the bankers' position. The State Department, in particular, housed prominent liberal academic thinkers such as Viner and Herbert Feis and many figures from Wall Street such as James Forrestal and Dean Acheson.[67] Representatives of the State Department and Federal Reserve would also find representation in the US delegation at the final Bretton Woods conference.

The strong opposition to White's proposals from Aldrich and bankers within the Administration who had been active supporters of Roosevelt reflected the still unresolved nature of New Deal financial politics. To a large extent, the support from these bankers for the New Deal had been motivated by the simple desire to remove the House of Morgan from its prominent position in the New York financial community.[68] Once Roosevelt's domestic financial reforms of 1933–5 had achieved this, their support for other radical initiatives in the financial area was very tentative. While some, such as Forrestal and Acheson, remained affiliated with the Administration, others such as Aldrich increasingly distanced themselves from the government, denouncing its excessive public spending and inflationary tendencies.[69] As one Russian delegate at Bretton Woods noted, Aldrich and the other American bankers at the conference 'regarded Mr. Morgenthau and Mr. White as representatives of a "different world" since they were in favor of the active intervention of the state in financial policy'.[70]

Interestingly those industrialists who had also provided Roosevelt with crucial business support in the 1930s were much more sympathetic to the need for capital controls to protect national Keynesian planning.[71] The Department of Commerce, a stronghold of these figures, showed interest in the idea of joint capital controls in its postwar blueprint published in 1943.[72] Similarly the Council for Economic Development created in 1942 by several of these 'New Deal industrialists' was strongly supportive of Keynesian strategies as well as sensitive to the need for capital controls to preserve policy autonomy.[73] Finally the choice of Alvin Hansen – one of the most active proponents of the new Keynesianism – to author the postwar monetary plans for the business-dominated Council for Foreign Relations reflected the growing acceptance of more unorthodox policies in industrial circles. Indeed his proposals were entitled 'Exchange Control: Structures and Mechanisms' and were 'patterned after the advice Keynes offered the British Treasury'.[74] This division between industrialist and banker on the question of the desirability of capital controls was one paralleled in other countries.

The opposition of the New York bankers had two principal impacts on the evolution of the Bretton Woods proposals concerning financial movements. First, the bankers sought to limit countries' right to control capital movements by pressing for the Agreement to state prominently that one of its objectives would be to promote the international movement of 'productive' capital.[75] Reflecting this pressure, White's 1943 revised draft, for example, stated prominently that one of the Fund's purposes would be: 'To reduce the use of such foreign exchange restrictions, bilateral clearing arrangements, multiple currency devices, and discriminatory foreign exchange practices as hamper world trade and *the international flow of productive capital.*'[76] To the British, this new clause was very threatening. By outlining an explicit *obligation* to reduce barriers to the flow of productive capital, this clause might be used to limit their *right* to control financial movements, particularly with exchange controls.[77] It was not just Keynes who strongly opposed this clause: the Bank of England also made it clear in early 1944 that this phrase would be unacceptable and insisted that an explicit guarantee of the right to use exchange controls to control capital be included in the final agreement.[78] The Bank's position must have been particularly discouraging to the New York financiers who were hoping to revive their pre-1931 political alliance with bankers in the City of London as part of a return to a more liberal and orthodox world. Instead of being an ally, Bank of England officials, along with other private financiers in the City, were siding with the restrictive proposals of Keynes and White. One reason for the Bank of England's stance was that, as chief administrator of Britain's exchange controls, it was aware of the extreme vulnerability of Britain's payments position. Equally important, however, was the fact that, in the wake of the 1931 crisis, the Bank had quietly reformulated its role to act as a leader of a protectionist sterling area.[79] This policy, begun immediately after the crisis, had been dramatically accelerated during the war when the loose arrangements of the sterling area were transformed into the more formal sterling bloc. By 1944–5, the Bank was proposing the consolidation and extension of this sterling bloc as a more effective way than the Bretton Woods proposals to preserve the international role of sterling and the City of London.[80]

Despite pressure from the New York bankers, the British successfully resisted any dilution of their right to control capital movements with exchange controls. In the Joint Statement by the British and US delegations in April 1944, the objectionable phrase relating to the need to promote 'productive' capital flows was eliminated. Moreover, in the final Agreement, Article 6-3 explicitly granted countries the right to use exchange controls to curtail financial movements: 'Members may exercise such controls as are necessary to regulate international capital movements.'[81] At the same time, the Article continued: 'but no member may exercise these controls in a manner which will restrict payments for current transactions or which will unduly delay transfers of funds in settlement of commitments'. After the Bretton Woods conference, it was argued by some (notably the Federal Reserve and State Department) that this wording – in addition to that of Article 8-2a which prohibited the imposition of 'restrictions on the making of payments and transfers for current international transactions' – had removed the right to institute a system of exchange controls as a way of controlling such financial transactions.[82]

Those involved in drafting the sections, however, had been explicit that this was not the correct interpretation. Instead, what had been introduced was a distinction between 'restrictions' on current account transactions which were *not* allowed and 'exchange controls' on current transactions which *were* allowed. It was clear that the latter could be used to search for capital movements as long as they did not 'restrict' current account payments. White had explicitly clarified this point under questioning during the conference before the clause had been approved.[83] Indeed, archival documents make it clear that the US bankers had failed to convince the US delegation at the Atlantic City conference before Bretton Woods to curtail the right to use exchange controls to make capital controls effective.[84]

The second proposal that the bankers tried to influence was more vulnerable. While they were unable to dilute the right to use exchange controls to control capital movements, they had more success in combating the proposal for obligatory cooperative controls. To the bankers, this proposal was particularly offensive since it might force the USA to adopt capital controls.[85] Their success in diluting it was first visible in White's 1943 draft, where cooperation in enforcing foreign government controls became required *only* when the IMF recommended it. Moreover governments were no longer required to hand over 'all property in form of deposits, investments, securities' of the nationals of a requesting country but only 'information' concerning this property.[86] By the time of the April 1944 Joint Statement, almost all mention of obligations to cooperate in controlling undesirable flows had been removed.

At the Atlantic City and Bretton Woods conferences there was considerable pressure from both the British and the Polish delegations to reinstate a provision concerning obligatory joint controls. The US delegation, however, strongly opposed these initiatives.[87] Not only were they fearful of 'having to bring before Congress a special law such as would be required to make black markets illegal', but also the bankers on the US delegation, such as Edward Brown, strongly opposed the proposals.[88] In the end, a compromise was reached. The final Agreement stated clearly that states were *permitted* to cooperate in controlling capital movements (Article 8-2b). They had, however, only two *obligations*. First, states were required on request to provide the IMF with information on financial movements and holdings (Article 8-5a). They were, however, under no obligation to do so to the extent that such information would disclose the affairs of individuals or companies.[89] Second, all members had to ensure that all exchange contracts contravening other members' exchange control regulations be made 'unenforceable' in their territory (Article 8-2b). This second provision, while appearing impressive, implied only a very weak notion of cooperation as the annotations of leading delegates at Bretton Woods made clear: 'This does not mean that one country owes any duty to police or enforce the exchange control regulations of another country.' Rather, it meant only that, 'if suit is brought within the courts of one country involving a contract which violated the exchange control regulations of another country, the courts of the former will not enforce the contract'.[90] As Joseph Gold, the IMF's long-time legal counsel, notes: 'The United States had seen the provision as one that...would protect it from any proposal that should introduce capital controls in the interests of other members.'[91]

Although the notion of cooperation had thus been preserved in the final Agreement, the USA had in effect extracted itself from explicit obligations to introduce capital controls. The US position was brought home effectively at the final press conference of the Bretton Woods meetings. Just as Keynes had finished announcing that the agreement 'provides that capital movements must be controlled, and indeed that is an essential condition', White interrupted to state that countries who wished to use capital controls were permitted to do so, but that 'the United States does not wish to have them'.[92] Moreover, just to be certain, the US delegation also succeeded at the Atlantic City conference in changing a clause which had allowed the IMF as late as the 1944 Joint Statement to 'require' the imposition of capital controls if its resources were being drained by a member for the purpose of financing a deficit stemming from speculative capital movements. Keynes and White had granted the IMF this power to ensure that its resources would be used only for the purpose of financing deficits on the current account or those stemming from productive capital movements.[93] Under US pressure, the

IMF's power was reduced to the extent that it could only now 'request' controls to prevent such use, with refusal to cooperate penalized by the member being declared ineligible to use the resources of the Fund (Article 6-1a). In the words of the US technical group at the conference, this change was made because 'the US does not want to be forced to control an export of capital'.[94]

In sum, despite opposition from the New York bankers, the final Bretton Woods documents retained the basic structure outlined by Keynes and White in their early drafts. Far from being a liberal document in the financial field, the Agreement embodied a restrictive approach to financial movements. To be sure, productive, equilibrating flows of capital were to be promoted by the activities of the World Bank and by the fact that IMF resources could be used to finance deficits connected with 'capital transactions of reasonable amount required for the expansion of exports or in the ordinary course of trade, banking or other business' (Article 6-1b(i)). The overriding 'norm', however, was that of controlling capital movements. States were given the explicit right to control *all* capital movements. Capital controls were also encouraged by the fact that IMF funds could not be used to finance a 'large or sustained outflow of capital' and by the way the Fund was empowered to 'request' (although not 'require') a member to implement controls to prevent such use of the Fund (Article 6-1a). Perhaps most significantly, however, the two mechanisms outlined by Keynes and White as necessary to make capital controls effective found their way into the final Agreement. States were permitted to use exchange controls to search for illicit financial movements and the Agreement endorsed the use of cooperative control mechanisms, although opposition from the New York bankers had prevented the most effective forms of cooperation from being required.

IV Conclusion

The Bretton Woods Agreement did not set the scene for the globalization of financial markets in recent years. While in the trade and exchange rate arenas the authors of the Bretton Woods Agreement turned their back on the unorthodox policies of the 1930s, in finance they built a multilateral order in which the capital controls and financial interventionism of 1930s might be consolidated. As we have seen, there were two sources of the restrictive financial provisions in the Bretton Woods Agreement. First, the upheavals of the 1930s and wartime gave political prominence to 'embedded liberals' who wanted to defend the policy autonomy of the new welfare state from international financial market pressures. At the same time, the alliance between bankers in New York and London which had dominated financial politics in the 1920s was left fractured and weakened. Second, there was a shared belief among bankers and 'embedded liberals' alike that a liberal financial system would not be compatible, at least in the short-term, with a stable system of exchange rates and a liberal trading system.[95] Seeing a liberal financial system as a less important feature of a liberal international economic order, they chose to sacrifice it in favour of preserving fixed exchange rates and a liberal trading order.

The move towards an open and liberal international financial order in recent years has marked the breakdown of this Bretton Woods order. To begin with, speculative and disequilibrating flows of capital have severely compromised the policy autonomy of the welfare state in the three ways that Keynes and White outlined. First, independent macroeconomic policy has been rendered very difficult. Not only is monetary policy disrupted by large movements of funds, but also capital flight has severely constrained governments, such as that in France during 1981–3, from pursuing a unilateral expansionary fiscal policy. Moreover independent tax policy has been made much more difficult. As Dornbusch puts it: 'Most international capital flows today involve tax sheltering or tax evasion rather than socially productive resource transfers.'[96] Second, the domestic financial regulatory structures that were central to postwar industrial and macroeconomic planning in many states have been rapidly eroded in recent years as domestic savers and borrowers have gained access to the offshore Euromarkets or the rapidly deregulating American and British financial systems. Finally the enormous volumes of short-term capital in the international financial markets have come to act as a strong disciplinary force on left-of-centre governments around the world.[97]

Speculative and disequilibrating financial movements have also severely disrupted the Bretton Woods international monetary and trading order in the way that many had feared in 1944. The collapse of the Bretton Woods fixed exchange rate system in the early 1970s at least partly reflected the increasing inability of states to counteract the rapidly escalating volume of speculative international financial movements in this period. Large and rapid financial movements in the 1970s and 1980s have also disrupted the international trading system. This was most dramatic after 1982 when enormous financial inflows pushed up the US dollar and led to, as Emminger puts it, 'distortions in foreign trade competition and protectionist tendencies'.[98] Echoing discussions at Bretton Woods, many have been left asking in the 1980s 'whether free trade is antithetical to capital liberalization'.[99] In the words of one Bank of England official: 'We have freed the capital side of the balance of payments at the expense of doing the opposite on the current account.'[100]

The history of the breakdown of the restrictive Bretton Woods international financial order has received much less attention than the breakdown of the Bretton Woods fixed exchange rate system or the erosion of the postwar international trading order. Although this is not the place to explain it, three points can be noted in the light of the discussion outlined in this chapter.[101] First, it has been greatly facilitated by the rebuilding of the alliance between bankers in New York and London after the latter turned away from a closed sterling bloc in the 1950s. This alliance was instrumental in creating the Euromarkets in the 1960s and encouraging financial liberalization in the 1970s and 1980s. Second, the breakdown has also been encouraged by an ideological shift away from Keynes and White's financial 'embedded liberalism' towards a more orthodox 'neo-liberal' position of the kind outlined by the New York bankers at Bretton Woods. The abolition of capital controls has increasingly been seen as necessary to promote efficient financial intermediation domestically and internationally, as well as to 'remove what is a substantial restriction on, and could become a threat to, individual liberty'.[102] Moreover capital movements have come to be seen as correctly 'disciplining' countries 'to impose sound monetary and fiscal policies as well as choose regulatory and tax policies that encourage business success'.[103] This ideological change grew out of the economic uncertainties of the 1970s and early 1980s and was promoted especially strongly by financial interests. Also significant, however, was support from large industrial corporations who became increasingly frustrated with capital control regimes as their interests became increasingly global in the 1970s and 1980s.

Finally the breakdown of the Bretton Woods financial order was also partly the result of difficulties states had in effectively controlling financial movements along the two lines outlined by Keynes and White. Exchange controls, for example, became increasingly ineffective in controlling illegal financial movements as technology advanced and economic interdependence grew in the postwar period. In this context, only very draconian measures could make controls effective, measures that states were unwilling to consider. The other mechanism for controlling finance proposed at Bretton Woods was that of cooperative controls. Although various initiatives were proposed up to the 1970s and 1980s for such cooperative action to stem the globalization of finance, each was scuttled by states who wished to preserve a regulation-free environment in order to attract international financial business to their territory. In this sense, collective action problems prevented the preservation of a *closed* financial system rather than an open one, as is the case in the trade sector.[104]

Although less attention has been paid to it, the breakdown of the Bretton Woods international financial order has been an equally, if not more, important upheaval in the global political economy than the breakdown of the Bretton Woods fixed exchange rate system or the erosion of the postwar international trading order. In the late 20th century, international private financiers have come to exert the kind of key influence within the international system that governments at Bretton Woods had sought to prevent. In the words of Tom Wolfe's famous Wall Street character in *Bonfire of the Vanities*, the bankers feel themselves to have become 'masters of the universe' rather than the 'servants' of Keynes and White's early plans.[105]

Notes

This chapter is based upon material from the author's forthcoming book, *The Reemergence of Global Finance* (Cornell University Press). Financial support for the research for this project was provided by the Social Sciences and Humanities Research Council of Canada. Helpful comments were received from Jennifer Clapp, Robert Denemark and Lou Pauly.

1. For an excellent overview, see Goodman and Pauly (1990).
2. Quotation from Gardner (1980, p. 76).
3. Bryant (1987, p. 152).
4. The classic historical texts on the Bretton Woods negotiations (eg. Van Dormael, 1978; Block, 1977; Gardner, 1980; Eckes, 1975) refer only sparingly to the discussions concerning international private finance. Somewhat more detailed, though still limited, discussions can be found in De Cecco (1979) and Gold (1977).
5. See, for example, Costigliola (1984), Hogan (1977), Leffler (1979), McNeil (1986), Maier (1975), Silverman (1982).
6. Costigiola (1972).
7. Quoted in Kunz (1987, p. 71). In addition to previous references, see Kindleberger (1973), Clarke (1967) for accounts of the crisis.
8. Hirsch and Oppenheimer (1976, p. 643). See also Kunz (1987), Aronson (1977, p. 41) for the structural break.
9. Feis (1964 [1930]), Viner (1951), Leffler (1979, pp. 122, 174–7), Einzig (1970, p. 286).
10. For Germany, see Child (1958). For Japan, see Dowd (1953).
11. Quoted in Hathaway (1984, p. 284). See Hyman (1976) on Eccles's pre-Keynes Keynesian views.
12. Williams (1939, pp. 18–20).
13. The volume of these inflows was enormous, with the Treasury estimating that during 1935–7, as much as $100 million was entering New York per month (Warren, 1937, p. 339). See also Bloomfield (1950) on European capital flight to the USA in the 1930s.
14. Bloomfield (1950, pp. 182, 186–8, 195), Williams (1939, pp. 20–21), Nurkse (1944, p. 165 fn. 1). Kindleberger (1987, p. 24) also mentions discussions in the Federal Reserve in 1938 on this issue.
15. Williams (1939, pp. 20–21).
16. Kindleberger (1943, p. 348), Bloomfield (1950, pp. 187–8).
17. Quoted in Van Dormael (1978, p. 52).
18. Quoted in Gardner (1980, p. 76).
19. Quoted from Eckes (1975, p. 152), Gardner (1980, p. 76).
20. Quotation from the American journalist I.F. Stone, Eckes (1975, p. 152).
21. White, quoted in Kees (1973, p. 79). He had become a convert of Keynesianism by 1937 (Kees, 1973, pp. 64–5).
22. See, for example, Kunz (1987, pp. 6, 189).
23. Cairncross and Eichengreen (1983, p. 22).
24. Ham (1981, chs. 4–5).
25. Keynes (1933, p. 758). See also his recommendations to the 1931 Macmillan Committee (Moggridge, 1986, p. 58).
26. Quotes from Horsefield (1969, p. 13), Van Dormael (1978, p. 7). See also Van Dormael (1978, pp. 6–7, 33), Pressnel (1986, p. 18).
27. Horsefield (1969, pp. 67, 66).
28. Quotes from Horsefield (1969, p. 32). In earlier drafts, White had also been concerned with the 'reserve position of the capital losing country' (Horsefield, 1969, p. 49). See also Keynes (1980b, pp. 16–17), Van Dormael (1978, p. 8).

29. This distinction between 'abnormal' and 'normal' movements was one frequently made at the time (Fanno, 1939; Bloomfield, 1950, pp. 33–5), although Keynes did not use the actual terms in his Bretton Woods plans.
30. Keynes (1980a, p. 149); see also pp. 212, 275–6.
31. Keynes (1980b, p. 17).
32. Horsefield (1969, pp. 31, 67).
33. Keynes (1980a, p. 149); see also p. 31.
34. Horsefield (1969, p. 67).
35. Ibid, p. 67.
36. Keynes (1930, p. 335).
37 Quotes from Van Dormael (1978, pp. 33, 10). See also White's concern with 'the rapidity with which the mechanism of adjustment in the balance of payments is operating' (Horsefield, 1969, p. 49).
38. Flanders (1989, pp. 230–31).
39. Nurkse (1944). See also Ohlin (1936, p. 82), Henderson (1936, p. 168), Robinson (1944, p. 436). See also the initiative by Morgenthau to encourage Blum to implement capital controls to prevent capital flight from forcing a devaluation of the franc in 1936 (Brown, 1987, p. 74).
40. Quoted in Robinson (1944, pp. 434–5). See also Bloomfield (1950, p. 182).
41. In White's words: 'The desirability of encouraging the flow of productive capital to areas where it can be most profitably employed needs no emphasis' (Horsefield, 1969, p. 46).
42. Horsefield (1969, p. 32, 11, 13).
43. Keynes, quoted in ibid., pp. 13, 32. For White, see ibid. pp. 176, 49–50.
44. Ibid. pp. 32, 46, 139, 176.
45. For a discussion of 'embedded liberalism', see Ruggie (1982).
46. Harrod (1969, p. 566; 1972, p. 8), for example, explains Keynes's lack of enthusiasm for encouraging 'productive' capital flows partially on this basis.
47. Ohlin (1936, p. 90). In his published PhD dissertation concerning the French balance of payments, White had also emerged sceptical of the classical liberal arguments applied to finance: 'The French experience in the matter of capital exports leads to the conclusion that the orthodox attitude toward unrestricted capital exports is open to criticism; the assumption that the capital exports benefit both the country and the world at large is not unassailable' (White, 1933, p. 301). See also Horsefield (1969, p. 67). Even Aldrich (1943, p. 16), one of the key New York bankers supporting a liberal financial order, argued that international investment was not vital to global economic prosperity because 'capital accumulation…is largely a product of domestic policy'.
48. Horsefield (1969, p. 13) (emphasis in original). White also endorsed the use of exchange controls to control financial movements (Horsefield, 1969, p. 63).
49. Ibid., p. 66. See also Nurkse's influential views at the time (1944, pp. 188–9).
50. Horsefield (1969, p. 13).
51. Ibid., p. 44. For Keynes's recommendation, see ibid., pp. 13,29,31–2.
52. De Cecco (1976, pp. 382–3;1979, p. 52), Enkyo (1989, p. 49).
53. See, for example, Brown (1944, p. 205), Riddle (1943, p. 32), Williams (1949, pp. 96–7;1943, p. 6).
54. Warren (1937, pp. 339–40); see also pp. 342–3 and Lutz (1943, p. 19), Riddle (1943, pp. 30–31)., advisor to Bankers Trust Co. of New York, Conolly (1936, pp. 367–8) of the BIS.
55. Johnson (1968, p. 282); see also Block (1977, p. 53).
56. Anderson (1943, p. 15).
57. American Bankers Association (1943, p. 13), Fraser (1943) and Riddle (1943), for example, all recommended basing international monetary cooperation around the BIS instead of the IMF. Chicago banker Edward Brown also strongly opposed the resolution to abolish the BIS at Bretton Woods (Van Dormael, 1978, p. 204).
58. Anderson (1943, p. 13).
59. Viner (1943, p. 103).

60. De Vegh (1943, p. 539) and quoted approvingly by Riddle (1943).
61. See, for example, *Wall Street Journal* editorial on 1 July 1944 (Eckes, 1975, p. 166), Riddle (1943) and Edward Brown (1944, p. 205) of Chicago banking community.
62. Williams (1936, 1943). Interestingly Williams himself did not share the bankers' opposition to Keynes and White's capital controls provisions. Not only did he favour the use of tight controls during the transition period, but he also supported the provision in Keynes and White's proposals that *permanent* capital controls would be needed in the postwar world. In his opinion, this 'modification' to the gold standard was necessary not only to prevent speculative flows from disrupting stable exchange rates, but also, as with Keynes and White, to preserve states' policy autonomy. Unlike the other bankers, he had become an advocate of active fiscal and monetary policy and he worried that 'national business cycles' could be disturbed by panic flights of capital as well as by capital movements which caused a 'spreading of booms and depressions, or of a boom in one country feeding upon deflation elsewhere' (Williams, 1944, p. 45).
63. Aldrich (1943, p. 11); see also Aldrich (1944, pp. 25–6).
64. By 1943, he was making a point of meeting intermittently with the bankers (Eckes, 1975, pp. 298 fn.29). See also Pressnel (1986, p. 21), Robbins (1971, p. 199), Howson and Moggridge (1990, p. 84).
65. Eckes (1975, p. 74), de Cecco (1979, p. 51), Robbins (1971, p. 199).
66. Johnson (1968, pp. 194–6, 212).
67. Acheson chaired the State Department's subcommittee on postwar monetary planning (Oliver, 1971, p. 15). He strongly opposed the US Treasury's support of the resolution to abolish the BIS (Howson and Moggridge, 1990, p. 190). For Herbert Feis's annoyance with the US Treasury international monetary proposals, see Howson and Moggridge (1990, p. 63). For Viner's views, see Viner (1926; 1943, p. 103), Oliver (1971, p. 18). As Viner (1947) put it later, 'The nineteenth century international flow of capital...was one of the many great blessings which cupidity has procured for mankind.'
68. See especially Ferguson (1984).
69. Aldrich resigned from the government-sponsored Business Advisory Council in 1935 (McQuaid, 1976, p. 179). See Aldrich speeches in Johnson (1968, p. 190–91, 210–11, 222).
70. Quoted in Johnson (1968, p. 292).
71. See Collins (1978) for general discussion of emergence of this group of industrialists.
72. Robinson (1944, p. 434).
73. See McQuaid (1982, p. 117) and Salant (1989, p. 46) on strong support for Keynesianism. See CED-sponsored research project by Duke economist Calvin Hoover (1945, pp. 26–8, 32, 42, 56–7fn.1) and official CED report (CED, 1945, pp. 7,20) on sympathetic approach to capital controls.
74. Quote from Schulzinger (1984, p. 68). See Hansen's (1946, pp. 38, 134–5) advocacy of regulation of international lending.
75. Both Secretary of State Hull and the ABA had pressed White strongly for measures to promote flows of 'productive' capital (as had Jacob Viner for the Council on Foreign Relations). See, for example, Hull's memo (NA, RG 56 'Records of the Assistant Secretary – Chronological Files of H.D. White', 29 June 1943) and the ABA resolution at its 5 September 1943 conference (NA, RG 82 'Records of Federal Reserve System' – 001.501–ABA 1939–46).
76. Horsefield (1969, p. 86) (emphasis added).
77. Kahn (1976, p. 18), Gold (1977, p. 13).
78. Pressnel (1986, pp. 140, 148–9), Van Dormael (1978, p. 114). Other important Labour figures such as Bevin also announced their refusal to consider any dilution of the right to control capital movements (Pressnel, 1986, p. 130).
79. Pressnel (1986, pp. 69, 72, 74, 142, 148); Strange (1971).
80. Pressnel (1986, pp. 72, 96–7, 141, 148); Van Dormael (1978, pp. 131–2).
81. Horsefield (1969, p. 194). This was first introduced at the Atlantic City conference, NA, RG 56 'Bretton Woods, Atlantic City', Document f-1, no.172.
82. Horsefield (1969, p. 195); Van Dormael (1978, pp. 229–39).

83. Department of State (1948, pp. 314, 598). This meaning was also clarified at the Atlantic City conference; see NA, RG 56, 'Bretton Woods, Atlantic City – Meeting of Subcommittee Two of Preliminary Agreement Committee, June 23, 1944'. See also Gold (1977, pp. 5, 14), Rasminsky (1972).
84. See debate within US delegation on this question at Atlantic City conference in NA, RG 56, 'Bretton Woods, Atlantic City – Meeting of American Technical Group, June 17, 1944 – Attachment D'.
85. See Aldrich (1943, 1944) and American Bankers Association (1943, p. 16).
86. Horsefield (1969, p. 96).
87. For Polish and UK proposals, see Department of State (1948, pp. 230, 334, 437); NA, RG 56, 'Bretton Woods, Atlantic City – Minutes of the Meeting, June 28, 1944'. Inexplicably, at one point in the negotiations, the USA did propose a draft with a clause requiring cooperation (Department of State, 1948, pp. 502, 542, 576), but the clause never reappeared.
88. Quote from Keynes (1980b, p. 138). For Brown's opposition, see Brown (1944, p. 205) and NA, RG 56, 'Bretton Woods, Atlantic City – Minutes of Meetings June 28, 1944; Meeting of the Financial Agenda Committee June 29, 1944'.
89. Horsefield (1969, pp. 196–7); Bloomfield (1946, p. 706fn.33).
90. Quoted in Gold (1986, p. 792fn.2).
91. Gold (1977, pp. 15–16). A good summary of the history of the drafting of Article 8–2b can be found in Gold (1982, pp. 429–38).
92. Van Dormael (1978, p. 185). Similarly Morgenthau announced to the Atlantic City conference, 'It is our intention…to restore the free movement of capital to and from the US', NA, RG 56, 'Bretton Woods, Atlantic City – Speeches Prepared for the Secretary'.
93. See Horsefield (1969, pp. 23, 49–50, 89–90, 133–4).
94. NA, RG 56, 'Bretton Woods, Atlantic City – Meeting of American Technical Group June 17, 1944'. Keynes had tried to convince US officials that the USA could be subject to considerable capital flight immediately after the war if it fell into depression (Bernstein, 1984, p. 15).
95. Although the New York bankers argued that such inconsistencies between the constituent parts of the liberal international economic order would be ironed out once economic and political stability could be restored, this would prove to be far from the case. As Henderson (1936, p. 166) effectively argued in 1936, the growth of speculative financial flows in the interwar period had not been related solely to such uncertainties. Also significant had been the growth of international securities transactions which would if anything increase in volume when a more stable monetary and economic order was restored.
96. Dornbusch (1986, p. 224).
97. For a recent discussion of these various effects of global financial mobility, see McKenzie and Lee (1991).
98. Emminger (1985, pp. 57–8) (translation).
99. Levich (1988, p. 218).
100. Quoted in Hamilton (1986, p. 237). See also Gilpin (1987, p. 367), Hamada and Patrick (1988, p. 130), McMahon (1985, p. 180), Wojnilower (1986).
101. For a history, see Helleiner (1991).
102. Quotation comes from a 1979 pamphlet of the British neo-liberal Institute for Economic Affairs advocating the abolition of capital controls to the new Thatcher government: Miller and Wood (1979, p. 68).
103. Quote from Nigel Lawson, British Chancellor of the Exchequer in the late 1980s, in *Financial Times*, 7 November 1988.
104. Helleiner (1992).
105. Wolfe (1987).

References

NA= US National Archives (NA), Washington, DC
  Record Group 56, General Records of the Dept. of Treasury
    Bretton Woods, Atlantic City Conference
    Records of the NAC
    Records of the Assistant Secretary (H.D. White)
  Record Group 82, Records of the Federal Reserve System

Aldrich, W. (1943), 'The Problems of Postwar Monetary Stabilization', Address to the American Section of the International Chamber of Commerce (April).
Aldrich, W. (1944), *Some Aspects of American Foreign Economic Policy* (September).
American Bankers Association (ABA) (1943), *The Place of the US in the Postwar Economy*, New York: American Bankers Association.
Anderson, B. (1943), *Postwar Stabilization of Foreign Exchange: The Keynes–Morgenthau Plan Condemned*, New York: Economists' National Committee on Monetary Policy.
Aronson, J. (1977), *Money and Power: Banks and the World Monetary System*, London: Sage Publications.
Bernstein, E. (1984), 'Reflections on Bretton Woods', in *The International Monetary System; Forty Years After Bretton Woods*, Boston: Federal Reserve Bank of Boston, Conference Series no.28.
Block, F. (1977), *The Origins of International Economic Disorder: A Study of the US International Monetary Policy from World War Two to the Present*, Berkeley: University of California Press.
Bloomfield, A. (1946), 'The Postwar Control of International Capital Movements', *American Economic Review*, **36**, 687–709.
Bloomfield, A. (1950), *Capital Imports and The American Balance of Payments 1934–39: A Study in Abnormal Capital Transfers*, Chicago: University of Chicago Press.
Brown, B. (1987), *The Flight of International Capital: A Contemporary History*, London: Croom Helm.
Brown, E. (1944), 'The IMF: A Consideration of Certain Objections', *Journal of Business of the University of Chicago*, **17**,(4), 199–208.
Bryant, R. (1987), *International Financial Intermediation*, Washington, DC: Brookings Institution.
Cairncross, A. and B. Eichengreen (1983), *Sterling in Decline: The Devaluations of 1931, 1947, 1967*, Oxford: Basil Blackwell.
Child, F. (1958), *The Theory and Practice of Exchange Control in Germany: A Study of Monopolitic Exploitation in International Markets*, The Hague: Martinus Nijhoff.
Clarke, S. (1967), *Central Bank Cooperation 1924–31*, New York: Federal Reserve Bank of New York.
Collins, R. (1978), 'Positive Business Response to the New Deal: The Roots of the Committee for Economic Development 1933–42', *Business History Review*, **52**,(3), 369–91.
Committee for Economic Development (CED) (1945), *International Trade, Foreign Investment and Domestic Employment*, New York: CED.
Conolly, F. (1936), 'Memorandum on the International Short Term Indebtedness', in *The Improvement of Commercial Relations Between Nations: The Problems of Monetary Stabilization*, Paris: International Chamber of Commerce.
Costigliola, F. (1972), 'The Other Side of Isolationism: The Establishment of the First World Bank 1929–30', *Journal of American History*, **59**, 602–20.
Costigliola, F. (1984), *Awkward Dominion: American Political, Economic and Cultural Relations with Europe 1919–33*, Ithaca: Cornell University Press.
Crotty, J. (1983), 'On Keynes and Capital Flight', *Journal of Economic Literature*, **21**, 59–65.
De Cecco, M. (1976), 'International Financial Markets and US Domestic Policy Since 1945', *International Affairs*, **52**,(3), 381–99.
De Cecco, M. (1979), 'Origins of the Postwar Payments System', *Cambridge Journal of Economics*, **3**, 49–61.

De Vegh, I. (1943), 'International Clearing Union', *American Economic Review*, **33**, 534–56.

Department of State, US Government (1948), *Proceedings and Documents of the UN Monetary and Financial Conference*, Washington: US Government.

Dornbusch, R. (1986), 'Flexible Exchange Rates and Excess Capital Mobility', *Brookings Papers on Economic Activity*, **1**, 209–15.

Dowd, L. (1953), 'Japanese Foreign Exchange Policy 1930–40', PhD dissertation, University of Michigan.

Eckes, A. (1975), *A Search for Solvency: Bretton Woods and the International Monetary System 1941–71*, Austin and London: University of Texas Press.

Einzig, P. (1970), *The History of Foreign Exchange*, 2nd edn, London: Macmillan.

Emminger, O. (1985), 'International Capital Transactions – Pacemaker or Disruptive Factor in the World Economy' in W. Engels, A. Gutowski and H. Wallich (eds), *International Capital Movements, Debt and the Monetary System*, Mainz: Hase and Koehler.

Enkyo, S. (1989), 'Financial Innovation and International Safeguards: Causes and Consequences of "Structural Innovation" in the US and Global Financial System: 1973–86', PhD dissertation, London School of Economics.

Fanno, M. (1939), *Normal and Abnormal International Capital Transfers*, Minneapolis: University of Minnesota Press.

Feis, H. (1964 [1930]), *Europe: The World's Banker 1870–1914*, New York: Augustus Kelley.

Ferguson, T. (1984), 'From Normalcy to New Deal: Industrial Structure, Party Competition and American Public Policy in the Great Depression', *International Organization*, **38**, 41–94.

Flanders, M.J. (1989), *International Monetary Economics 1870–1960*, Cambridge: Cambridge University Press.

Fraser, L. (1943), 'Reconstructing the World's Money', *New York Herald Tribune*, 21 November, Section 7, p. 12.

Gardner, R. (1980), *Sterling–Dollar Diplomacy in Current Perspective: The Origins and the Prospects of Our International Economic Order*, New York: Columbia University Press.

Gilpin, R. (1987), *The Political Economy of International Relations*, Princeton: Princeton University Press.

Gold, J. (1977), *International Capital Movements Under the Law of the IMF*, Washington: IMF, Pamphlet Series no.21.

Gold, J. (1982), *The Fund Agreement in the Courts, Vol.2*, Washington: International Monetary Fund.

Gold, J. (1986), *The Fund Agreement in the Courts, Vol.3*, Washington: International Monetary Fund.

Goodman, J. and L. Pauly (1990), 'The New Politics of Global International Capital Mobility', Working Paper no.29, International Business and Trade Law Program, University of Toronto Faculty of Law.

Ham, A. (1981), *Treasury Rules: Recurrent Themes in British Economic Policy*, London: Quartet Books.

Hamada, K. and H. Patrick (1988), 'Japan and the International Monetary Regime' in T. Inoguchi and D. Okimoto (eds), *The Political Economy of Japan, Vol.2: The Changing International Context*, Stanford: Stanford University Press.

Hamilton, A. (1986), *The Financial Revolution*, New York: Free Press.

Hansen, A. (1946), *America's Role in the World Economy*, New York: Penguin Books.

Harrod, R. (1969), *The Life of John Maynard Keynes*, New York: Augustus Kelley.

Harrod, R. (1972), 'Problems Perceived in the International Financial System' in A. Acheson (ed.), *Bretton Woods Revisited*, Toronto: University of Toronto Press.

Hathaway, R. (1984), 'Economic Diplomacy in a Time of Crisis 1933–45,' in W. Becker and S. Wells (eds), *Economics and World Power: An Assessment of American Diplomacy Since 1789*, New York: Columbia University Press.

Helleiner, E. (1991), 'American Hegemony and Global Economic Structure: from closed to open financial relations in the postwar world', PhD dissertation, London School of Economics.

Helleiner, E. (1992), 'States and the Future of Global Finance', *Review of International Studies*, **18**, 31–49.

Henderson, H. (1936), 'Memorandum on New Technical Arrangements for Postponing Stabilization' in *The Improvement of Commercial Relations Between Nations: The Problems of Monetary Stabilization*, Paris: International Chamber of Commerce.

Hirsch, F. and P. Oppenheimer (1976), 'The Trial of Managed Money: Currency, Credit, and Prices 1920–70', in C. Cipolla (ed.), *Fontana Economic History of Europe: The Twentieth Century: Part 2*, London: Fontana.

Hogan, M. (1977), *Informal Entente: The Private Structure of Cooperation in Anglo-American Economic Diplomacy*, Columbia, Mo.: University of Missouri.

Hoover, C. (1945), *International Trade and Domestic Employment*, New York: McGraw-Hill Book Co.

Horsefield, J.K. (1969), *International Monetary Fund 1945–65*, vol.3, Washington: International Monetary Fund.

Howson, S. and D. Moggridge (1990), *The Wartime Diaries of Lionnel Robbins and James Meade 1943–5*, London: Macmillan

Hyman, S. (1976), *Marriner S. Eccles*, Stanford: Graduate School of Business, Stanford University.

Johnson, A. (1968), *Winthrop W. Aldrich: Lawyer, Banker, Diplomat*, Boston: Harvard Graduate School of Business Administration, Harvard University.

Kahn, R. (1976), 'Historical Origins of the International Monetary Fund', in A. Thirwall (ed.), *Keynes and International Monetary Relations*, London: Macmillan.

Kees, D. (1973), *Harry Dexter White: A Study in Contrast*, New York: Coward, McCann and Geghegan.

Keynes, J.M. (1930), *A Treatise on Money*, London: Macmillan.

Keynes, J.M. (1933), 'National Self-Sufficiency', *Yale Review*, **22**, 755–69.

Keynes, J.M. (1980a), *The Collected Writings of J.M. Keynes: Vol.25 – Activities 1940–44: Shaping the Postwar World, The Clearing Union*, ed. by D. Moggridge, London: Cambridge University Press.

Keynes, J.M. (1980b), *The Collected Writings of J.M. Keynes: Vol.26 – Activities 1941–46: Shaping the Postwar World, Bretton Woods*, ed. by D. Moggridge, London: Cambridge University Press.

Kindleberger, C. (1943), 'Planning for Foreign Investment', *American Economic Review*, **33**, 347–54.

Kindleberger, C. (1973), *The World in Depression, 1929–39*, Berkeley: University of California Press.

Kindleberger, C. (1987), 'A Historical Perspective', in D. Lessard and J. Williamson (eds), *Capital Flight and Third World Debt*, Washington: Institute for International Economics.

Kunz, D. (1987), *The Battle for Britain's Gold Standard in 1931*, London: Croom Helm.

Leffler, M. (1979), *The Elusive Quest: America's Pursuit of European Stability and French Security, 1919–33*, Chapel Hill: University of North Carolina Press.

Levich, R. (1988), 'Financial Innovations in International Financial Markets', in M. Feldstein (ed.), *The US in the World Economy*, Chicago: University of Chicago Press.

Lutz, F. (1943), *The Keynes and White Proposals*, Princeton: Princeton University Press.

Maier, C. (1975), *Recasting Bourgeois Europe*, Princeton: Princeton University Press.

McKenzie, R. and D. Lee (1991), *Quicksilver Capital: How the Rapid Movement of Wealth Has Changed the World*, New York: Free Press.

McMahon, C. (1985), 'The Global Financial Structure in Transition: Consequences for International Finance and Trade', in J. McClellan (ed.), *Global Financial Structure in Transition*, Lexington: Lexington Press.

McNeil, W. (1986), *American Money and the Weimar Republic*, New York: Columbia University Press.

McQuaid, K. (1976), 'The Business Advisory Council of the Department of Commerce 1933–61: A Study of Corporate/Government Relations', in P. Uselding (ed.), *Research in Economic History, Vol.1*, Greenwich: JAI Press.

McQuaid, K. (1982), *Big Business and Presidential Power: From Roosevelt to Reagan*, New York: William Morrow and Co.

Miller, R. and Wood, J. (1979), *Exchange Control For Ever?*, London: Institute for Economic Affairs.

Moggridge, D. (1986), 'Keynes and the International Monetary System 1906–46', in J. Cohen and G. Harcourt (eds), *International Monetary Problems and Supply-side Economics*, London: Macmillan.

Nurkse, R. (1944), *International Currency Experience: Lessons of the Interwar Period*, Princeton: League of Nations.

Ohlin, B. (1936), 'International Economic Reconstruction', in *International Economic Reconstruction*, Paris: International Chamber of Commerce.

Oliver, R. (1971), *Early Plans for a World Bank*, Princeton: Princeton University, Studies in International Finance, No.29.

Pressnel, L. (1986), *External Economic Policy Since the War: Vol.1. The Post-war Financial Settlement*, London: HMSO.

Rasminsky, L. (1972), 'Canadian Views', in A. Acheson, J. Chant and M. Prachowny (eds), *Bretton Woods Revisited*, Toronto: University of Toronto Press.

Riddle, J.H. (1943), *British and American Plans for International Currency Stabilization*, New York: National Bureau of Economic Research, Our Economy in War Occasional Paper No.16.

Robbins, L. (1971), *Autobiography of an Economist*, London: Macmillan.

Robinson, J. (1944), 'The US in the World Economy', *Economic Journal*, **54**, 430–37.

Ruggie, J. (1982), 'International Regimes, Transactions and Change: Embedded Liberalism in the Postwar Economic Order', *International Organization*, **36**, 379–415.

Salant, W. (1989), 'The Spread of Keynesian Doctrine and Practice in the US', in P. Hall (ed.), *The Political Power of Economic Ideas: Keynesianism Across Nations*, Princeton: Princeton University Press.

Schulzinger, R. (1984), *The Wise Men of Foreign Affairs: The History of the Council on Foreign Relations*, New York: Columbia University Press.

Silverman, D. (1982), *Reconstructing Europe After the Great War*, Cambridge: Cambridge University Press.

Strange, S. (1971), *Sterling and British Policy*, London: Oxford University Press.

Van Dormael, A. (1978), *Bretton Woods: Birth of a Monetary System*, London: Macmillan.

Viner, J. (1926), 'International Free Trade in Capital', *Scientia*, **39**, 39–48.

Viner, J. (1943), 'Two Plans for International Monetary Stabilization', *Yale Review*, **33**, 77–107.

Viner, J. (1947), 'International Finance in the Postwar World', *Journal of Political Economy*, **55**, 97–107.

Viner, J. (1951), 'International Finance and Balance of Power Diplomacy 1880–1914', in J. Viner, *International Economics*, Glencoe, Illinois: Free Press.

Warren, R. (1937), 'The International Movement of Capital', *Proceedings of the Academy of Political Science*, **17**, 357–44.

White, H.D. (1933), *The French International Accounts 1880–1913*, Cambridge: Harvard University Press.

Williams, B. (1939), *Foreign Loan Policy of the US Since 1933*, A Report to the Twelfth International Studies Conference, Bergen, 27 August–2 September.

Williams, J. (1936), 'International Monetary Organization and Policy', republished in J. Williams, *Postwar Monetary Plans and Other Essays*, New York: Alfred A. Knopf (1947).

Williams, J. (1943), 'Currency Stabilization: The Keynes and White Plans' republished in J. Williams, *Postwar Monetary Plans and Other Essays*, New York: Alfred A. Knopf (1947).

Williams, J. (1944), 'Postwar Monetary Plans' republished in J. Williams, *Postwar Monetary Plans and Other Essays*, New York: Alfred A. Knopf (1947).

Williams, J. (1949), 'International Trade with Planned Economies', republished in J. Williams, *Postwar Monetary Plans and Other Essays*, Oxford: Basil Blackwell (1949).

Wojnilower, A. (1986), 'Japan and the US: Some Observations on Economic Policy', in H.

Patrick and R. Tachi (eds), *Japan and the US Today*, New York: Center on Japanese Economy and Business.
Wolfe, T. (1987), *Bonfire of the Vanities*, New York: Bantam, 1988.

PART II

THE POLITICS OF TRANSNATIONAL FINANCE IN A MORE OPEN WORLD

3 The deregulation and re-regulation of financial markets in a more open world

Philip G. Cerny

In the 1980s, many states entered upon a process of modifying the system of regulation of their financial markets, including both banks and securities markets. The dynamic behind these changes, which often cut across traditional political cleavages, was a complicated blend of several different but interrelated political and economic factors. In the first place, an ideological backlash against state economic interventionism in general became the central characteristic of right-wing politics, especially in the form of Thatcherism in Britain and Reaganomics in the United States. Secondly, there had developed in the 1970s a widespread perception that the welfare state and Keynesian demand management had reached a plateau of effectiveness and were leading to a vicious circle of stagnation and inflation – a perception shared by significant elements of the Left as well as the Right. Finally the pressures of a world economy characterized by increasingly complex and volatile international capital flows – and the impossibility of insulating national economies at both macroeconomic and microeconomic levels – forced states to experiment (sometimes proactively, but more often reactively) with a variety of measures, from neo-mercantilism to promoting even further openness, designed to improve their competitive advantage in a relatively open world. Finance was therefore at the very heart of the 'competition state'.

In the regulatory sphere, this process was usually labelled 'deregulation'.[1] However this term has usually masked a complex process of regulatory change at several levels. For example, regulations cannot merely be 'lifted'. The very operation of market economies is dependent upon the existence of *a priori* rules, as well as of a range of mechanisms to deal with market failure. These rules concern property rights, contracts, currencies and other basic elements embedded in the nature of the modern capitalist state. Changing regulations has sectoral, macroeconomic and transnational effects far removed from the original intentions of policy-makers.[2] Consequently so-called 'deregulation' has not simply resulted in a reduction of regulations or of the overall weight of state interventionism, but has generally led to a complex process of drafting new regulations. These new regulations, because they are untried and untested in practice, can not only be more onerous in their effects, but can entrench new vested interests, distorting markets still further.[3]

Finally, 'deregulation' really means the attempt by the state to impose upon market actors – and upon itself – *new market-oriented rules*. Small private capital markets do not become dynamic sources of efficient capital allocation overnight; indeed, deregulation may, especially in a more open world, force upon them a new vulnerability which can be highly detrimental to the existing financial sector, to industrial sources of capital and to the state. Exposure to new winds of market change can require even more complex safety nets, especially in the form of prudential regulation[4] (from insider trading to capital adequacy controls) or the extension of 'lender of last resort' facilities to a range of newly-troubled financial institutions (as in the US Savings and Loans crisis).[5] All in all, then, financial market 'deregulation' can perhaps be more usefully conceptualized as a process of *re-regulation*.

This process of re-regulation, furthermore, seems to have two phases: the first is the drawing up and imposition of the new market-oriented rules; the second is the subsequent readjustment of those rules, from pro-market fine-tuning to the resort to traditional bureaucratic constraints to deal with the new distortions and market failures which result from phase I. This chapter is mainly concerned with analysing the process of phase I financial market re-regulation, but will also consider the implications of this analysis for a phase II which is already well under way in the 1990s.

I   The context of financial market re-regulation

Since the first 'financial revolution' of the late 18th and early 19th centuries, government intervention in the operation of financial markets has been driven by the imperatives of the nation-state and the state-based international system. The first imperative has been the consolidation and expansion of the state apparatus itself, which has required secure sources of capital, especially during periods of fiscal crisis, most spectacularly in times of war.[6] Thus governments have promoted and guaranteed domestic banking systems and, in a more uneven way, securities markets. This analysis differs from the standard explanation given by economists for the development of financial markets: that 'whatever the location, they were formed in response to an increase in the number of people anxious to dispose of some sort of financial asset and of buyers prepared to put their savings into them'.[7] (Indeed, government demand for finance, especially to cover growing budget deficits, is still a major factor in the expansion as well as the regulation of markets, as has been argued for US, Japanese[8] and French[9] deregulation in the 1980s.[10])

The second imperative has been economic competition between nation-states themselves, which has required the expansion of national wealth more generally and the development of new production and consumption processes. Thus governments have provided direct finance to industry through subsidy, procurement and public ownership. They have attempted indirectly to channel private sources of finance to selected sectors, and manipulated monetary and fiscal levers. And they have supported the development of 'finance capital' or 'organized capitalism' in the era of corporate integration characteristic of the 'Second Industrial Revolution' (from the late 19th to the middle of the 20th century). Different national systems of regulation have generally consisted of policy measures and enforcement structures which represent varying balances between the above goals. These balances reflect the interaction of three main dimensions of differentiation between states: endogenous state capacity, or the ability of particular states to intervene effectively; the nature of national economic structures; and the degree of vulnerability of the national economy to transnational market (and other economic and political) forces and pressures. Essentially two competing models of capitalism have emerged – relatively open, market-driven systems and relatively closed, state or corporate-driven systems[11] – although these analytical distinctions blur somewhat in practice.

The first type has tended to be characterized by what has been called 'arms-length' financial systems,[12] combining active financial markets and a diversified banking system providing relatively short-term credit with a view to financial returns.[13] The second type, often called 'strategic' or 'developmental', has tended to be characterized by structures which give a greater developmental role to long-term debt rather than equity or short-term debt, and which integrate industrial and financial decision-making under the aegis of structured linkages between the state, the banks and extended corporate networks. It is often argued that the character of the spread of modern capitalism is the result of the leading position (or hegemony), during key phases of capitalist development, of certain states characterized by arms-length financial systems, especially Britain in the 19th century and the United States since the Second World War.[14] The role of finance is crucial. The stability of the production and trading system under the gold standard was guaranteed by the dominance of London as a financial and commercial centre (rather than by Britain as the industrial 'workshop of the world'), by the willingness of the British state to back up its financial institutions, and the willingness of British individuals and institutions to export capital.[15] In turn, the stability of the post-Second World War period was guaranteed by American support for the Bretton Woods system and the dollar exchange standard, along with a willingness to alleviate the postwar dollar shortage.[16] Had the Axis powers not been defeated, and had the Soviet centrally-planned model not been 'contained', state-led financial systems might well have been dominant.[17]

In both 'arms-length' and 'strategic' types of system, however, the main regulatory framework for financial markets as capitalism developed resulted from the desire of national governments to protect domestically based institutions. Finance was widely seen as a vital strategic industry, too important, especially in the context of postwar macroeconomic management, to be left to the market alone. In the 'arms-length' systems of Britain and the United States, despite different mixes of statutory supervision and 'self-regulation', financial regulation developed incrementally, generally as the result of market failures and exogenous shocks. The American framework, from the establishment of the Federal Reserve System in 1913 to the post-Depression reforms, was a particularly *ad hoc* structure, reflecting the fragmented sovereignty of US bureaucracy as well as the diversified structure of the financial system itself.[18] In both cases, the main principle of regulation was compartmentalization. To prevent endogenous market failure, this involved the separation of different financial 'markets' to prevent failure in one from creating a chain reaction through the others, as had been seen to happen in 1929. The types of compartmentalization, however, differed: in the United States, commercial banks were prevented from dealing in securities; in Britain, stockbrokers were prevented from trading on their own account, while 'jobbers' (market-makers) were prohibited from trading directly with the public.

More widely, in the context of the Keynesian welfare state (broadly defined), governments established a set of buffer mechanisms to prevent exogenous shocks from setting off domestic chain reactions. Capital controls, interest rate controls and other monetary policy instruments, exchange rate stabilization, lender of last resort facilities and the like depended ultimately on the capacity of transnational regimes and the financial strength of the international 'hegemon' to underwrite the liquidity and stability of the system. Wider financial stability, in turn, made it possible for governments to 'fine-tune' national economies in order to maintain the economic expansion necessary to manipulate the levers of the welfare state. Maintaining and increasing the flow of credit to the economy enabled capitalist economies to go beyond the bounds of fixed capital and physical monetary reserves in expanding the production system in a way which was compatible with greater openness and interdependence in production and trade.

The postwar expansion of the welfare state, then, was dependent upon the maintenance of the financial regulatory mechanisms which had developed in reaction to the breakdown of the pre-First World War international financial structure in the 1930s. However this was itself still dependent upon maintaining, protecting and guaranteeing the nationally based financial systems which had originated in the first financial revolution. This became increasingly difficult to do, however, especially as those systems were more and more being called upon to perform transnational tasks in the rapidly expanding world of international integration of production and trade. Now the so-called 'second financial revolution' of the 1980s and 1990s, if it is indeed a new financial revolution, is widely seen to be the consequence of this structural contradiction. Financial market 'deregulation' is, then, a response to the inadequacy of such nationally based regulatory systems to deal with the new internationalization of finance.

These changes raise a number of issues for the analyst. In the first place, it is important to examine whether or not this new, transnational financial structure is likely to work well *as a financial system*: (a) whether it will lead to a more or a less *efficient* allocation of capital in the world economy, promoting or constraining economic growth, trade and so on;[19] and (b) whether it will be a *stable* or unstable system, given the increasing volume and volatility of capital flows and the destabilizing effect which they have had on previous international financial arrangements. At the present time, complex competing interpretations have emerged and the debate is very much open – for example, as to whether the October 1987 world-wide stock market crash, the mini-crash of October 1989, the Tokyo crash of 1990 and so on were indicators of underlying destabilization, or whether they were simply sharp 'corrections' of price levels, allowing the markets to consolidate without interrupting long-term growth. The onset of recession since 1989 has often been linked by observers with financial deregulation in both the USA and the UK. These more technical questions will not be dealt with here, although the basic shape of the new structure, and some of the more central hypotheses about its functioning, will have significant consequences for the other issues dealt with in this chapter.

A second concern is to look more closely for explanations of change. An understanding of the different factors which have played a role in shaping the new financial system is crucial, not only for an analysis of the actual responses of different states, but also for an understanding of the possibilities for and limitations on state actions in the future, that is, for current and future policies and processes of deregulation and re-regulation. The present writer has suggested elsewhere a range of explanatory factors with a wider application,[20] the implications of which for the financial sector will be briefly considered here. The third issue is the wider question of the future of financial regulation in particular – and its relationship with state economic intervention in general – as transnational structures constrain the activities of states and, more specifically, that cluster of activities making up the postwar welfare state.

This chapter will look at a range of state responses in the light of linkages between particular responses and different types of state structures. It will examine the ostensible scope of action/reaction in different state settings, the effectiveness of particular instruments of state action and the ways in which these state responses have interacted with changing transnational structures, not only to alter the balance of power between states in the international system, but also to channel and shape the development of the international political economy itself. Particular attention will be focused upon the process of 'regulatory arbitrage', in terms of both domestic political processes and international shifts in the pattern of competitive advantage. It will be argued that, while states which more or less fit the model of the 'competition state' may be better able to manage and manipulate shifts in competitive advantage than those which do not, in the long run the power of *all* states to manage their economic affairs will be structurally constrained by the emergence of an 'integrated, 24-hour global financial marketplace'.

II   Re-regulation and changes in financial market structures

The major changes in financial market structures which have involved deregulation and re-regulation are (a) decompartmentalization, (b) disintermediation and securitization, (c) financial innovation, (d) the marketization of government involvement in the markets themselves, and (e) globalization. At one level, each of these changes has been closely intertwined with broader changes in state regulatory frameworks, whether proactive or reactive, not only in lifting old regulations and devising new regulatory frameworks to promote marketization (phase I re-regulation), but also for responding to the unanticipated consequences of structural change, market failure and so on (phase II re-regulation). Taken together, however, they make up a differentiated, interlocking system which has altered the structured field of action within which states operate, constraining in new ways the range and scope of choices open to policy-makers in the future. We will look briefly at each, and then consider how they interact.

Decompartmentalization

As pointed out above, compartmentalization was long a fundamental element of the regulatory responses of different states to financial market failure. This approach has been intended (a) to prevent failures in one sector of the market affecting other sectors (the economy as a whole), (b) to protect weak (or politically powerful) sectors of the market from destabilizing competition ('cozy clubs of stockbrokers'), and (c) to prevent conflicts of interest (including 'insider trading') which might injure smaller, private investors and thereby damage business confidence. This was crucial not only to the American financial system, which was seen by New Deal policy innovators as being at the centre of the process which caused the Depression of the 1930s, but also to the USA-guaranteed welfare states elsewhere as they emerged from the Second World War. Compartmentalization could operate at a number of levels: in terms of geographical or hierarchical limitations within a particular financial sector, as with the prohibitions on interstate banking in the USA; between different financial sectors, such as separating commercial banking and securities markets; between different functions *within* sectors, such as restrictions on 'universal banking',[21] the delineation of boundaries between brokers and market-makers, the requirement that different functions within firms be rigorously separated (what are called 'Chinese walls' in the UK and 'firewalls' in the USA), or 'polarization';[22] or involving the protection of professional structures within each sector, especially the setting of minimum commissions but also other prudential regulations such as capital adequacy rules, prohibitions on manipulation of customers' accounts by brokers to their own advantage (including 'front running' and 'churning') and so on, tailored to the particular problems of each sector.

The essence of compartmentalization, of course, is the restriction of competition, and restrictions on competition only retain their efficacy when other market actors are bound by analogous restrictions or do not have the market power to challenge the restrictions. When other outlets exist for obtaining funds at lower margins or investing them for higher returns, then the compartmentalized sectors will be squeezed. Preventing their decline may require effective changes in the regulatory regime to avoid loss of competitiveness. That regime would, in theory, need to be made either more restrictive and/or more inclusive, the first in order to prevent what is sometimes seen as 'free-riding' on the stability provided by the regime (and to protect the positions of existing institutions and state interests), the second to loosen the regime itself to force those institutions and interests to adapt to changed competitive conditions. Of course, the acceptance of some loss of competitiveness may also be an option, especially in the short term. But where loss of competitiveness is the result of longer-term changes in the *exogenous* structure of competitiveness – whether because of the growth of new institutional structures or financial innovations which exploit loopholes and/or develop new forms of business within the territory covered by the regime, or because of the impossibility of insulating domestic markets from changes abroad – then action in the form of deregulation/re-regulation will usually be unavoidable. And unless the state can change or effectively counteract the competitive conditions themselves, then an overly *restrictive* approach to re-regulation may well result in further competitive decline. The crucial factor is the *mix* of restrictive and inclusive (market opening) measures taken.

This results in a complex economic and political process of regulatory arbitrage in which the policy communities representing financial sector interests and the regulators themselves, in 'competition state' fashion, seek to reform the regulatory regime in the light of the new conditions.[23] The obvious danger is that the removal of restrictions on competition will lead to either (a) a new instability or volatility which undermines potential gains in competitiveness (chaotic competition) or (b) a new distortion of markets – or both. In the second case, the new situation may simply allow those market actors best placed to take advantage of the new structured action field to use their market power to restrict competition in different *de facto* ways, using new economies of scale and transaction cost advantages to entrench their dominance.[24] What begins as opening can turn into closing. Structural changes in the US airline industry in the 1980s – after 'deregulation' – are frequently taken as exemplifying this process.[25] Thus deregulation has inevitably been accompanied by various forms of re-regulation, aiming not only to impose (and reinforce) more efficient, transnationally oriented market-type behaviour, but also to control new sources of market failure and new forms of market distortion (as with the explosion of insider trading regulation).

In the recent history of financial markets, the pattern has been one of 'decompartmentalization', in order to allow national financial institutions, faced with loss of competitiveness, to resist, and this has required both deregulation and re-regulation. The growth in the 1960s and 1970s of the unregulated markets in London for loans and other financial instruments denominated in currencies other than sterling – dubbed 'Euromarkets' – has provided a familiar story in the literature on transnational regulatory change.[26] These were vastly expanded: first as dollars spread abroad in the 1960s to avoid regulatory restrictions in the United States;[27] next as the new regime of floating exchange rates in the early 1970s required huge new private capital flows to hedge against changes in the value of currencies; and then as 'petrodollars' were recycled through London, in particular, after the first 'oil shock' of 1973–4.[28] The Euromarkets are usually cited as the single most important structural change, creating permissive conditions which in turn forced other financial markets to react to the new structures of competitiveness which emerged. The pattern of cause and effect is complicated. Several factors in the 1950s and 1960s – pressure from expanding American finance capital for more open financial markets, US expenditure abroad (both public and private), expansion of international trade in the 1950s and 1960s, and the growth of multinational corporations – all put the Bretton Woods system under strain. The Euromarkets, however, brought all of these factors together in the mid-to-late 1960s, before the Bretton Woods system actually broke down, and then expanded dramatically in the wake of its collapse.

The impact of the Euromarkets was twofold. In the first place, huge amounts of funds flowed through a relatively unregulated market, free, for example, from US or UK exchange controls and domestic interest rate controls (which the British government avoided in order to maximize income to UK institutions and maintain their traditional international role), at interest rates which were significantly more attractive than those available in the domestic markets. This meant not only that the Euromarkets were price-competitive, but also that they could attract the market actors (borrowers and lenders) with the greatest financial market power, including US commercial and investment banks, multinational corporations, governments seeking finance, large public sector firms, and one source of funds with unprecedented power, the member states of the Organization of Petroleum Exporting Countries (OPEC). Demand for sovereign loans from states with inadequate financial systems themselves, from the USA and France to Third World countries seeking development capital, gave the structure the impression of both growing demand and relative stability. A second aspect of the Euromarkets, however, was probably more important for the specific issue of decompartmentalization, and only came on stream with the Third World debt crisis of the 1980s and the drying up of international syndicated loans; this was the central role the Euromarkets played in shifting the *composition* of financial exchanges away from loans to negotiable securities, which will be dealt with below.

The trend toward decompartmentalization has been uneven. In the United States, basic legal prohibitions on interstate banking still exist and so do the restrictions on commercial banks trading in securities, but these have been largely eroded by the advent of money market funds and a whole host of exceptions and legal changes.[29] The ability of American financial institutions to shift their operations abroad since the 1960s forced many early changes, and the strength of American investment banks, powerful institutions which grew up in the grey area between commercial banking and stockbroking, has been a key factor in levering change at the political as well as the market level.[30] Although it is often considered that the erosion of the Glass-Steagall Act (that part of the Banking Act of 1933 which separated commercial banking from securities trading) is the result of the commercial banks' attempts to get into the securities business, in fact much of the pressure comes from investment banks and other institutions which want to undertake traditional banking business in order to diversify their activities and develop into 'financial supermarkets'. In the United Kingdom, the 'Big Bang' of 1986 basically removed a whole system of restrictions on the securities markets, but this was only part of the overall picture following the lifting of exchange controls in 1979 and credit controls thereafter, once again giving new opportunities to non-bank institutions as well as to banks to engage in a wide range of financial activities. In the securities markets in both countries, closed self-regulation gave way to greater legal regulation, with the state pushing as well as international competitive pressures pulling the staid sector of equities towards greater openness.[31]

In France, the state has taken a strong lead in undermining previous state-sponsored restrictive practices and in imposing decompartmentalization on other – often reluctant – market actors,[32] both to counter the loss of market share to London and to gear up for the coming of the Single European Market at the end of 1992.[33] In Germany, where universal banking was already the rule, *geographical* compartmentalization (rooted in the German federal system) effectively insulated the financial system from systematic pressures for deregulation until the early 1990s;[34] however the power of the Bundesbank, the fact that there is a single regulator for both banks and securities markets, and the dominant role of the banks in the securities markets themselves have in fact meant that there has been little hindrance to *ad hoc* changes in practice which have made Germany a powerful player, especially on the growing bond markets.[35] But in the European Community generally, the growing freedom of capital movements may handicap more rigid systems of financial regulation by starving them of both borrowers and investors, as capital flows towards less compartmentalized centres such as London. And in Japan, financial institutions have been adapting not so much through deregulation at home, although regulatory reform has been gaining momentum in recent years, as through the capacity of the huge Japanese institutions, now dominant internationally, to operate in deregulated markets outside Japan.[36]

Compartmentalization has traditionally meant that borrowers and investors have had to choose between markets which are normally characterized by higher returns and more risk, such as share markets, and those usually characterized by lower returns and less risk, such as intermediated loans. At the same time, as market actors have been restricted as to the particular 'playing field' in which they were permitted to compete, there has been a secondary regulatory effect of making it easier controlling market distortions: fraud, unfair competition, monopolization and so on are easier to detect within a smaller, more insulated arena. Decompartmentalization has meant that, while a wider range of institutions and market actors have been able to go after higher returns, it is more difficult to control risk. But it also becomes more difficult to control market distortions. This is why the most salient issue for the public which has arisen out of the decompartmentalization process – and apparently (but in many ways misleadingly) out of the deregulation process as a whole – has been that of 'insider trading'. Unlike the situation in the United States, insider trading has not been illegal in most countries until relatively recently (1980 in the UK) and the passing of 'privileged information' has been a normal practice not seen as morally wrong (a situation which still more or less holds in places like Germany and Japan); indeed some economists believe that insider trading actually improves the allocative efficiency of markets through increasing the total amount of information. But in a decompartmentalized market system, insider trading is now usually seen as the source of much more serious market distortions which have knock-on effects through the crucial mechanisms of arbitrage between 'different' but inextricably interlocking markets. Financial markets operate through a continuous process of recurrent contracting. Money is not (or, at least, no longer) a physical phenomenon, traded only for other 'things'; it is the representation of an abstract standard of value, and can be most quickly and easily traded for other forms of money. However the very abstraction of financial markets multiplies the significance of information, as distinct from specific physical assets, in determining the pattern of economies of scale and transaction costs in the industry. In the terms used by transaction cost economists, the asymmetric control of information can quickly lead to opportunism and a small-numbers exchange condition which together have the effect of replacing efficiency prices with arbitrary prices.[37] This means that a few actors can dominate the market for their own ends, so that prices no longer reflect the most accurate information about potential supply and demand; that is, they can no longer be relied upon as indicators of the efficient allocation of resources and factors of capital.

At the same time, as we have noted earlier, profits gained in financial markets have a problematic relationship with the 'real economy'. Financial markets are usually seen as a 'strategic industry', and governments support and regulate them in order to maximize their wider wealth-creating rather than their rent-seeking function. Their rationale and purpose, in public policy terms, is to provide finance to service the physical economy. Financial markets, therefore, in order to maximize their wider allocational functions, need to be even more open – based on a 'level playing field' in terms of information and characterized by a large-numbers exchange condition – than other markets. Yet monopolization based on informational asymmetries is more of a threat than in other markets; the temptation to 'corner the market' is ever-present.

Therefore there is a strong argument that 'deregulated' financial markets must be controlled by new, *pro-competitive* regulations and restrictions such as Chinese walls. Indeed the breach of these restrictions is widely seen as a major scandal, distorting not only the financial markets themselves but also, and more importantly, the real economy too. But insider trading is, of course, notoriously difficult (if not impossible) to control, like the prohibition of alcohol in the United States in the 1920s. What its public exposure does do, however, is to distract attention in counterproductive ways away from deeper structural issues and towards anecdotal instances of personal malfeasance – good as news or as Hollywood plots, but bad as analysis. The re-regulation which has resulted from insider trading scandals, the most public face of re-regulation (cutting across phase I and phase II), identifies a crucial ongoing issue but turns it into a sideshow.[38] A much more important form of re-regulation has been the attempt to evolve new sets of controls relating to other interrelated processes the structural significance of which is much greater in a more decompartmentalized world.

Disintermediation and securitization

The second major change in transnational financial market structures has involved the twin processes of disintermediation and securitization. Although each might be seen to have some different dynamics, the main dynamic has been the intertwining of the two processes themselves. Disintermediation concerns either the slower growth of, or the fall in, the supply of intermediated bank credit (essentially loans), caused first by the impact of negative real interest rates in the 1970s and then by the Third World debt crisis of the 1980s. Securitization involves the growth of negotiable securities issues and trading, especially in the 1980s. In effect, whereas loan finance was traditionally seen to be less risky even if generating lower returns (because the intermediary – a bank – with its diversified deposit base acted as a buffer against failure) and securities had higher returns but more risk, both elements seemed to move in favour of securities in the 1980s. Banks also needed to reduce their exposure to bad loans ('non-performing assets') not only by cutting back on loans in general, but also by finding new sources of funds when failures undermined investor confidence in the banks themselves.

Furthermore securities had three major advantages over loans. In the first place, they could be packaged in a variety of new ways which increased both borrower and investor demand (see comments on financial innovation, below). As securities markets became more liquid – as buyers and sellers became more plentiful – primary issues could be tailored to a more segmented and sophisticated market. Secondary trading, too, could cover a much greater variety of instruments which might be matched to the specific requirements of a wider range of market participants, especially those with transnational linkages and market power. Secondly, they opened up new sources of finance for governments, especially the United States but also Japan and France, which were dealing with rapid rises in national budget deficits (see comments below on government market operations). Finally they could be traded more and more easily on an international level than ever before, especially given the rise of the Euromarkets and deregulation of domestic securities markets (partly in reaction to Euromarket competition). Thus securities became far more liquid than loans *at the level of major institutions operating transnationally.* Sovereign governments (including major public enterprises) and blue-chip firms, dealing only in very large volumes, stopped borrowing through banks and started issuing new debentures or shares (or mixtures of the two); firms could, in effect, lend directly to other firms, with banks and other institutions acting only as brokers and/or guarantors.

Meanwhile, of course, new financial institutions grew to meet the demands for specialization which these developments entailed, sometimes subsidiaries of the banks themselves, sometimes entirely new institutions, and sometimes the result of complex mergers and takeovers in the financial world, all being permitted in the decompartmentalized environment described above. These institutions were dependent, not on a deposit base, but on a new range of brokerage and market-making activities, raising funds on the markets themselves for customers and making profits from commission income and the spread between buying and selling prices rather than from interest income. Such institutional developments interacted with the process of decompartmentalization in a mutually reinforcing way, making new institutions into key market actors and decompartmentalization into what economists would call a 'sticky' structural development: that is, one difficult to reverse. This of course does not mean that disintermediation will continue unchecked. Efforts by major states to control their budget deficits, the gradual unravelling of the Third World debt crisis (as banks attempt to cut their losses) and the volatility of some securities markets (as manifested in the October 1987 stock market crash) all fed into an upturn in traditional bank lending after 1988 and a certain stagnation on many securities markets, with the rising volumes and prices of the mid-1980s a fading memory. But this is unlikely to reverse the process overall, especially in the context of the current recession with its combination of a 'credit crunch' and falling demand for loans. One significant aspect of securitization in this sense is the way it has interacted with the process of financial innovation, the third major change in financial market structures.

Financial innovation
There is an extensive and growing literature on the innovation of financial instruments which is too complex to go into here.[39] Suffice it to say that the overwhelming trend has been in the area of securities and 'off-balance-sheet' instruments in which the role of institutions is essentially a brokerage role and income is basically commission and spread income rather than interest income. The movement towards variable interest rate bonds, new instruments such as perpetual floating rate notes which are virtually the same as capital (although rules vary from country to country), warrants, convertibles, revolving underwriting facilities, futures, options, swaps, commercial paper and so on has done what 'flexible manufacturing systems' have done for steel, automobiles, electronics and a range of other industries.[40] It has permitted a segmentation of financial markets in which volumes can be increased by increasing the tailoring of instruments to the needs of borrowers and investors – although this means in practice the largest borrowers and investors such as sovereign governments and multinational

corporations.[41] This interacts with the technological revolution of electronic systems which permit instant information retrieval, integrated global trading and so on – what economists call 'process' innovation (in addition to 'product' innovation).

In other words, contrary to previous forms of financial exchange – intermediated loans and traditional securities trading – the combination of market segmentation and the relatively cheap (and flexible) capital investment required by electronics systems[42] has meant the simultaneous development of increasing diversification and economies of scale at the same time. Again this form of industry organization might suggest, in Williamson's terms, the presence of an extremely effective 'governance structure', maximizing both strategic control and operational deconcentration at the same time. Because transaction costs (including informational and monitoring costs) are such a dominant element in the structure of the financial sector, their minimization will have a disproportionate impact upon the maximization of structural efficiency. In the process this has also meant a change in the financial labour market, from large numbers of staff to deal with extensive branch banking to enlarge a relatively inelastic deposit base to smaller numbers of highly skilled staff working from trading rooms and the like. Such developments will never replace traditional intermediation, of course, because (a) deposit bases are still important sources of capital and (b) many borrowers (sometimes the most important ones for deep, rather than just wide, economic development) are too small or have too low ratings to operate to their maximum efficiency in the securities markets.

However, even here, the transformation of intermediated loans such as mortgages or car loans into packaged negotiable securities traded between institutions has further integrated different financial markets. Finally, the trading of negotiable securities internationally is easier and sometimes actually safer than the expansion of loan activities, because markets are more liquid. This means that debt can be recycled at a discount in secondary markets – rather than having to be rescheduled or written off, as we have seen with the Third World debt crisis, with the consequent instability of major institutions. The markets have, with strong government support of course, shrugged off various financial crises since October 1987 without disturbing other markets for more than a short time; in early 1993 the US and UK securities markets are not far off record highs, despite periods in the doldrums, and even the Japanese stock market and property crash since 1990 has not had significant knock-on effects in other markets. Thus, with the vast expansion of financial innovation and the huge increase in the velocity of trading as well as its volume in the 1980s, securities markets have come to dominate processes of structural change internationally. Even the 1990s recession has not seen a reversal of this trend, but, rather, its continuance.

This is often attributed to another feature of financial innovation, the increased possibilities for portfolio diversification, and therefore the hedging of risk which diversification creates. At the same time, of course, reckless portfolio diversification can also increase risk, as the US Savings and Loans (S&L) crisis shows.

Government involvement in the markets

The fourth major change in financial market structures concerns the changing role of governments, not merely as regulators, but as participants in the markets themselves. This involves the quality as well as the quantity of state intervention. For governments are not simply interested in preventing market failure (indeed it is doubtful if this ever was the case, if we look for analogies in earlier periods such as the 'first financial revolution'). They have three further goals: ensuring their own solvency; manipulating monetary and fiscal levers; and promoting the international competitiveness of home-based firms and/or the benefits to the national economy of other transnational linkages. These goals are fused, of course, in the search for economic growth and a viable tax base. And all three have involved the expansion and increased structural complexity of 'open market operations' at different levels – the marketization of the state itself.

In recent years governments have increasingly pursued the first of these three goals by looking to new types of state issues and new structures to handle them, especially issues and structures which will appeal to sources of relatively easy liquidity abroad (partly in order to avoid 'crowding out' domestic sources of investment, but more often to finance budget deficits inflated by low-tax or high-spending policies like Reaganomics). Short-term instruments such as US Treasury Bills have become key building-blocks in the development of new transnational financial structures, and the expansion of 'primary dealerships' in government securities has been a significant source of both growth and structural leverage for internationally expanding financial institutions. In France and Japan, too, budget deficits have provided a major impetus to deregulation, although at quite different time periods (Japan in the mid-1970s, France in the mid-1980s). Even in the UK, where the Thatcher Government first reduced and then eliminated the Public Sector Borrowing Requirement, the Big Bang led to an expansion of firms operating in the gilts market and strong competition between them where there had been a narrow, closed structure previously.

In terms of the second of these goals, the search for policies to end stagflation in the late 1970s led to the fashion for more active and interventionist government monetary policies, and this in turn has involved the more extensive use of open market operations to manipulate interest rates to control the money supply. Monetary policy was to some extent successful in

Britain and the United States in 1981–2, although at the price of a very deep recession. But attempts to manipulate interest rates also provoked transnational monetary movements which undermined crude monetary policy, as funds flowed in from abroad to take account of higher interest rates and decontrol of credit, undermining the capacity of interest rates themselves – the main instrument of monetary policy – to control the money supply effectively. This also had a perverse impact on exchange rates, which undermined the effects of investment and helped to increase imports. (Germany is suffering from a similar predicament at the time of writing.) Only a conscious policy of currency devaluation by Britain in 1983–6 and by the USA in 1985–7 counteracted this tendency. Combining tax cuts and monetary policies has been one of the most problematic issues of recent years, in different ways in different countries.

In terms of the last goal, we come to the fuzzy boundary between deregulation and re-regulation in the marketization of state intervention itself. In the context of increasing transnational financial integration, governments have acted either defensively, to attempt to stem outflows of capital seeking higher returns elsewhere, or offensively, to support home-based institutions attempting to find such increasing returns and to gain market share abroad, or both at the same time in different ways and in different financial sectors. Manipulation of monetary and fiscal policies and structures, altering mechanisms of open market operations, support for financial innovation, decompartmentalization and so on have all been part of the state's growing armoury to support competitiveness, usually through the restructuring of the financial system rather than by attempting to protect uncompetitive national financial sectors. Of course, with the possible exception of major bank failures like that of Continental Illinois in 1984 or the waves of thrift bankruptcies, or losses in a major stock market crash, there are not many votes to be lost through government-promoted financial restructuring, in contrast to the destruction of capital and the increase of unemployment involved in the manufacturing sector. Therefore governments find it easier to continue deregulating than to try to 'buck the markets'.

Domestic sociopolitical constraints on the capacity of the competition state to undermine cozy clubs of stockbrokers are fewer than those on the creation of rust belts. And, when taken together with increased state involvement with a range of financial markets in its pursuit of other policies, government promotion of financial market decontrol reinforces both the emerging character of the state as a market actor and its growing predilection to impose internationally oriented market-rational behaviour on other market actors too. The main problem is, of course, that this increased marketization of state interventionism significantly increases the international constraints on non-financial economic policy. An expansive fiscal policy of the sort which is meant to stimulate private supply-side investment and the financial markets via tax cuts (as in the USA in 1981–2 or the UK in 1987–9) tends to lead not to significant structural investment but to increased spending on imports, not unlike the impact of increased government spending in Keynesian France in 1981–2. It also turns monetary policy from a tool of fine-tuning into at best a blunt instrument, sometimes destroying wide swathes of capital (as in the UK in 1979–82 and since 1989), and an ineffective one at worst, especially given its perverse effects on the exchange rate.

Finally, running through the whole issue of the marketization of state financial operations, we can discern a change of kind, rather than of degree, which is having far-reaching ramifications for macroeconomic policy in general. In effect several factors stemming from financial transnationalization have together altered not only the scope but also the substance of government intervention. In the first place, it is by now well known that growing transnational constraints have undermined Keynesian demand management policies through adverse effects on capital flows, the exchange rate and so on. Monetary policy (in its various guises) has become the main instrument of macroeconomic control.[43] Yet, at the same time, these very 'exogenous' constraints have increasingly meant that monetary policy instruments have become blunted and that to work they are required to 'overshoot', reinforcing boom–slump cycles. These tendencies are continually being reinforced in complex ways through the increasing dynamic of financial globalization, as we shall see below. The consequence is that governments, even where they seem to be able to live beyond their means (as in the United States), must increasingly measure their performance according to criteria acceptable to the financial markets; that is, they must be either 'strong' or 'sound', in order to retain the confidence of the transnational financial community. Rather than a system of 'embedded liberalism',[44] then, what we have today is a system of 'embedded financial orthodoxy' which sets an international 'bottom line' for government economic intervention more broadly. Globalization is a two-edged sword.

Globalization

The final dimension of change in financial market structure is of course globalization, which is intertwined with each of the changes discussed above. Without the crystallization of transnational linkages between them at key points in time, decompartmentalization, disintermediation/securitization, financial innovation and government marketization would not have been able to take off, and each would have been strictly limited in its development. We have already mentioned, then, many of the key mechanisms through which financial markets have become integrated at the global level: the emergence of virtually unregulatable interest rate competition through the Euromarkets; the breakdown of the Bretton Woods system and the multiplication of international currency flows after 1971 (much exacerbated by the oil shocks of 1973–4 and 1979–80); inflation and the fiscal crisis of the state, followed by deflationary monetary policies; the Third World debt crisis; the knock-on effects of limited deregulatory measures through policy competition (regulatory arbitrage) between states; the emergence of new kinds of financial institutions; and, allowing these linkages to develop through a new material infrastructure (new 'forces of [financial] production?'), the development of electronics and information technology which permit financial flexibilization and more complex decision-making processes to operate efficiently.

It must be pointed out, however, that the end result of these processes is not an evenly 'integrated, global 24-hour financial market-place', as media images would have it. Of course, gross financial exchange transactions, estimated at 60–70 trillion dollars a year in the mid-1980s, dwarf exchanges of goods and services, which then totalled around only 4 trillion; and gross capital exchanges between the United States, Europe and Japan (excluding intra-European exchanges) grew at an average annual rate of 54 per cent per year between 1980 and 1986, while trade grew at an average of only 8 per cent per year over the same period. But, as research by international management consultants McKinsey points out, the development of transnational financial market structures has been very uneven, leading to 'the emergence of distinct world markets for each type of instrument ... depending closely on the complex nature of the risks which determine the price of each instrument in different countries'.[45] Thus, although the major trends are still toward global integration, some markets are highly globalized, some still essentially national with some transnational linkages, and others a mixture.

For example, in currency and short-term capital markets, instruments are relatively simple, forward markets liquid, and information about the main price signal – interest rates – easy to obtain. Furthermore analysts have noted a long-term convergence of interest rates, when controlled for inflation expectations.[46] In this context, technological developments make complex arbitrage profitable with low transaction costs from minimal spreads; price changes have an immediate impact across markets. It is easy to see why the move to floating exchange rates provided a lever for the internationalization process. In partial contrast, risk assessments are far more complex in bond markets, especially private sector bond markets; these are more integrated at the level of primary markets, where interest rate levels and ratings provide more comparable international price signals than in secondary markets. Nevertheless it was the role that the Euromarkets played in improving price signals and reducing risk transnationally in this sector which provided the main linkage between transnational capital flows, securitization and eventually the process of regulatory arbitrage which helped to undermine compartmentalization. Finally markets for shares are still relatively nationalized; although there has been some globalization in secondary markets for purposes of portfolio diversification, there have been few genuinely international issues,[47] despite a gradual growth in Euroequities and an increasing tendency to offer a proportion of shares or of a rights issue in foreign markets. The main impact of the 1987 stock market crash, in fact, was on the share markets, where it led to a process of 'coming home' – a trend towards investors preferring to buy domestic shares again.

Most share markets have been stagnant compared to their performance prior to the crash, but they have not fallen further and indeed have touched on or surpassed pre-crash highs in several cases.[48] Following the Gulf War in 1991, equities climbed strongly for a time in the United States, although the Japanese market is still running at less than 50 per cent of its pre-1990 levels. Bond markets, which signalled the onset of the 1987 crash, benefited from a 'flight to quality' and from government support; indeed probably the main impact of the 1987 crash on state/financial market relations was the decision taken informally by the finance ministers of the Group of 7 to increase liquidity to the markets after the crash. Currency and short-term capital markets have been relatively healthy; in fact the recent crisis in which Britain withdrew sterling from the European Exchange Rate Mechanism demonstrated the power of the currency markets in a recessionary period. Changing financial market structures, then, have proved remarkably resilient, and government action has in general reinforced, or even initiated, patterns of restructuring – a trend which is continuing today.

III   Regulatory arbitrage and the state: explaining change
Any analysis of the interaction of financial market structures and the state in the contemporary world must go beyond the sort of taxonomy which we have established and consider the nature of the dynamic process of change. Most of the financial and economic literature dealing with changing financial market structures is either descriptive or practical, often aimed at market actors or financial analysts.[49] Where it does not fit this picture, it tends to be based on the assumption that markets are expansionary by nature, and that as the world economy in general has expanded in recent decades it has required financial markets to become 'freer' and more expansionary also, in order to maintain (and, indeed, increase) allocative efficiency. This mainstream version of the market explanation is in contrast, of course, to the school which sees markets as inherently unstable, with the need of owners and controllers of capital continually to increase accumulation in the face of a long-term tendency for the rate of profit to fall; in this case, market expansion and the development of *more complex* regulatory regimes are in uneasy relationship

with each other, leading to recurrent cyclical effects, in this case 'credit crunches'.[50] In addition to these market-based explanations, of course, are a range of institutional/technological and political explanations.[51]

Certainly for the mainstream market approach, the changes in financial market structures outlined earlier represent the 'turning' and ultimately the undermining of an international financial system which was constructed around the crucial allocative blockages described above (and by Eric Helleiner in the previous chapter). Declining financial competitiveness was seen by mainstream economists as a central factor in declining competitiveness in manufacturing and in other services. National regulatory systems were subjected to strong pressures for structural change, although a fully transnational alternative has not been available in what is often called an 'anarchic' international system. In this perspective, October 1987 was not a crisis but a market correction, demonstrating that open markets can still be stable without compartmentalizing regulation. For the instability school, in contrast, the 1987 crash was counteracted by a new *de facto* transnational regulatory regime, in which key government officials in all of the leading powers, through a series of formal and informal signals, by consensus, undertook coordinated action to lower interest rates and provide strong guarantees to financial institutions which might be faced with failure.

Our earlier discussion of the structural characteristics of financial markets and institutions has foreshadowed key aspects of institutional/technological explanations of change, especially the capacity of financial market actors and institutions to combine size and flexibility in ways that other sorts of firms cannot. In such a context, financial economies of scale can be rapidly adjusted to a global level in order to maximize competitive advantage, exploiting the possibilities of financial innovation and regulatory arbitrage presented at the international level. Thus an infrastructure can be built using contemporary information technology, putting these organizations in a position where they no longer require traditional financial intermediaries and can relatively easily find ways around many of the constraints built into regulatory frameworks. However this is not relevant only to financial firms *per se*; it also grows out of the financial activities of multinational corporations, which dwarf not only traditional banks and stock exchanges (especially where the financial system is highly protected) but states too. Such developments as computerized program trading are frequently reactive attempts by markets to develop mechanisms which can approach transnational finance capital in market power; Black Monday demonstrated the fact that financial *markets* have not yet developed the capacity to do this, despite deregulation, re-regulation and all the rest.

The third set of explanatory categories is the political: on the one hand, the political process, and on the other hand, the state. The political process approach focuses on the competition between interest groups and policy communities, and especially the crystallization (or lack of it) of reform-minded coalitions of 'modernizers' or others which can bring about reform, usually in the face of institutional inertia. The best known political analysis of the process of transport deregulation in the United States focuses on the alliances formed across party lines in Congress in the 1970s, and Michael Moran argues that it was the presence of such coalitions in the USA and UK, and the lack of them in Germany, which led to financial market deregulation in the former but hindered it in the latter.[52] With regard to analyses which focus on the 'state', several levels of explanation can be identified.

First, the state requires financing and, like companies or individuals, requires credit to finance its activities in a modern society where the state's version of 'physical money', that is its tax revenue, is inadequate for its tasks. Second, a category of state actors develops,[53] key members of which oversee and interact with financial institutions and markets in several guises; they often develop a sense of the public interest, or at least a belief in their own lack of self-interest, which gives them an *esprit de corps* which in turn influences the wider pattern of state/market imbrication in each system. American officials may have to operate through persuasion and bargaining – controlling a complex and relatively open system of access and competing centres of power – while Japanese officials can issue rather more powerful 'administrative guidance'. Nevertheless they all, in effect, seek to shape the behaviour of market actors through the structured action field of the state. And third, of course, the form of financial regulation itself – whether through the delegation of 'self-regulatory' authority to stock exchanges and so on, or through the imposition of direct statutory control – can be the focus of interest; it is the formation and decay of various types of *corporatist* as well as bureaucratic structures which become the key analytical issue.

Political approaches point to a number of important explanatory factors in the process of financial market deregulation/re-regulation. They are often even more selective and concrete than either market or institutional/techno-logical approaches, as they take into account not merely contextual changes in the economic or institutional/technological environment, but also real decision-making processes, policy decisions and patterns of implementation. Thus, for example, it is easier to understand why in *dirigiste* or 'strategic' states like Japan or France, the 'coalition of modernizers' is actually composed predominantly of state actors rather than of institutionally-driven investment bankers or market-driven stockbrokers. In turn it is easier to understand why a non-*dirigiste* state with such a fragmented, entropic political process as the USA[54] requires a long process of political access-gaining and bargaining by a classic coalition of modernizing interests, or why a centralized but private-dominated non-*dirigiste* state like the United Kingdom can undertake the most extensive reform of all, the Big Bang, on the basis of a private agreement worked out at the narrowest elite level between a 'modernizing' Secretary of State for Trade and Industry, Cecil Parkinson, and a 'modernizing' Chairman of the London Stock Exchange, Nicholas Goodison.

But this does not tell us why the governments in all of these countries have decompartmentalized (in different ways), gone along with disintermediation and securitization, and supported – and often forced – the pace of financial innovation. The state-oriented political approach tells us more, for example, about why governments have turned to the markets to finance the state, but the political process approach does not. Political approaches of either kind, however, perhaps tell us least about the dimension of globalization, unless, of course, we firmly locate them in the context of the 'competition state', which is itself a product of globalization. Essentially the argument underlying this chapter is that to a large extent states have had to cope, and cope in somewhat contrasting ways, with similar forces which none the less affect each of them in differential fashion. There is a dialectic of convergence – not so much convergence in terms of simply becoming alike, but rather emphasizing being in a *common situation* – and divergence. The common situation is itself multi-layered and uneven; and states have differential endogenous capacities to deal with different layers.

There are two basic dimensions to the differences in the ways in which the leading states have interacted with the changing structures of financial markets. The first of these is the distinction between financial market (or 'asset-based') systems and credit-based (or 'overdraft') systems.[55] The second concerns the responsiveness of the policy-making process to wider international changes: whether the response has been a defensive and essentially tactical one, or whether it has involved an offensive strategy in pursuit of world market share. In each case, the cultural peculiarities of the policy-making process provide a filter through which these dimensions operate; at the same time, however, given the differential international 'structural power' of each state, the impact of a seemingly small change in one national context can trigger off what seem to be larger and more comprehensive changes in other contexts.

Whatever the differences in responses, however, the similarities are perhaps more important. In the first place, in each case, the role of the state appears to be far more important for initiating or promoting adaptation than market or institutional/technological approaches might suggest; and in the second place, the impact of policy and structural changes taken together has introduced new, common dimensions to state/financial market interaction, on one level reducing the power of the state in terms of its ability to plan and to operate in a *dirigiste* fashion, but at the same time drawing the state into the processes of promoting competitive advantage in a more complex inter-stitial way.

In the United States, the process of state response was one of piecemeal adaptation, but one which had wide reverberations because of the financial power of the USA, first as creditor, later as borrower. As Strange has asserted,[56] the process of financial change in the USA was one in which the major decisions were taken as a defensive reaction in an attempt to head off external pressures which reflected America's declining capacity to underpin and guarantee the postwar international monetary system, with the 1971 decision to come off the gold exchange standard, followed by a vacuum of policy as the world moved to floating exchange rates *faute de mieux*. This triggered off a massive expansion of international capital flows which, along with other changes, underscored the relative weakness of America's domestic capital markets. Nevertheless, as Moran points out,[57] this did not in itself lead to domestic deregulation of financial markets. More important was the political process which first put pressure on Congress and the Executive to abolish the minimum commission structure previously maintained by brokers – the famous May Day 1975. The impact of more recent reforms has left the USA with a patchwork regulatory structure, divided up between different statutory and self-regulatory bodies covering different sectors with no overall policy and conflicting interests.[58] Proposals for reform of banking regulation sent to Congress by the Bush Administration in 1991 seemed to be quite sweeping in certain areas, but they were eviscerated in the legislative process.[59]

Of course, at the same time, a key element in the decisions of other states to adapt or reform their financial regulatory systems has been the attraction of the United States for foreign capital. The size and structure of US financial markets gives them a clear competitive advantage internationally. When American stock markets are deregulated, even partially and unevenly, other markets must deregulate too in order to prevent capital flowing abroad; the same has been true for the setting of interest rate levels, although recent falls in US rates to combat the recession have reversed the focus. When the USA develops short-term instruments for financing its budget deficit, other countries must innovate in order to compete for funds to finance state as well as private borrowing. Thus the United States may be a poor 'competition state' in many ways, as its trade deficit in particular shows; but in its own incoherent way it has set many of the parameters which other countries now follow, starting chain reactions. Its defensive approach to deregulation and re-regulation has had offensive consequences for the rest of the world.

The British response also began as a defensive one, partly reflecting domestic concern with the lack of investment in British industry in the 1970s, but more significantly in reaction to the lack of competitiveness experienced by City financial institutions in the wake of the removal of exchange controls by the Thatcher Government in 1979. The investigation of the London Stock Exchange by the Office of Fair Trading for restrictive practices could have led to a long-drawn-out court battle. However, in 1983, as we have already mentioned, the Goodison–Parkinson agreement opened the way to the Big Bang by abolishing minimum commissions and leading to the elimination of the incompatibility rule between brokers and jobbers – not only breaking down demarcation lines between domestic financial institutions but also allowing foreign institutions to purchase stakes in and eventually to take over UK financial firms. An entirely new 'self-regulatory' structure, but with a great deal more statutory content, was instituted with the 1986 Financial Services Act.

Thus the 'arms-length' British financial market system did not constitute a major obstacle to state-initiated, but consensual, reform. Negotiation at elite level produced not so much a compromise as an offensive strategy aimed at capitalizing on the main strength of the British financial market structure, its very high level of internationalization.[60] Whereas internationalization is a new element in financial markets elsewhere, it has long been characteristic of the UK markets, as the Euromarkets have so recently re-emphasized. It also reflects the long-standing cozy relationship between the City of London, the Bank of England and the Treasury which has underpinned London's role as a world financial centre since the 19th century. Britain, then, is well placed as a competition state in the financial sector, even in spite of the increased level of statutory re-regulation since the Big Bang in 1986; however its capacity to play such a role in other sectors, especially in manufacturing, is in serious doubt, and that uncertainty is reinforced by both the traditional internationalism of the financial community and the close relationship between finance capital and the state.

France, in contrast to both Britain and the United States, has been characterized in the past by a dominant state-led, credit-based financial system, one which during the years of expansion in the 1960s and early 1970s was the core of French industrial policy.[61] Capital markets were small, highly restricted and heavily undercapitalized. Although minor reforms had been initiated in the 1970s, both Right and Left in France assumed that they could use the *dirigiste* financial system to promote industrialization, as had been the case throughout the postwar period. It was the failure of that approach under the Socialists after 1981, plus the good performance of a stock market paradoxically deprived of its biggest but often most sluggish companies by a major nationalization programme, which laid the groundwork for deregulation. In effect, the Socialist Government wished both to maintain the traditional system and to make the financial markets somewhat more efficient at the same time.

But the French 'overdraft' system had been under pressure since the collapse of the Bretton Woods system in the early 1970s, and from 1984, as the entire *dirigiste* industrial programme was suffering from budget cutbacks and a growth in the fashion for managerial autonomy, the new Socialist finance minister, Pierre Bérégovoy, was convinced by his advisors that the only way that he could confront a range of short-term and long-term problems which he faced at the same time – to prevent French capital from continuing to flow abroad, to counteract the strong pull from the incipient Big Bang in London and the financing needs of the US budget deficit (among other factors), as well as to reduce interest rates to industry in an overintermediated and costly banking system, to finance the French budget deficit, and even, perhaps, to encourage new sources of investment capital to come out of the woodwork for the benefit of both public and private sectors – would be to promote reform of the financial markets. The source of the deregulatory response was essentially defensive, therefore, as France struggled to recover from the deep recession of 1981–2. However, as analysts such as Michel Crozier and Stanley Hoffmann have shown in an earlier era, once the red tape is cut and the inhibitionist tendencies of the French bureaucracy have been overcome by an impetus of reform, that reform can often be designed and implemented in a throroughgoing strategic manner, thanks to the centralized structures of the state.

Now given the extremely protected nature of the stockbrokers' traditional monopoly, plus the restrictions placed on their operations by the existing system of financial market regulation, there was little impetus for that cozy world to adapt. French banks did not take the lead, either, despite their large size and international standing, because, although they might have wanted more market business, it would have meant significant restructuring for them, and also the loss of their own protected relationship with the state. In this context, then, we have an apparent paradox. This was not a pluralistic political process such as is found in the USA, nor was it a consensual agreement between the state and powerful private market actors, as in the UK. Instead the state took the leading role in imposing a far-reaching set of reforms, starting with the legalization of new financial instruments. Whatever was not specifically permitted had to be legalized, given the legal position of the Ministry of Finance and other agencies, ranging from bank certificates of deposit to commercial paper and a range of new short- and long-term government securities.

Although this process was more gradual than in Britain, it has unfolded with a certain logic, leading to a phased end to the brokers' monopoly by 1992, the development of a full range of financial services, the shift of the government itself from quantitative money supply and interest rate controls to an open market system, the lifting of exchange controls, banking reforms, the establishment of futures and options markets and so on.[62] Thus France has seen a process of state-led deregulation/re-regulation, imposing market practices and a market culture not only on the state, but on the often reluctant market actors themselves. Furthermore defence is meant to turn into offence when the Single European Market for financial services is completed in 1992, although the Paris Bourse is still undercapitalized, fragile and prone to seemingly minor scandals. But perhaps the most important impact is on the structure of the French state itself. In making such a complete turnaround from a state-led credit system to an incipient financial market system, the state has also altered its tools for intervention in other economic sectors. It will no longer be able to direct investment flows in the way that it once could, and that suits the higher civil servants; it is said that the greatest free-marketeers in France are the bureaucratic elite trained in the civil service's own *grandes écoles*.

It is hoped that a slimmed-down banking system will take up the demand for investment funds for small businesses, while larger companies – including the major firms privatized under the right-wing government between 1986 and 1988 as well as the nationalized industries, which have been experimenting with mixed debentures/ preference shares for several years now – will get their funds from the market. But these markets are not, in fact, necessarily French, as the reforms have not stemmed the tendency of the shares of the most important French firms to be traded in London rather than in Paris. Thus France, having had an early form of competition state which by the 1980s seemed mired in the 'Second Industrial Revolution' legacy of inflexible and insufficiently internationalized 'national champions', has altered the structural basis of state/financial market relations to a highly significant degree. Nevertheless the embryonic financial market system there does not seem up to the task of proving itself to be a dynamic source of new capital, especially in the recession. The hopes of deregulating policy-makers now explicitly ride on Paris becoming a major financial centre in the Single Market, and it is internationalizing rapidly. Thus the competition state may need to restructure its own *dirigisme* in a more open world.

Such is less likely to be the case in Japan, although, as with trade, it is important not to underestimate the extent to which Japan has liberalized in terms of actual regulatory restrictions, rather than cultural resistance. As in the United States and France (but not in Britain), a major impetus to deregulation since the mid-1970s has been the need for the state to finance large budget deficits in new ways. This began to undermine the system of interest rate controls, which has played such a critical role in the state-led, credit-based Japanese financial system at the heart of the 'developmental state'.[63] Exchange controls and a range of other regulations have been eased in order to permit Japanese financial firms to expand abroad and Japanese surplus capital, which is in oversupply, to be exported to those countries where demand for capital exists, especially in the United States.[64] But, while a token number of foreign firms have been allowed greater access to Japanese financial markets themselves, these have changed very little despite expanding rapidly to the point where, prior to the 1990 Tokyo stock market crash, its capitalization was greater than that of New York.

Instead, it has been the expansion of Japanese financial institutions abroad, where they are able rapidly to gain market share in the deregulated financial environments of New York, London and elsewhere, that has been most analysed and commented upon.[65] This has led, as with Japanese industrial expansion abroad, to the emergence of a certain 'scare' literature, analysing the interlocking nature of Japanese institutions and industrial firms, and applying phrases like the 'termite strategy'[66] to the dangers of Japanese financial expansion. But Japan's financial position has potential weaknesses. Internally, for example, while the availability of capital increased in the late 1980s, this has been partly because industrial investment started to decline and more people began to save in an ageing population with a poor pension system (Japan is likely to have a higher proportion of retired people than any other major industrial country around the turn of the century). A major shift took place in the 1980s from traditional bank credit to the stock markets, and this for a while made Tokyo the largest stock market in the world in terms of capitalization, although its value even then was often thought to be excessively inflated. And Japan's position as a leading creditor nation has attracted pressure from other countries, pressure which is often credited with forcing some of the most significant deregulatory inroads, including the 1984 Yen–Dollar Agreement.[67]

With many of the formal structures of state/market relations also changing in Japan, it is still a matter of conjecture whether such factors as cultural resistance to foreign products and firms, the archaic nature of the Japanese internal distribution system, or the continued influence of 'administrative guidance' (which played a major role in countering the effects of the October 1987 Wall Street crash) will continue to make Japan the only leading economic power which could expand its financial markets, innovate and deregulate without really internationalizing them. During 1991–2, furthermore, the recession has hit not only Japan's stock markets and property markets, but also the banking system, which is squeezed from several angles. Already Japanese banks are said to be having problems meeting the international Basle capital adequacy standards, partly because of the decline of their stock market holdings; and the problem of bad loans, common to all countries in the slump, has hit Japan too. The recent changes to the Securities and Exchange Law will need to be analysed more closely *after* they have been fully implemented and put into practice, before an answer to the question of internationalization can be attempted.[68]

Longer-term prospects are not all favourable, either. If Japan's financial success proves to have been dependent on continued rapid industrial expansion, whether at home or abroad, then the slowdown may have yet more serious consequences. In addition, as the ageing of the population progresses and as the Japanese government becomes more responsive to demands (both internal and external) for increased levels of domestic expenditure, Japan's famous surplus of capital may be redirected into consumption at home rather than capital exports abroad. Finally, if the Japanese domestic financial system itself is under strain, the glue which has held the 'strategic state' together may begin to dissolve. Robert Gilpin's view of Japan as a rising financial hegemon may rest on fragile grounds by the year 2000.[69] The internationalization of Japanese finance may make Japan more vulnerable rather than more financially powerful.

In the meantime, however, Germany has been able to resist pressures for both deregulation and internationalization because of the structural strength of its banking system, although the coming of the Single Market, with its principle of allowing financial service firms to operate according to the rules of the home rather than the host nation – along with the *Konzept Finanzplatz Deutschland*[70] – may undermine this in the future. The United States, Britain and France have both deregulated and internationalized and, as Japan's economy comes under pressure, it may be hard to resist the development of a greater degree of financial internationalization too. But the one major obstacle is the huge surplus of capital still available from domestic savings and foreign earnings, which create a natural protective barrier against market forces, and that barrier does not look likely to shrink in the short term.

The hegemonic powers of the last two centuries in the capitalist world economy have combined the roles of leading military power and leading creditor nation, but these are increasingly being separated. This is particularly true for major potential powers like Japan and Germany, as the experience of the 1991 Gulf War clearly shows. Borrowers may also have influence, but that influence is negative, rather than positive, in a more open financial world, whatever the appearance of military prowess of a financially strapped state like the USA. Furthermore creditor nations have always eventually been forced to internationalize, whether because of internal pressures from institutions, market actors, political processes or state actors, on the one hand, or because of exogenous and/or transnational pressures from international markets, powerful international firms, and other states, on the other. In the long run, even Japan will find it difficult to remain insulated.

IV   Conclusions

Financial market deregulation and re-regulation, in their various guises, have come to constitute a major developmental trend, not only in the world economy, but also in world politics. Processes of regulatory arbitrage, market expansion and the development of the competition state in a more open world, among other factors, have led to a range of intertwined structural changes which are usually referred to oversimplistically as the 'integrated, 24-hour global financial market-place'. That series of changes has had an uneven impact upon different states (and different kinds of state and market structures); nevertheless it has constrained the actions of policy-makers everywhere. In analysing the interaction of changing financial market structures and changing state structures, then, it is impossible to rely on any one form of explanation – market, institutional/technological or political – or to focus on any one level of change, such as the state or international regimes or the global system, as the predominant structural or systemic level of analysis. Indeed there are two paradoxes here. In the first place, market change is also inextricably political change, through processes like regulatory arbitrage; and in the second place, political change in response to transnationalized economic structures and pressures alters the nature of politics itself.

States are like lumbering giants, vastly powerful when roused, but often easy to get around, disable with a hundred darting blows from different directions (or a few well-aimed stones from a slingshot) and topple over in a dazed condition. This is especially true given that the state is not usually a true Leviathan, but an unevenly developed and organized structure in which the right hand does not know what the left hand is doing and the coordinating function does not usually resemble a brain. Increasingly globalized, diversified and active financial markets in a more open world are not easy for states to regulate effectively, yet they also depend on states, in the absence of strong transnational regimes, to guarantee their structures, prevent or compensate for market failure and carry out a range of other tasks which can vary widely from state to state. However *all* states have found that their capacity to make policy has become more and more constrained by the increasingly transnational dynamic of financial market structures. Their attempts to cope through regulatory reform, whether offensive or defensive, whether in arms-length financial market systems or credit-based systems, and whether the country in question is internationally strong or weak in financial terms, have been pushed, pulled and shaped by a major shift of power, albeit of an apparently diffuse and reactive kind, to financial markets.

Governments have all found their capacity to intervene in the domestic economy significantly altered, reducing their power to pursue comprehensive economic strategies and differentiating and complicating the kind of market interventions which they are led or forced to adopt. They have all found themselves having to pursue financial policies which imbricate their state structures more and more closely in transnational financial structures, even where this allows all states to some extent, and some states more than others, to manipulate these structures to their own competitive advantage. The interaction of changing financial market structures on the one hand and states on the other has done more than production, trade or international cooperative regimes to undermine the structures of the Keynesian welfare state and to impose the norms of the competition state, while at the same time narrowing the parameters of competition still further. In this context, the competition state itself has become the main vehicle, the preeminent carrier, of 'embedded financial orthodoxy'. Indeed the key question becomes whether we have reached the end of Polanyi's 'Great Transformation', or whether (and how) the politics of financial market regulation, too, is shifting, however unevenly or equivocally, to the transnational level.[71] More than that, however, this complex relationship between states, financial markets and the international political economy indicates that international relations do not so much involve the juxtaposition of an 'anarchical' international system and a 'hierarchical' state; rather it underscores the multi-level, plurilateral, even polyarchical, nature of the contemporary world.

Notes

1. The concept of deregulation is considered in a wider theoretical and analytical context in P. G. Cerny, 'The Limits of Deregulation: Transnational Interpenetration and Policy Change', in Cerny (ed.) *The Politics of Transnational Regulation: Deregulation or Reregulation*, special issue of the *European Journal of Political Research*, **19**, (2&3), (March/April 1991), pp. 173–96.
2. Susan Strange, for example, regards many of the changes involved in the 'deregulation' process as the unintended structural consequences of such conjunctural decisions as the American withdrawal from the Bretton Woods fixed exchange rate system in 1971; see *Casino Capitalism*, Oxford: Basil Blackwell, 1986.
3. For example, the 'Big Bang' in British financial markets has led to the drawing up, under the umbrella of the Financial Services Act of 1986, of a far more complex set of state-imposed rules for the regulation of financial markets than existed under the previous cozy self-regulatory regime. Cf. Maximilian Hall, *The City Revolution: Causes and Consequences*, London: Macmillan, 1987 and W.A. Thomas, *The Securities Market*, London: Philip Allan, 1989.
4. Prudential regulation generally refers to regulations aimed at ensuring that market actors themselves – individuals and institutions – do not engage in certain risky or illicit – 'morally hazardous' – practices when entering into market transactions. They can be *a priori* regulations, such as those requiring practitioners to be properly qualified or requiring institutions to be adequately capitalized; or they can be *a posteriori* regulations, such as those sanctioning practices like insider trading. However prudential regulations are not intended directly to structure the markets themselves or the processes of transacting business as such. Often the process of 'deregulation', then, involves the removal, or at least the alleviation, of direct structural regulations, but at the same time toughening the penalties for cheating or taking more extreme risks.
5. In the most thorough journalistic investigation of the S&L crisis, the authors generally use the word 'deregulation' which they present as creating permissive conditions for the crisis; however they later make a distinction between 'deregulation' and 'unregulation',

the first of which may be necessary if treated 'like brain surgery', while the latter will lead to market distortion, corruption and market failure: Stephen Pizzo, Mary Fricker and Paul Moulo, *Inside Job: The Looting of America's Savings & Loans*, New York: Harper Collins, 2nd edn, 1991, p. 494.

6. Cf. Geoffrey Ingham, *Capitalism Divided? The City and Industry in British Social Development*, London: Macmillan, 1985, pp. 42–50, and Philippe Sassier and François de Witt, *Les Français à la corbeille*, Paris: Robert Laffont, 1985, pp. 15–104.

7. Thomas, *The Securities Market*, p. 1.

8. Cf. Robert Alan Feldman, *Japanese Financial Markets; Deficits, Dilemmas, and De-regulation*, Cambridge, MA: MIT Press, 1986 and James Horne, *Japan's Financial Markets: Conflict and Consensus in Policymaking*, Sydney, London and Boston: Allen & Unwin, 1985.

9. P. G. Cerny, 'The "Little Big Bang" in Paris: Financial Market Deregulation in a *dirigiste* System', *European Journal of Political Research*, **17**, (2), (March 1989), pp. 169–92.

10. Although British deregulation took place mainly in the context of a reducing deficit, a significant proportion of this reduction resulted from the sale of state assets in the markets through the privatization process, which was in turn a major element in the expansion of UK financial markets in the mid-1980s.

11. See P. G. Cerny, 'Modernization and the Fifth Republic', in John Gaffney (ed.), *France and Modernization*, Aldershot: Avebury/Gower, 1988, pp. 12–14.

12. John Zysman, *Governments, Markets, and Growth: Financial Systems and the Politics of Industrial Change*, Ithaca, NY: Cornell University Press, 1983.

13. The American system is probably the most diversified system of this type. American commercial banking, despite the imposition of various national regulatory structures since 1863 and the long influence of large investment banks (especially J.P. Morgan), is still influenced by its early emphasis on 'free banking'; see Benjamin J. Klebaner, *American Commercial Banking: A History*, Boston: Twayne, 1990.

14. For a wider argument which is compatible with this interpretation, see Angus Maddison, *Phases of Capitalist Development*, Oxford: Oxford University Press, 1982.

15. Ingham, *Capitalism Divided?*

16. Cf. Richard N. Gardner, *Sterling–Dollar Diplomacy in Current Perspective*, New York: Columbia University Press, revd. edn. 1980 and Fred L. Block, *The Origins of International Economic Disorder*, Berkeley and Los Angeles: University of California Press, 1977.

17. In the 1930s, of course, the autarchic/bureaucratic model, not only in its German, Japanese and Soviet versions, but also in trends visible in more open economies affected by protectionism (Britain, France and others) and in the less developed world (Brazil, Argentina) seemed to be on the way to dominance; only war defeated it, and US political dominance of the economic reconstruction process in the West played a major role in ensuring that shattered capitalist economies did not again close.

18. See P. G. Cerny, 'Money and Power: The American Financial System from Free Banking to Global Competition', in Grahame Thompson (ed.), *Markets*, vol. 2 of *The United States in the Twentieth Century*, London: Hodder and Stoughton for the Open University, forthcoming 1994.

19. The relationship between the financial system and the 'real economy' is a key issue for economists. 'Keynes's subtle point [in chapter 12 of the *General Theory*] was that *inefficient* financial markets are necessary for the efficient working of the rest of the economy. The argument starts with Adam Smith's "invisible hand": if people seek to maximize their own welfare, social welfare will be maximized as a consequence. In pursuit of personal gain individuals will be motivated to "invest in better mousetraps" and otherwise satisfy and improve the lot of their fellow citizens. However, financial markets distort incentives. Once a developed system of financial markets exists, by far the best method of getting rich is likely to be in finance. Hence financial markets will be overdeveloped and other industries neglected. Both British and American firms have echoed this by complaining that an excessive proportion of highly skilled and/or trained

labor goes into finance. Moreover, many forms of finance are "rent-seeking" rather than "wealth-creating", to use the terminology of the ultra pro-marketeer Buchanan – i.e., no-one else gains as a consequence of the individual's profit (share dealing being one of the examples he cites)' David H. Gowland, 'Privatization and Deregulation in Finance', paper presented to the Interdisciplinary Conference on the Culture of Dependency and the Culture of Enterprise, Institute for Research in the Social Sciences, University of York, November 1989.

20. Cerny, 'The Limits of Deregulation', pp. 185–94.

21. In universal banking systems, banks can undertake virtually any kind of financial services business; compartmentalization is not practised.

22. 'Polarization' refers to the requirement, set out in the Financial Services Act of 1986, that financial institutions selling products to the public must *either* sell only their own products to the exclusion of the products of other firms, *or* must sell a wide enough range of products provided by *other* firms to be able to provide 'best advice' while *not* being permitted to sell their own products.

23. Soichi Enkyo, Senior Research Economist at the Bank of Tokyo, develops the notion of 'structural arbitrage', adapting Joseph Schumpeter's analysis of innovatory cycles to the regulatory process and integrating state actors into this process: 'Financial Innovation and International Safeguards: Causes and Consequences of "Structural Innovation" in the US and Global Financial System, 1973–1986', unpublished PhD dissertation, London School of Economics and Political Science, 1989.

24. On the relationship between economies of scale and transaction costs as factors in economic organization, see Oliver P. Williamson, *The Economic Institutions of Capitalism*, New York: Free Press, 1985.

25. After deregulation in the late 1970s, new entrants to the airline market in the USA such as People Express, led to a phase of intense competition through both price wars and route wars. In the late 1980s, however, after huge structural changes in the airlines themselves (bankruptcies, mergers, 'taming the unions', the adoption of the 'hub-and-spoke' system which reimposed quasi-monopolies at *airport* level rather than through national regulation and so on), the stronger airlines (especially American and Delta) saw off the new entrants and even reinforced their oligopoly position *vis-à-vis* traditional rivals like Pan American and TWA.

26. See R.B. Johnston, *The Economics of the Euro-Market: History, Theory and Policy*, London: Macmillan, 1983, for background. A section on the growth of the Euromarkets has become *de rigueur* for studies of the deregulation process, although there is not space for more than brief comment here.

27. Enkyo is particularly good on this: 'Financial Innovation and International Safeguards'.

28. See, especially, Strange, *Casino Capitalism*.

29. Useful surveys can be found in Enkyo, 'Financial Innovation and International Safeguards' (although this does not cover changes since 1986) and Sarkis J. Khoury, *The Deregulation of the World Financial Markets: Myths, Realities, and Impact*, London: Pinter, 1990, chs 2 and 7. See also P. G. Cerny 'Global Finance and Governmental Gridlock: Political Entropy and the Decline of American Financial Power', in Richard Maidment and James A. Thurber (eds), *The Politics of Relative Decline*, Oxford and New York: Polity Press and Basil Blackwell, 1993.

30. See Michael Moran, 'Deregulating Britain, Deregulating America: The Case of the Securities Industry', paper presented to the Workshop on Deregulation in Western Europe, Joint Meetings of Workshops, European Consortium for Political Research, Amsterdam, April 1987; and Moran, *The Politics of the Financial Services Revolution: The US, UK and Japan*, London: Macmillan, 1991.

31. The changing character of corporatist self-regulation in the securities markets is the central focus of Moran, *The Politics of the Financial Services Revolution*.

32. See Cerny, 'The "Little Big Bang" in Paris'.

33. For the impact of financial liberalization stemming from the Single European Market, see Peter A. Vipond, 'The Liberalization of Capital Movements and Financial Services

in the European Single Market: A Case Study in Regulation', in P. G. Cerny (ed.), *The Politics of Transnational Regulation*, pp. 227–44.

34. Michael Moran, 'A State of Inaction: The State and Stock Exchange Reform in the Federal Republic of Germany', Manchester Papers in Politics: University of Manchester, Department of Government, September 1987.

35. In early 1992, however, German Finance Minister Theo Waigel published a far-reaching plan for regulatory reform, the *Konzept Finanzplatz Deutschland*. Although some preliminary steps toward the integration of trading on the different regional stock exchanges have been taken in late 1992, further steps are more controversial and it will be some time before its various elements are negotiated and implemented. See *Financial Times – Financial Regulation Report* (hereinafter referred to as *FT–FRR*) February 1992, pp. 1–8; *FT–FRR*, July 1992, pp. 19–20; the *Financial Times*, 8 October 1992; and *FT–FRR*, October 1992, pp. 10–13.

36. Cf. Richard W. Wright and Gunter A. Pauli, *The Second Wave: Japan's Global Assault on Financial Services*, London: Waterlow, 1987; Enkyo, 'Financial Innovation and International Safeguards', ch.III.1, and Khoury, *The Deregulation of the World Financial Markets*, ch. 4. During 1992, however, new legislation has been passed which may lead to significant 'deregulation', although the key role of the Ministry of Finance has been maintained; see *FT-FRR*, March 1992, p. 14; *FT-FRR*, July 1992, pp. 25–7; *FT-FRR*, October 1992, p. 28.

37. Cf. Williamson, *The Economic Institutions of Capitalism*, and Charles E. Lindblom, *Politics and Markets*, New York: Basic Books, 1977.

38. This is a major weakness with otherwise fascinating and thoroughly researched commentaries such as Pizzo *et al., Inside Job*, which focuses on the issue of corruption (including Mafia control), undoubtedly a problem which needs to be dealt with urgently, but one which leads the authors to confuse causes with effects.

39. In this section 'financial innovation' is used not in the wider sense employed by Enkyo, but in the narrower one of the development of specific new financial instruments. Cf. Marcia Stigum, *The Money Market*, New York: Dow Jones Irwin, 2nd edn, 1983; Marcello de Cecco (ed.) *Changing Money: Financial Innovation in Developed Countries*, Oxford and New York: Basil Blackwell, 1987; and a long list of articles in such publications as *Euromoney, Institutional Investor*, the *Revue Banque* and the financial press generally.

40. On flexible manufacturing, cf. Robert B. Reich, *The Next American Frontier*, New York: Times Books, 1983 and Michael J. Piore and Charles F. Sabel, *The Second Industrial Divide: Possibilities for Prosperity* (New York: Basic Books, 1984). Reich focuses more closely on the way these factors affect more abstract forms of 'symbolic analysis' – although not financial systems in particular – in his recent book, *The Work of Nations: Preparing Ourselves for 21st-Century Capitalism*, New York: Alfred A. Knopf, 1991.

41. In doing so, it has also created (or left behind) a range of 'niches' for small firms catering, at much higher margins, to small investors and borrowers, although the significance of this end of the flexibility chain, so important for the proponents of flexibility in manufacturing, is widely debated. This is particularly true, for example, with regard to debates about the real significance of the 'popular capitalism' spread by the privatization of nationalized industries in the UK and other countries in the 1980s.

42. Compared with fixed industrial investment.

43. There are different kinds of 'monetarism'. Unlike the fashionable monetarism of the early 1980s, however, which emphasized direct manipulation of the money supply itself – a task which proved virtually impossible in more open markets – monetarism today has reverted to an older type, which focuses primarily on the manipulation of interest rates. But any monetary policy in an open economy pits the goal of controlling the domestic economy against that of controlling the exchange rate, a conflict which also destroyed the gold standard.

44. A term elaborated in John G. Ruggie, 'International Regimes, Transactions, and Change – Embedded Liberalism in the Post-War Order', *International Organization*, **36**, (3), Autumn 1982, pp. 379–415.

45. Philippe Giry-Deloison and Philippe Masson, 'Vers un marché financier mondial: les rouages de la globalisation', *Revue Banque*, no. 485, July–August 1988, pp. 725–9.
46. Mitsuhiro Fukao and Masaharu Hanazaki, 'Internationalization of Financial Markets and the Allocation of Capital', *OECD Economic Studies*, no. 8, Spring 1987, pp. 36–92.
47. Giry-Deloison and Masson, 'Vers un marché financier mondial'.
48. The Tokyo market, which weathered the 1987 crash fairly well, of course had its own crash in 1990, but this did not have drastic consequences for the Japanese economy or elsewhere.
49. Khoury, *The Deregulation of the World Financial Markets*, is a typical example of a book with many useful lists of facts and some commonsense observations, but with an insufficient and uneven theorization of change; what theorization he attempts (beyond orthodox references to the superiority of market allocation), however, is not incompatible with the 'regulatory arbitrage' approach taken in this chapter: Khoury, ch. 8.
50. Robert Guttmann, 'Instability and the Regulation of the Post-war US Monetary Regime', unpublished paper, Hofstra University, February 1988.
51. As noted above; see Cerny, 'The Limits of Deregulation'.
52. Martha Derthick and Paul Quirk, *The Politics of Deregulation*, Washington, DC: Brookings Institution, 1985; Michael Moran, 'Deregulating Britain, Deregulating America' and 'A State of Inaction'.
53. The conceptual category of 'state actors' is most systematically examined in Eric A. Nordlinger, *On the Autonomy of the Democratic State*, Cambridge, MA: Harvard University Press, 1981.
54. P. G. Cerny, 'Political Entropy and American Decline', *Millennium: Journal of International Studies*, **18**, (1), Spring 1989, pp. 47–63; see also Cerny, 'Regulatory Arbitrage and Divided Government: The Reregulation of US Financial Markets in a More Open World', paper presented to the annual meeting of the American Politics Group of the Political Studies Association (UK), Bristol, 4–6 January 1991.
55. Françoise Renversez (ed.), *Les systèmes financiers*, Paris: La Documentation Française, January–February 1986, *Les cahiers français*, no. 224; also Zysman, *Governments, Markets, and Growth*. Probably the most comprehensive case study to explore the difference between these two types of financial system is Michael Loriaux, *France After Hegemony: International Change and Financial Reform*, Ithaca, NY: Cornell University Press, 1992.
56. *Casino Capitalism*.
57. 'Deregulating Britain, Deregulating America'.
58. The analysis in Enkyo, 'Financial Innovation and International Safeguards', ch. II.2, is excellent.
59. See Cerny. 'Global Finance and Governmental Gridlock: Political Entropy and the Decline of American Financial Power', in Richard Maidment and James A. Thurber (eds), *The Politics of Relative Decline: the United States at the End of the Twentieth Century*, Oxford and New York: Polity Press and Basil Blackwell, forthcoming 1993.
60. London is the only major financial market where trading in foreign shares predominates over domestic ones.
61. Cf. Loriaux, *France After Hegemony*, and John Zysman, *Political Strategies for Industrial Order: Market, State, and Industry in France*, Berkeley and Los Angeles: University of California Press, 1977.
62. Cerny, 'The "Little Big Bang" in Paris'.
63. Chalmers Johnson, *MITI and the Japanese Miracle*, Stanford, CA: Stanford University Press, 1982.
64. See Edward M. Graham and Paul R. Krugman, *Foreign Direct Investment in the United States*, Washington, DC: Institute for International Economics, 1989.
65. Cf. 'Yen Power', *Time*, 8 August 1988, and Al Alletzhauser, *The House of Nomura: The Rise to Supremacy of the World's Most Powerful Company*, London: Bloomsbury, 1990.
66. Wright and Pauli, *The Second Wave*.
67. Cf. Enkyo, 'Financial Innovation and International Safeguards' and Khoury, *The Deregulation of the World Financial Markets*, ch. 4.

68. See above, note 36.
69. See Robert Gilpin, *The Political Economy of International Relations*, Princeton, NJ: Princeton University Press, 1987.
70. See above, note 35.
71. For an argument along these lines, see Geoffrey R.D. Underhill, 'Markets Beyond Politics? The State and the Internationalization of Financial Markets', in P. G. Cerny, (ed.), *The Politics of Transnational Regulation*, pp. 197–226; Karl Polanyi, *The Great Transformation*, New York: Rinehart, 1944.

4 Global finance, monetary policy and cooperation among the Group of Seven, 1944–92

Stephen Gill

> Since the end of World War II, the world has been split between capitalist and communist, North and South. Today, as these old divisions fade in significance, a new one arises.
>
> From now on, the world will be split between the fast and the slow.
>
> In fast economies, advanced technology speeds production. But this is the least of it. Their pace is determined by the speed of transactions, the time needed to take decisions (especially about investment), the speed with which new ideas are created in laboratories, the rate at which they are brought to market, the velocity of capital flows, and above all the speed with which data, information and knowledge pulse through the economic system. (Alvin Toffler[1])

This chapter considers recent literature in the field of international political economy (IPE) which seeks to explain the dynamics of present-day capitalism and the conditions for international macroeconomic cooperation, with special reference to money and finance. The chapter poses the question, how are we to explain the latest phase in attempts between the major capitalist nations to cooperate in matters of international macroeconomics? Part of the answer suggested below is that we now appear to be in a post-hegemonic, hierarchical, market-determined system, dominated by the scale and power and swift reflexes of internationally mobile capital, and this largely explains the nature and shortcomings of the G7 process, rather than the often cited decline of US hegemony and leadership.

Thus as the global political economy is becoming transformed in a 'Third Revolution' in production and finance, international economic diplomacy between the leaders of the world's largest capitalist nations appears to be caught in a conceptual and institutional time-warp. The annual Group of Seven (G7) economic summits, which began in the economic crisis of the mid-1970s (in 1975) are the most politically visible of the various forums in which political leaders and their senior economic ministers and heads of central banks meet and seek to develop economic cooperation. However these meetings rest on knowledge systems and institutional arrangements which were developed in a era of slower change.[2]

In this sense, the G7 process reflects a wider contradiction between the growing power, scale, mobility, speed and innovatory capacity of the vanguard global economic forces and the relatively underdeveloped political arrangements through which the world economy is governed and potentially stabilized. This is despite the apparent success of some attempts at initiatives of international economic cooperation and crisis management, for example the Mexican debt rescue of 1982[3], the G5 Plaza Agreements of September 1985[4] and the 1987 central bank rescue following the global stock market collapse of October 1987.

The G7 process, of course, serves some interests more than others. Ostensibly the stated aims of the G7 process, broadly defined, are to promote the provision of the 'international public goods' of sound money, 'sustainable' economic growth and financial stability. In practice, however, these goals have not been achieved and, indeed, the nature and definition of these public goals are highly political.[5] From the vantage point of late 1992, historical time appears to have accelerated, particularly in the light of the momentous changes in Europe associated with the collapse of the USSR. However, as the quotation from the futurologist Alvin Toffler suggests, the diffusion of knowledge and the speed of socioeconomic change is uneven and is generating both new forms of discipline and new forms of social inequality, as well as new problems for the regulation of global economic activity. Thus, as in Orwell's farm, some agents are more disciplined than others in the brave new world of international finance and money in the 1980s and 1990s.

I   Some theoretical issues

The theme of hegemony, order and stability in the global political economy presupposes answers to a number of other questions: (a) what sort of hegemony are we talking about and how do we conceptualize it? (b) what sort of economic order are we discussing? What are its major characteristics and dominant forces? Who benefits from such an order? (c) what form of stability is being pursued and how is it sustained?

Let us first of all note how these questions are raised in the bulk of the IPE literature. Here it is widely suggested that in the 1980s there was a liberal international economic order which has increasingly been threatened by mercantilist forces, including those which have surfaced in the post-hegemonic United States – partly reflected, for example, in the upsurge in protectionist bills in the Congress during the 1980s, in the potential uses of the 1988 US Trade Act, and in the populist–nationalist rhetoric used by certain US politicians and business persons (such as the 1992 Presidential candidate Ross Perot), much of it directed against Japan. On a wider plane, it is feared that the consequences of a spreading economic nationalism will be a disintegration of the world economy, probably into regional blocs each dominated by an economic hegemon and, more broadly, the prospect of an age of economic and political incertitude.

In this context, much of the IPE literature on international macroeconomic questions has been built, almost axiomatically, around the fashionable 'theory of hegemonic stability' (THS). The broadest versions of the THS suggest that a necessary condition for international economic stability and fruitful international economic cooperation, especially in matters of money and finance, is the existence of a hegemonic state. The hegemon is able and willing to lead others in the system and to act, for example, as an international lender of last resort (ILLR) and a leader of cooperation in the event of a financial crisis or panic. Thus attempts at collective forms of macroeconomic steering, as reflected in the existence of forums such as the G7, are associated with a situation of growing instability, explained in large part by the relative hegemonic decline of the USA, and the shift from a 'hegemonic' system of international money and finance towards a 'negotiated', or 'non-system'.[6]

Much of the THS literature has taken inspiration from the writing of Charles Kindleberger and in particular his arguments that the Great Depression of the 1930s was in large part due to the absence of hegemonic leadership on the part of the United States.[7] In the absence of leadership or hegemony, other states will tend to follow a *sauve qui peut* strategy. The liberal international economic order and its associated monetary arrangements may then disintegrate, unless other leading capitalist nations are willing to share more of the burdens of its management and leadership. Failing the emergence of a positive form of international collective action, international regimes will corrode and a tendency towards either economic Gaullism or regional blocs may prevail. This argument is paralleled by arguments concerning military 'burden-sharing' and 'free-riding' between the USA and its European and Japanese allies.[8]

Thus, 'after' American hegemony there may be more conflict and disorder in the international political economy. For Robert Keohane,[9] if there is a solution to this problem, it lies in the flexible strengthening and extension of international collective goods, regimes and institutions. Regimes can provide a more favourable environment for cooperation through enhancing communication and altering perceived pay-off structures for different actors, and making them consider the longer-term repercussions of their actions, by extending the 'shadow of the future'. In this context, there has been a growth in the use of game theory as a means of understanding the conditions which best promote rational self-interested cooperation and a lengthening of political time-horizons.

This neo-utilitarian application of the rational calculus of states now forms part of an American conventional wisdom. The concept of hegemony which shapes this outlook is based upon the ancient Greek or realist one of the preponderance of a state with extraordinary material might, dominating or exerting power and influence over others. It is worth emphasizing, therefore, that this view has itself become hegemonic in a deeper ideological sense: the neo-realist rational choice perspective serves to condition the limits of what is considered possible. It helps to generate the conceptualization of the American position in the international economic order in academic debates in political science and economics – and to a certain extent in policy-making circles – in the United States (although less so elsewhere).

Moreover, as Andrew Walter has argued,[10] the THS sees the main source of instability in international money as mainly 'political' in the narrow sense that instability is due largely to either the absence of, or decline in, hegemonic power and leadership of states in the inter-state system. THS theorists base their arguments on three major cases: British hegemony in the 19th century; the non-hegemonic interwar period; and the hegemony of the USA between 1945 and 1970, in the Bretton Woods system which, it is normally argued, collapsed in 1971 when President Nixon ended the convertibility of the dollar into gold. The decline of US hegemony since the early 1970s has resulted in, among other things, ineffective macroeconomic cooperation between the major states and 'undersupply' of international public goods associated with stable and sound money (including the prudential regulation and supervision of banking and financial services) – although this is also seen as due to the proliferation of competing financial centres. This type of argument is associated with writers such as Gilpin and Keohane.[11]

Recent work by a range of scholars from different perspectives[12] indicates that hegemony, defined in realist terms as the preponderant power of one state over others in the system, is merely one variable in complex historical situations, in which a range of socio-historical forces need to be taken into account in any explanation. Hegemony, thus defined, is neither necessary nor sufficient for the provision of the 'international public good' of international macroeconomic stability. For example, Walter has demonstrated, along with others, such as de Cecco,[13] however, that the historical evidence is not consistent with the arguments of the THS: the 19th-century world economy was by no means crisis-free and did in fact exhibit considerable instability. Further the evidence is mixed that Britain enforced the rules of the international gold standard (IGS) either consistently or alone. Indeed the UK did not possess sufficient gold reserves to act as ILLR (France and Russia bailed out the UK in both 1890 and 1907). Whereas the UK and the USA attempted to restore a rule-governed monetary and financial order in the interwar period, they did so with obsolete concepts (reflecting the dominance of laissez-faire thinking) and inadequate institutional infrastructures (the US Federal Reserve was in its infancy, having been created in 1913), they made inept decisions (especially the UK) and, most importantly, their reform efforts were bound to fail because of deeper structural problems which stemmed from the social and political transformations of the time.

Of the first importance here is that the interwar period brought a 'great transformation', in Polanyi's term,[14] in the relations between state and civil society. This meant that the policies of orthodox deflation required to resurrect the IGS were incompatible with the politics of the times (although orthodoxy was still attempted in a number of countries after the Wall Street Crash). The interests of money or *rentier* capital, which sought to restore orthodoxy, were at odds with those of productive capital and organized labour who pressed for increased state intervention and protection from international market forces. The (partial) triumph of productivist forces was reflected not only in the New Deal in the USA, but also in the range of corporatist, including fascist, forms of state which began to emerge.

These sociostructural forces, along with persistent instability in the realm of international security,[15] rather than the lack of a hegemon *per se*, are perhaps the key to explaining the near-breakdown in international money and trade (as well as the failure to restore a viable system of international credit and clearance after 1931) and are central to any explanation of the interwar crisis. Indeed, as Robert Cox has shown,[16] these conditions set the stage not only for postwar Keynesianism, and some domestic control over international capital mobility and international finance, but also for the 'welfare-nationalist' form of state to develop in the postwar advanced capitalist states. In most writing on hegemony and the international economic order, in contrast to the idea of historical structures which is suggested above, an individualist sense of structure is used and IPE is defined as the investigation of the interaction between territorial states and potentially global markets. This tends to suggest a system of balances and equilibria or disequilibria, but rarely discusses or allows for structural transformation. In this prevailing view, recently synthesized into what can be called neo-realist liberalism, structures are seen in methodological individualist terms as aggregations of atomized actors or agents, rather than as wider generative elements which serve to condition both the relationships between, and behaviour of, agents. In the conceptualization of structure used here, the focus is more on its historical, that is cumulative and dialectical aspects, themselves largely the product of the individual and collective actions of different agents. Thus in the interwar years blocs of sociopolitical forces began to struggle in self-defence against the power of international market forces and the special prerogatives of money capital. In this context they were able to press for the reconstruction of the form of state and to promote economic policies which prioritized production, rather than finance.

The conceptual contrast between historicist and methodological individualist concepts of structure is important partly because it implies that the mainstream approaches may lack a sense of structural contradiction. An exception to this is seen when attempts are made to incorporate cyclical dynamics (for example in neo-classical economics in terms of the transition from one equilibrium to another; in neo-realist and world systems theory in terms of the rise and decline of hegemony and international monetary orders).

What is needed, then, is an historicist approach which is less state-centric than the THS, and one which is more sensitive to the complex interplay of historical forces. The approach used here builds on an integral conception of the global political economy (developed in more detail elsewhere) and from Robert Cox's influential analysis of social forces (defined in terms of ideas, institutions and material capabilities), forms of state and world orders, and relates developments in money and finance to concepts of structural power and production.[17] These are synthesized in new forms of historical materialist analysis of concrete historical formations.[18]

In this sense, hegemony may be redefined as a congruence between social structures and predominant forms of state in a given world order. Hegemony is thus defined as a social, economic and political process, where the most powerful classes give weight to the interests of subordinates in shaping institutional arrangements and in major decisions. In this sense, hegemony is a universal, albeit momentary politico-economic and ideological synthesis of the universal interests of the dominant class forces, or historic blocs of the major states, both within and across nations. This definition implies a quite different approach to the analysis of historical forms of world order, as Cox proposes: 'The hegemonic concept of world order is founded not only upon the regulation of inter-state conflict but also upon a globally-conceived civil society, i.e. a mode of production of global extent which brings about links among social classes encompassed by it.'[19]

In addition, this concept of hegemony, inspired by the writings of Antonio Gramsci,[20] implies a consensual balance between different social forces and political interests as well as a coercive capacity which can help stabilize this set of relationships over time. It also implies a particular form of sociopolitical order whose processes are largely perceived to be legitimate by the dominant groupings in a range of societies. The world order would need to have a universal quality in both material and ethico-political terms for it to be a politically stable one. Thus, with regard to the concept of a public good, this would mean that the pursuit of sound money would not be principally to the benefit of *rentier* elements in society, but demonstrably to the general benefit of society.

From this perspective, the widely perceived crisis in American hegemony of the late 1960s and 1970s reflected a lack of congruence between the main social forces at the global level, as well as a decline in the ethico-political appeal of certain aspects of the civilizational model associated with the *pax americana*. American leadership was now more likely to be perceived in ambiguous terms by people in other allied countries: as much 'malevolent' as 'benevolent' in its effects (for example reflected in the criticisms of US monetary policies for their 'malign neglect' of the interests of the rest of the world during the 1970s and 1980s). In the context of the 1980s, in part because of the restructuring of forms of state allied to the tendency towards more deep-seated global economic integration and the increased mobility of (especially financial) capital, the socioeconomic foundations of the postwar liberal international economic order are being eroded and reshaped. This, then, is not a crisis in US dominance as such, but a crisis of hegemony defined in Gramscian terms, and involves the shift away from the 'embedded liberalism'[21] of the welfare nationalist era towards the dominance of transnational capital in a neo-liberal, market-based disciplinary order.[22]

II   Postwar cooperation, structural change and the emergence of the Euromarkets

The discussions at Bretton Woods were influenced by the ideas and arguments of Lord Keynes, the British negotiator, and by Harry Dexter White, who led the US team which was dominated by officials from the US Treasury, which had been a bastion of New Deal thinking. There was a similarity of views between Keynes and White on the need for state intervention in a 'mixed economy' in order to compensate for market failures and the distributional consequences of the operation of unfettered market forces. In particular, each considered that there needed to be some control over money capital, notably in the form of speculative, or 'hot money' flows of internationally mobile funds, which they felt would be destabilizing for national economic policy-making. These flows of hot money ('vicious flows') were differentiated from those which were used to sustain and promote production ('virtuous flows'). In this context, it was argued, finance should be made the 'servant' rather than the 'master' of production; that is, finance would be channelled (through capital controls) so that it would lubricate flows of goods and services and promote the development of the 'real' economy.[23]

Indeed, as noted above, these views were themselves premised upon the 'welfare-nationalist' form of state which had developed partly as a reaction to the dominance of international finance in the 1930s with its corresponding subordination of domestic economic activity to the imperatives of international market forces and the defence of currency parities, often at overvalued levels. Keynes, therefore, had spoken of the 'euthanasia' of the *rentier*, and of the need to construct a multilateral and publicly regulated international financial system, with control 'at both ends', that is by countries sending and receiving capital flows, with mutual adjustment of balance of payments.[24] The role of the IMF was seen to be crucial to this process. Nevertheless, as Eric Helleiner (see Chapter 2, above) has shown, the New York financial community, and some of its counterparts in Western Europe, succeeded in forcing a compromise on the issue of capital controls, allowing for the transatlantic circuit of money capital to be restored after the Second World War. The only controls that Wall Street was prepared to accept were temporary ones and they opposed the use of public institutions to monitor and control capital flows unless they were modelled on the Bank for International Settlements (BIS, see appendix). The IMF's resources were limited and it failed to develop as originally envisaged.[25]

The process of international payments and international monetary cooperation under the gold–dollar fixed exchange rate standard was initially almost totally dominated by the USA between 1945 and 1960 (a 'hegemonic' monetary system in the conventional terminology, with the dollar itself fixed in terms of the price of gold, at $35 per ounce). The working of the system proceeded under conditions largely determined by the USA, after the US government forced a structural change in the economic landscape in Europe, using capital flight to change exchange rate parities in return for new stabilization loans in the late 1940s. The USA encouraged investors to get out of European currencies (notably sterling) to force devaluation, and threatened to stop flows of Marshall aid if the UK did not adhere to US demands.[26] A total of 25 countries followed the UK in devaluing their currencies, and this transformed European economies into export economies: 'An "exporters' lobby" of increasing importance came into existence in all European countries which prevented meaningful adjustments of European currencies until 1971.'[27] In this context, and in the light of the military occupation of, and constitutional reform in, the former Axis powers, the USA was able to oversee the process of postwar reconstruction in post-1945 Western Europe and Japan. Convertibility of the main European currencies was restored in 1958, the same year as the EEC was formed.

Nevertheless the appearance of stability and order in what, in retrospect, was a 'golden age' of global economic growth was occasionally disturbed by public squabbles between the USA and its allies, who remained, however, dependent on US military power in the East–West confrontation. For example, intense French criticism of the USA surfaced in the mid-1960s for allegedly flooding the world with (inflationary) dollars, and later in the decade when President de Gaulle criticized the USA's 'exorbitant' monetary privileges and the abuse of these privileges to finance the Vietnam war internationally by imposing an inflation tax on the holders of US dollars.

Developments in the 1950s and 1960s coincided with the birth and expansion of the Euromarkets which became a key means through which the City of London could sustain its position as an international financial centre, as well as a means for US banks to develop their international business and avoid many of the capital controls imposed in the USA in the 1960s.[28] The Euromarkets were the first relatively free international capital and money markets to be created after the Second World War, and their emergence is crucial to the internationalization of money capital which has been a feature of recent economic history. As both Susan Strange and Jeffry Frieden[29] have shown, the creation and growth of this market was a product of government policy, that is of the US and UK governments. The offshore markets now constitute a gigantic pool of mobile capital, which is serving to erode the 'international and domestic, economic and political underpinnings of the postwar world order'.[30] What Frieden is referring to is the way that international financial mobility has served to unravel and undermine the system of embedded liberalism, and with it some of the socioeconomic foundations of the postwar international order:

> The Euromarkets arose in the 1950s and came to dominate international finance in the 1960s. They were in large part a result of attempts by American bankers and politicians to avoid the domestic political furore that American foreign lending caused before World War II. As American international banking began to clash with domestic economic goals, policymakers attempted to postpone the conflict by allowing financial institutions to squeeze through the cracks in national regulations. The ultimate result was to accelerate the expansion of a free-wheeling international financial system of unprecedented size.[31]

Part of the political support for the offshore markets in the 1960s stemmed from their growing importance in the short- and long-term financing of the operations of transnational firms, many of whom had influence in US politics in the 1960s. Because of the openness of the City of London the markets grew quickly, creating a similarity of interests between the City and New York finance similar to that of the 1920s. Moreover, as Helleiner argues,[32] the Eurodollar market was a means for the US government to allay fears concerning seigniorage gains accruing from the dollar, because the market was outside the direct control of the USA (and thus interest on deposits was not subject to ceilings imposed by the USA) as well as a way of preserving its policy autonomy (by encouraging foreigners to keep their deposits in dollars, stopping the drain on US gold). The Eurodollar market became attractive in the 1970s to the oil-exporting states, who deposited their massively increased earnings in the London offshore markets, whose value expanded 'to over $1 trillion ($1000 billion) by 1984. Its appeal for the oil states was that it was apparently beyond the reach of the US government; it was movable, it was secret; and it paid a handsome and floating rate of interest'.[33] The growth of the markets was paralleled by an enormous explosion in the demand for and supply of credit, even when real interest rates rose dramatically in the 1980s.

Thus, with improvements in telecommunications and information processing, increased trade and the internationalization of production, and the specific effects of the oil price rises of the 1970s, the offshore markets became massive, and more integrated with 'national' financial markets, as not only firms, but also states began to draw heavily upon them to finance budget and balance of payments deficits in an era of slower growth, punctuated by recessions of increasing severity. Nevertheless, as Susan Strange has noted,[34] the changes in question had contradictory effects, since the rapid credit expansion was to sow the seeds of the subsequent monetarist deflations of the 1980s.

As a number of authors have pointed out,[35] the rise in capital mobility served to undermine the fixed exchange rate system. Also of importance was the inflationary effect of US government expenditures to finance the Great Society at home and the war in Vietnam. Some US political leaders also came to accept the idea that the international monetary system was becoming more unstable because of the contradictory role of the dollar: as US deficits increased, confidence in the dollar could be restored if the US reduced its budgetary deficits. However to do so would deprive the rest of the world of international liquidity. Nevertheless the situation of dollar shortage in the world economy (1944–58) rapidly became a dollar glut, provoking General de Gaulle's attacks on US abuses of the system.[36]

Earlier the Belgian theorist Robert Triffin[37] had argued that US policies were incompatible with the maintenance of the international monetary system, given the unsustainability of convertibility when US reserves were shrinking and external deficits were growing. Taken together, these elements helped to motivate President Lyndon B. Johnson's moves to exploit seigniorage while he could and to internationalize the financing of the Vietnam war. These developments set the scene for the 'collapse' of Bretton Woods and the emergence of the regime of floating exchange rates configured around the superexorbitant privileges of the USA in the international monetary system.

Eric Helleiner has given a persuasive account of these developments.[38] He shows how the 'breakdown' was caused by a combination of growing payments imbalances among the major OECD countries and a widespread feeling among market operators that the central banks were defending unsustainable fixed exchange rates but doing so with a combination of inadequate reserves and porous capital controls. With confidence in the dollar in the markets declining, there was an increase in speculative flows, as well as in hedging, swaps, futures and other methods as a means to offset currency risks. Attempts were made to cooperate among the G10 (see appendix), who agreed to reduce placements of funds in the Euromarkets in 1971 to stem their growth, a strategy which was undone as the markets were soon flooded with petrodollars after the oil price rise, and thus the G10 governments turned to the offshore markets for payments financing. France advocated cooperative capital controls, but this was totally and successfully opposed by the USA, favouring a liberal regime in finance as a means to increase the structural power of the dollar and US financial interests in the system.[39]

The key contrast at this time was between the USA and the other major states. The USA wanted to implement a more fully liberal financial system, whereas the others favoured collective action and more substantial international cooperation. The USA sought to devalue its foreign debts via a dollar depreciation and force other countries to expand to absorb increases in US exports (this, the 1971 strategy, was repeated in 1985, and again in 1992). Other countries were forced to accept the implications of the new US unilateralism, because of the renewed centrality of the USA in the global political economy. More specifically it was because of US centrality in the international *financial* system caused by the international role of the dollar as the major reserve currency and international unit of account, by the depth and liquidity of the US financial markets, and the fact that the offshore markets were largely Eurodollar markets.[40]

Thus, via more aggressive, unilateral means, the USA was able to sustain its ability to pursue a relatively autonomous macroeconomic policy, with foreigners underwriting US deficits by holding dollars, as well as to internationalize the costs of US adjustment to the oil shock. Indeed Helleiner cites a CIA report of the time arguing that the USA would receive the majority of OPEC funds for precisely those reasons, and that therefore OPEC, like Europe and Japan in the 1960s, would in effect support US policy autonomy.[41] Other authors have noted the way that the USA was seeking to mobilize its structural power in the American-centred postwar capitalist system.[42] A recent study of G2/G3/G5/G7 cooperation has also shown how the USA was frequently able to use these forums to force other governments to accept dollar depreciation and to pay for central bank intervention to attempt to stabilize the system. The USA was also able, with the UK, to structure regulatory efforts so that they accommodated the globalization of financial markets.[43]

The social basis for this shift in US policies in a more aggressive, unilateralist neo-liberal direction, away from the New Deal social compromise, and from embedded liberalism, lay partly in the transnational expansion of US capital and a shift of identity on the part of American corporations who were restricted in their overseas expansion by US capital controls and thus sought access to more liberal international markets and, in an unholy alliance with neo-liberal academics and financial interests, supported the strategy of 'benign neglect'.[44] As Robert Gilpin noted in the mid-1970s,[45] no longer was there any simple correspondence between the domestic interests of the US population and the needs of international business, a key element in the fragmentation of the New Deal corporate liberal coalition, a fragmentation which accelerated after the recessions of the 1970s and 1980s. Thus, to a certain extent, US policies let the genie out of the bottle. The rest of the 1970s saw the rapid growth of the offshore markets in a much more liberal financial system. This created a new force-field of constraints on the policy autonomy of all states (for example, the UK in 1976, France in 1981), including the USA itself during 1978–9, during the dollar crisis which emerged as a result of unilateral US expansionary policies and attempts to force other countries to expand by trying to talk down the dollar.

However the rise in US inflation which went with this strategy meant the prospect, in David Calleo's words, of a 'catastrophic liquidation' in the international value of the dollar, prompting European discussions on the creation of the European Monetary System (EMS) to offset the repercussions of US monetary policy.[46] These developments prompted a draconian response, with the Federal Reserve tightening monetary policy and exerting a savage deflation on the US and world economy, as real oil prices and interest rates rose following the fall of the Shah of Iran (the 'Volcker shift'). This policy was only reversed in 1982, when the threat of domestic and international financial collapse became manifest. Systematic cooperation to control the Euromarkets amongst the BIS members was apparently discussed but was opposed by New York finance and the main Euromarket countries (UK, Switzerland and Luxembourg) and the idea finally ran out of steam when the Bundesbank withdrew its initial support because it did not have the constitutional mandate to control the overseas operations of German banks.[47]

Indeed the recessionary and unstable macroeconomic conditions of the 1970s and especially the 1980s have been part of a period of structural transformation in the postwar political economy away from the political compromises and socioeconomic balance between domestic and international aspects of world order. The Volcker shift of 1979 (so called after the newly-appointed Chairman of the Federal Reserve, Paul Volcker), involving a switch to tighter monetary policies and leading to a dramatic rise in American interest rates, was a critical turning-point in intensifying the financial pressures which accelerated change, because of the way the change in US monetary policy precipitated the most severe global recession since the 1930s. Several structural aspects of this transformation can be identified: below we merely sketch three interrelated developments which are important to our main argument.

First, in the OECD region, intensified global competitive pressures led to an eclipse of many of the older ('Fordist') industries, whilst there was a rise of dynamic, more 'flexible' production systems and knowledge-intensive or 'dematerialized' forms of production. There was also a shift to services, and a rise in the importance of global finance, for example in the offshore markets, as a means for firms and states to raise funds. Despite unprecedented levels of real interest rates, these and other financial markets were able to meet the apparently insatiable demand for credit in the roller-coaster years of the 1980s.

Second, there have been attempts to redefine and where possible restrict the role of the state in the political economy. This has been partly for reasons of ideology, and partly because virtually all governments in the system (federal, provincial, local) have experienced substantial fiscal problems in an era of slower growth. The onset of fiscal crisis, following a long period of the expansion of the role of the state in the context of the postwar boom, has caused, amongst other things, attempts to set off state assets and shift the burden of taxation towards indirect, regressive forms of taxation. The ability of governments to regulate their economies has been undermined by changes in the financial markets (propelled by innovation), such that even defining, let alone controlling, the money supply has become an ever more difficult task.

Related to the above, a general tendency has emerged whereby the effectiveness of national regulatory systems has been transformed and the global conditions under which transnational firms operate have been increasingly liberalized, partly because governments had increased their competition to attract scarce foreign capital for investment and to finance government operations, and partly because of the ability of capital to circumvent capital controls through the use of offshore centres and myriad forms of innovation. Financial liberalization can be understood as both cause and effect of the above. Nevertheless many of the major liberalization initiatives stemmed from regulatory changes in the USA. This forced other states to respond, in order to sustain the competitiveness of their domestic economies in a global competition for supplies of capital. This has led to a shift from the welfare-nationalist form of state towards a more neo-liberal 'competition state'[48] in the OECD and elsewhere. Thus older forms of inward-looking mercantilism have broken down in a more internationally competitive era. Now a more outward-looking, competitive mercantilism has come to characterize the foreign and economic policies of most governments in the global political economy.

Third, the USA has become increasingly integrated into, and therefore central to, the global political economy over the last 20 years or so. In the 1970s and 1980s many assumed that the rising economic and political importance of Japan and Western Europe would pose challenges to US supremacy and that this might lead to intensified alliance conflicts with the USA. However the end of the Cold War and the crisis of Stalinist and Leninist communism has left the USA as the unchallenged military superpower. Moreover, because of greater economic interdependence, developments in one part of the world may have swift and significant repercussions elsewhere. In particular, economic forces and policies stemming from the United States are of growing significance to most, if not all, other nations because of the size and weight of the American economy and because of the need for access to the world's biggest market in an era of slower growth. The structural centrality of the United States, underlined by its position in international monetary affairs under a dollar standard, has been further reinforced by the integration of American and global capital markets, encouraged by well-developed financial institutions, first-rate communications and transport facilities, and a liberal orientation to most forms of foreign investment. As the Latin American debt crisis of the 1980s revealed clearly, the United States is also a safe haven for flight capital.

III   Aspects of G5 and G7 cooperation

The immediate context for the formation of the G5 as it is understood today, then, was the international economic crisis of the early 1970s, which saw the break-up of international monetary arrangements alongside an apparently intractable combination of slower growth and higher inflation. In addition the early 1970s saw the specific financial and broader economic problems associated with the economic shock to the world economy of much higher oil prices. Between 1971 and 1973 there was intensive international discussion of monetary issues, involving not only the shift towards flexible exchange rates but also domestic economic policies. New European monetary arrangements were created from the early 1970s onwards; the European currencies floated in a block against the US dollar, with parities adjusted in the so-called 'Snake' and later, after 1979, in the Exchange Rate Mechanism (ERM). At the same time, a selective review of G7 discussions during the 1970s and 1980s reflects a steady shift away from macroeconomic policies premised upon Keynesian approaches and fixed exchange rates, and towards a 'market monetarist' paradigm, associated with flexible exchange rates and financial liberalization.

Under US pressure, from the mid-1970s onwards, the G7 generally prioritized policies to deliver lower inflation, supply-side ideas associated with more flexibility in labour and other markets, and the wider adoption of a more monetarist, market-oriented approach to policy. The scene had been set for these policy shifts earlier in the 1970s. For example, at Rambouillet in 1976, the French government finally gave up its efforts to re-establish fixed exchange rates, in return for pledges from the USA that its government would 'act to counter disorderly market conditions or erratic fluctuations in exchange rates'. However the USA did little to intervene in the markets to bring about this aim. At the 1976 summit in Puerto Rico, Canada attended for the first time, to make up the G7. At this meeting there was agreement that high unemployment would be allowed if this was needed to defeat inflation.[49]

A major exception to the shift away from Keynesianism appeared to be the 1978 Bonn Summit, which declared the arrival of the 'locomotive theory', whereby the West German and Japanese economies were to increase growth in order to 'pull' the expansion of the rest of the world. However this episode proved to be extremely controversial in West Germany, since it was associated with an inflationary surge which did much to discredit the idea of international economic cooperation, especially in German policy-making and academic circles.

The Tokyo summit of 1979 was mainly concerned with the second oil shock, and disagreements over energy policy surfaced between the participants. After 1979, the G7 macroeconomic debate was transformed by the 'Volcker shift', which, allied to the the budgetary expansion of the Reagan Administration, caused a situation in which the bulk of the world's surplus savings were sucked into the US economy to finance the soaring US budget and balance of payments deficits. This led to a contradictory situation for the other G7 leaders: on the one hand, US expansion meant growth in the major market for their exports; on the other, the tight money policy and deficits of the USA meant that, in the more globally integrated financial and money markets, interest rates in other G7 countries had to be kept higher to prevent even greater amounts of internationally mobile funds from moving to the USA. This meant, especially in Europe, that the recession hit hard, and it took longer to shake off than in the USA, which began to boom in 1983.

The Reagan economic team appeared to have little interest in matters of international economic cooperation and instead stressed its favourite themes of 'market-place magic', the 'supply-side revolution' and 'domesticism', that is, a focus on the US economy. Reaganomics was accompanied by a massive appreciation of the dollar between 1981 and 1985, and both the President and several key advisors associated the strength of the dollar with the strength of the United States. One unforeseen effect of Reaganomics was to worsen rapidly the Third World debt crisis, with the Mexican default of 1982 almost precipitating a collapse of the US and the global banking systems.

At the G7's 1982 Versailles summit, the original inner group of five decided to do more detailed work on international finance and currency relationships and the finance ministers met regularly in private during 1983 and 1984, with no secretariat. Eventually President Reagan was persuaded of the need to stop the appreciation of the dollar, mainly because of growing domestic political pressure from US industry whose competitiveness had been severely undermined by the strength of the dollar. These developments, among others, eventually led James Baker, the Treasury Secretary of the USA, to invite the other G5 finance ministers to the Plaza Hotel in Manhattan in September 1985 to institutionalize their meetings by making a public declaration, and then to the 1987 Louvre Accord on exchange rates. In the latter, the key individuals were Karl-Otto Pöhl, the President of the Bundesbank, and Jacques de Larosière, the head of the Banque de France and former Managing Director of the IMF (the key figure in directing the IMF response to the 1982 debt crisis).[50]

The Baker initiatives of 1985 focused on exchange rate realignment and on a plan to provide liquidity to Third World debtors (especially in Latin America) to alleviate their debt burdens. These initiatives were, to a certain extent, in contrast to the policy pursued by Donald Regan at the Treasury (1981–4) which was more in tune with Susan Strange's casino image of financial capitalism,[51] based on a more aggressive free-market orientation not disposed to international economic cooperation. The policies of 'benign neglect' (called by some 'malign neglect') of the dollar, and the laissez-faire orientation to the debt crisis embodied in Reagan's Treasury policies, can be interpreted as undermining the political cohesion of the G5/G7 forums: whilst European and Japanese exporters benefited from the Reagan expansion, the deflationary impact of these policies in the rest of the world undermined the consent of the United States' major allies.

The Baker initiatives perhaps reflected some awareness of structural forces, and the need for some limited cooperation in order politically to manage their effects. Baker sought to promote cooperation in order to minimize the unintended consequences of the structural power of mobile money capital. The shift towards a more negotiated set of policies in the emerging market-based system was also partly linked to the perception of a diffusion of economic and political power within the G7 grouping, with Japan and West Germany becoming more powerful. Thus coordination of policies was also bound up with a struggle over the leadership of the world economy, as well as with the search for agreement on ways to achieve policy consistency. In this regard the Japanese government has been much more willing to accede to US pressure than has the German government, for example in the Yen–Dollar Committee (set up in 1984) and more recently in the Strategic Impediments Initiative. These forums have enabled the USA to gain access to the financial services market in Japan, and to press for microeconomic reforms and expansionary macroeconomic policies.

The emerging view at the start of the 1990s in ruling circles concerning the sustainability of payments imbalances among the G3 was changing: the German surpluses are melting away with unification; the US deficits, whilst very large in absolute terms, have fallen as a proportion of GDP in the context of sustained growth; and Japanese surpluses are anticipated to decline in the 1990s partly as a result of a reorientation of economic growth more towards domestic activity (although Japan's politically sensitive trade balance has grown with the recent slowdown in growth). This has taken the steam out of any attempts to accelerate a more systematic and less *ad hoc* coordination process in the macroeconomic sphere (the propensity to cooperate here seems to be a function of the perception of the degree of systemic risk). So has the quickening of the momentum of the European unification process at the same time as the launch of new programmes for the reconstruction of Eastern Europe and the former USSR, under the aegis of the IMF, the EEC and the European Bank for Reconstruction and Development (EBRD).

Nevertheless, struggles still rage over the priorities in, and the means to achieve, the G7 agenda for cooperation. This agenda is large and includes, for example, global and regional macroeconomic management; microeconomic reforms designed to increase the efficiency and transparency of markets under regulated conditions; the restructuring of production relations (for example, by the restoration of labour markets and sectoral reforms); and the launching of international initiatives and strategies designed to restructure the economies of heretofore mercantilist, protectionist and state socialist countries, thereby integrating them more comprehensively into the ambit of the most powerful OECD economies and the forces which prevail within and across those economies. More generally, then, the aim, particularly on the part of the USA, is to deepen the world-wide appeal of market values and market forces to weaken nationalist–mercantilist states and economic structures, especially if they are opposed to the penetration of foreign capital and the liberalization of finance and associated services. Nevertheless contestation of the agenda and the policies to achieve it is still substantial among the G3, and this has tended to give a sense of G7 immobilism in the early 1990s.

International cooperation, in this sense, can be understood as a relatively limited attempt to provide a steering mechanism for stabilizing political change and, if possible, the world economy. To date the success of these initiatives appears to have been limited, and even contradictory in nature. For example, it is still not clear whether G7 actions caused or cured the massive 1987 stock market crash. Also at issue is whether, under G7 pressure, Japan expanded its money supply and lowered interest rates after the crash, resulting in the asset inflation in the stock and property markets thereafter. Moreover the key problem since 1989 has been a protracted and apparently intractable recession, which appears to be unique in postwar terms because it is linked to a severe, if unevenly distributed, debt deflation. This problem follows on directly from the financial liberalization and innovation of the 1980s, allied to the myopic lending of banks in an era of speculative excesses. This was especially the case in the UK and the USA, where indebtedness at all levels has grown, and in Japan, where the Finance Ministry and the Bank of Japan have sought to deflate the asset inflation characteristic of its 'bubble economy'. In the USA in late 1992, consumer and business confidence was so low that, despite the lowest levels of real interest rates since 1963, economic activity has failed to revive substantially.

In addition, the fiscal and inflationary costs of German unification have meant that there has been a very tight monetary policy in Germany, which has exerted a deflationary effect throughout Europe, and especially on members of the ERM. The former communist states in Europe have seen a catastrophic decline in economic activity, and the economic situation in Latin America, where there were some signs of a revival in the early 1990s, has to be set against the so-called 'lost decade of the 1980s'. Most of Africa has been in a spiralling decline for 15 years. In other words, where we may avert a repetition of the financial collapse of the 1930s when the last great debt deflation occurred – in part because of a more cooperative and institutionalized structure of postwar capitalism, at least when compared to the interwar years – the record of G7 cooperation in terms of economic growth and stability does not look too impressive.

Moreover the thrust of the current array of neo-liberal market monetarist policies is globally deflationary, and there is little to suggest from the most recent G7 summit in Munich in July 1992 that the leaders of the G7 have the imagination, the collective will or indeed the capacity to do much about it. The financial press has taken to suggesting that the G7 process reflects a preoccupation with domestic economic problems and that the G7 now play the (Frank) Sinatra doctrine, and do it 'My Way'. In this sense, the G7 meetings in the aftermath of the collapse of Soviet communism may come to be seen as the low point of capitalist internationalism since 1945. The plans for the restructuring of the Russian economy have been devolved to the IMF, which is applying a drip-feed form of credits according to its conditionality criteria, in a programme modelled on the 'shock therapy' applied by the IMF in Poland in 1990, a treatment which may prove to be more severe than the original disease. The resources devoted to the task by the G7 are meagre, given the size and the strategic importance of a country which has massive nuclear weapons and a large number of Chernobyl-type nuclear reactors which are in dire need of being decommissioned and made safe. The USA has designated 0.2 per cent of its GDP to the plan, compared to 1.2 per cent devoted to the Marshall Plan. Indeed it might be more appropriate to conclude that, at least for some members of the G7, the transnational political process of restructuring in the former Soviet Union is akin to an attempt to demobilize the enemy.

The G7 process has reflected and presided over the shift away from Keynesian style, closed-economy macroeconomic policies in a system of fixed exchange rates which prevailed in the 1950s and 1960s towards supply-side, market monetarist policies in a system of flexible exchange rates since the 1970s, policies which have tended to reward the economically fittest and to punish the weak. G7 meetings and communiqués have served to legitimate and support these policies and to press, where appropriate, for constitutional guarantees for the emergence of a market-based, disciplinary system of money and finance.

Beyond the inability to respond to the needs of a historically unprecedented situation, there is a wider contradiction between the relatively underdeveloped internationalization of political authority and the globalization of economic forces. This failure is reflected in the ongoing problem of sustaining the systemic integrity of the global financial system, and in the apparent inability of G7 macroeconomic cooperation to ensure stability in the markets, or to sustain global economic growth. This is the case not only with regard to the OECD countries but also in the poorer parts of the globe; much of the Third World has been in economic depression for about ten years, and many of the former communist states, not only the former USSR and Poland, are experiencing catastrophic economic decline in the early 1990s.

IV   Concluding reflections

Turning now to the potential contours of future international economic cooperation, this depends on how we understand changes within the world political economy. It can be argued that there is still a substantial gap between some of the prevailing conceptualizations of, and emerging changes in, the structural nature of the world economy. At the level of policy, consideration needs to be given to the way policy-makers conceive the political economy, as well as to the institutions and processes through which they seek to cooperate.

There is, as yet, very little empirical research which has been carried out on the ideological process which is bound up with these questions. In addition, there is very little work on the formal and informal social networks which link domestic forces in the United States with those elsewhere, and which may serve to internationalize the outlook of important political and economic groupings (although the present writer's own research on the Trilateral Commission was an attempt to trace some of these connections).[52]

Much more needs to be understood about not only the techniques though which cooperation between these national and international forces might take place, but also the political, social and ideological conditions which allow for the possibility of international communication and cooperation. One of the rare efforts in this direction is the work of Harvard's Robert Putnam on the economic summits.[53] He points out that the most successful summits (judged in terms of level of cooperation) of the 1970s and 1980s were those when a number of participating governments were internally divided on significant questions. Their divisions, however, instead of generating a sense of immobilism, actually provided a possibility for a transnational coalition of interests to form and thereby enhance cooperation.

In the future, if transnational forces become more salient in *domestic* politics among the summit powers, this might imply more propitious conditions for macroeconomic cooperation in the future to bring about greater stability and growth. That is to say, while it is correct to see national structures and attitudes – including the legacy of state interventionism, welfarism and mercantilism – as creating obstacles to such cooperation, the dialectical processes outlined here offer clues as to how these structures might gradually change. One of these is the internationalization of the United States. In this circumstance, and in so far as the United States has to compete with other states for portfolio and direct investment, it can be seen as no longer 'exceptional'. Like other states, America needs injections of foreign capital and technology in order to bolster its levels of productivity growth. However the United States is still exceptional in its ability to act as a social and economic magnet. As a result, whether the United States is or is not labelled a hegemon, its unique centrality is likely to continue well into the next century.

This special position of the United States may be seen as part of a movement towards a wider transnational hegemony. Hence, in response to the political question, 'hegemony for whom?', the answer for the next century could well be internationally mobile capital. This should be commodiously interpreted to include financial flows, direct investments and even flows of highly skilled labour ('human capital'). It is the transnational corporations which best embody and organize these constituents of economic power. Since these corporations will necessarily compete on a global level, their rise towards hegemony will have a contradictory and perhaps unstable quality, and will never be complete in a Gramscian sense. For example, banking transnationals may have a shorter time-horizon than high-technology manufacturing firms. Such differences and divisions may themselves contribute to difficulties in achieving cooperation, if international economic cooperation is taken to include not just state apparatuses but also private economic agents, including the representatives of labour.

What is less politically stable about the situation in the 1980s and 1990s – at least when compared with the 1950s and 1960s – in the OECD nations is that social democratic political forces and traditional trade unions have been weakened and marginalized from influencing the process of policy formation, the process Gilpin earlier identified in the American context as a long-run consequence of the export of capital from the United States.[54] This means that one of the domestic pillars of the original postwar economic order of embedded liberalism has been eroded (although embedded liberalism is still strong in continental Europe, especially in the social market system of post-unification Germany). Thus the emerging order which would accompany such a transformation would necessarily differ significantly from the liberalizing international economic order of the third quarter of the 20th century.

Returning to political and ideological conditions for international economic cooperation, what is suggested here is that a long-term effect of the transnationalization process may well be a greater international congruence of outlook and interest amongst important political actors and the domestic populations of the major states in the global political economy. However the major obstacle to this may well be the failure of American political leaders to adjust their concepts of the world economy and, as a consequence, the United States would continue to engage (perhaps periodically) in unilateral and inward-looking economic policies (for example, 'benign' or 'malign' neglect of the dollar), partly because of the nature of domestic politics in the USA.

Nevertheless market forces, plus the formation of a countervailing integrated monetary bloc in a more unified EEC and a more assertive Japan, might change the balance of international forces in the G7 forum. Thus the US government might be more subject to the forms of discipline which fall on other G7 governments. It might then be predisposed to cooperate on matters of macroeconomic policy on more equal terms with Europe and perhaps Japan in a new G3 (US–EC–Japan). In this situation, the EMS might provide some guidelines for G7 macroeconomic cooperation, in the sense that, to be effective, a relatively fixed exchange rate regime implies a willingness to agree upon and to share priorities, as well as to forgo some monetary autonomy. The sterling crisis and British withdrawal from the ERM in September 1992, however, merely underline the problems inherent in attempting to maintain a fixed exchange rate regime in a world of highly internationalized financial markets.

Indeed the constraints on US policy autonomy have increased during recent years. This is because of a range of factors, the most important of which are the size of its budget and balance of payments deficits; the fact that the USA has become the world's largest international debtor and will have to service its debts; increasing signs of the US dollar's relative decline as a reserve currency; and the growth of America's economic interdependence with the rest of the world as its relative self-sufficiency is eroded. Thus global economic interdependence is becoming less asymmetrical, that is less skewed in favour of the USA. For example, the USA has increasingly come to rely on European and Japanese financing and is likely to continue to need further substantial funds from these sources throughout the 1990s:

> Ironically, while it might be said that US policy since the Nixon years has been driven by the desire to maximise US autonomy *vis à vis* the rest of the world, the result may have been to increase the constraints upon US freedom of manoeuvre both relative to its major allies and to international financial markets.[55]

Nevertheless the USA is still the world's unchallenged military superpower, and it is likely to use this power in negotiations with its G7 partners to secure its objectives. Thus EC cooperation on defence questions, and the move towards an integrated European military capacity, are of importance not just for the provision of security, but also to strengthen the hand of an enlarged EEC in bargaining with the USA over macroeconomic and trade matters in the 21st century.

Thus, whilst G7 macroeconomic cooperation analogous to that practised in the EMS seems to be a distant possibility, long-term changes associated with transnationalization may eventually serve to bring about such cooperation in a G3 framework, perhaps in the next century. Whether these conditions will emerge is, of course, a moot point, as is the question whether the knowledge system and institutional apparatus of policy-making can be redeveloped so as *politically* to steer the contradictions of a more rapid, fully transnationalized system of global finance and production.

Appendix: other forums of international economic cooperation, 1944–92

The main institutions for cooperation and coordination of policies in the field of international money and finance – apart from the G3, G5 and G7 – are the International Monetary Fund (IMF), the Bank for International Settlements (BIS; set up in 1930 to help organize German reparations) and the Organization for Economic Cooperation and Development (OECD, founded in 1961, the successor to the Organization for European Economic Cooperation (OEEC), founded in 1948).

Created as an agency of the UN system, the IMF was originally seen by its Bretton Woods founders as an institution which would help to guarantee global financial stability and monitor and help to sustain the system of fixed exchange rates based on the US dollar fixed in price in relation to gold. Its sister UN institution, the World Bank, was intended to focus its efforts on development aid and technical assistance. The IMF mandate was inspired by the desire to avoid competitive devaluations of currencies and beggar-thy-neighbour policies, and involved specific conditions under which adjustments in parities could be made by countries: that is, when it was deemed to be a case of 'fundamental disequilibrium', and only if the IMF approved of the change (in practice most of the important changes made up to 1973 were made without consulting the IMF).

The role of the IMF has changed with the transformations in the global monetary system, following the final abandonment of fixed exchange rates in 1973. Since then, the Fund has focused increasing effort and resources on indebted countries, especially in the Third World, and, in the 1980s and 1990s, the former communist states of Eastern and Central Europe and the former Soviet Union. The IMF has also made important loans to G7 members, most notably to Britain in 1976. When funds are provided, the Fund attaches what is called 'conditionality': that is, a set of economic policy requirements which are designed to bring about future solvency and thus the ability to repay international debts.

During the 1960s the Group of Ten (G10) of finance ministers and heads of central banks (the so-called 'rich men's club') assumed growing importance.[56] However, the G10 lost significance as a forum because of US opposition following President Nixon's decision, in August 1971, to end the convertibility of dollars into gold and thus to terminate the regime of fixed parities, or pegged exchange rates anchored around the US dollar. Attempts to return to fixed exchange rates (as at the Smithsonian meeting of December 1971) quickly failed and the world moved towards a floating regime or, more accurately, a regime of flexible exchange rates: after 1973 some rates have often sunk quickly whilst others have risen. Some of the G10's work in the monetary sphere was taken up by the IMF's Interim Committee, which has 22 members, with half drawn from developing countries. This committee has met biannually since 1974, and was developed from the IMF's so-called Committee of Twenty. It advises the Board of Governors of the IMF. The latter was formed in 1972 and comprises central bank governors and finance ministers.

The BIS, located in Basle, has been described as a 'Holy-Roman-Empire kind of place for central bankers to meet'.[57] Its role was minimal after the 1931 global financial collapse, until it helped organize the postwar intra-European payments systems. In 1961, in response to flows of speculative funds following the revaluation of the Deutschmark, the BIS members concluded the informal Basle Agreements intended to counter speculative pressures on currencies and reserves. These involved networks of official swaps or short-term (3–6 month) credits. These were reciprocally linked to the US

Federal Reserve, which only began to participate fully in BIS deliberations in 1960.

The UK drew heavily on the system of central bank cooperation to support sterling in the 1960s, and so did France in the 1970s. The Bank of England relied on a huge $5.3 billion credit on 7 June 1976 from the other G10 central banks, along with Switzerland and the BIS. This paved the way for the UK IMF Drawing of December 1976. Concerted efforts were made to defend the US dollar in November 1978. In the early 1980s, the BIS moved into pre-financing of IMF deals, in concert with other central banks, in Hungary, Mexico, Brazil and Yugoslavia. The G10 plus Switzerland now meet 10 times a year in the BIS to coordinate policies. The BIS is also the key source for information on the Eurocurrency markets. It provides the secretariat for the process of international banking supervision and regulation under the so-called Cooke Committee, established in 1974. Under the initiative of the UK and USA, in 1987 this committee established internationally agreed rules for the capital adequacy of banks in order to shore up the foundations of the international financial system, and it meets regularly to monitor international developments.

The OECD is governed by a Council in which member countries are represented; it meets annually at ministerial level. The most important committees are the Economic Policy Committee (EPC), which meets biannually and which focuses on general macroeconomic issues, and Working Party Three (WP3), which focuses on international monetary questions and balance of payments imbalances. WP3 membership is restricted to the G10 minus Belgium plus Switzerland.

Notes

1. Toffler (1990, p. 389).
2. The members of the G7 are Canada, Germany, France, Japan, Italy, the United Kingdom and the United States. Since 1977 they have been joined at the Economic Summits by the President of the European Commission. The G7 deputies' meetings, which take place more frequently, involve not only finance ministers (and their deputies) but also the heads of central banks from these nations.
3. The bail-outs associated with the debt crisis, and also in support of domestic banks in the 1980s have been associated with the term 'moral hazard', which suggests that individual economic agents (such as lenders and borrowers) will not behave according to the disciplines of the market because they anticipate that the government is likely to come to the rescue to avert a financial collapse or panic: that is, the government will act as lender of last resort. Thus a purely market-based form of discipline as advocated by F.A. Von Hayek is difficult to envisage simply because governments actually exist. Thus the ordo-liberals of the Freiburg school in Germany stress the need for independent central banks: that is, the discipline of an independent public institution to enforce monetary discipline in the 'social market', or a combination of public and private discipline through IMF conditionality and leadership of the private banking sector in managing debt workouts.
4. Of course G2 (United States and Japan), G3 (G2 plus Germany), G5 (G3 plus France and the United Kingdom) and G7 meetings are not solely devoted to 'economic' ques-

tions, narrowly defined: they are also highly political, since they are part of a wide-ranging set of political processes which seek to develop collective strategy on the part of the G7, for example with regard to not only the oil crisis of the 1970s and the debt crisis in the 1980s, but also the political, economic and social restructuring of the former Soviet Union in the 1990s. In the case of the G2, for example, the United States and Japan seek to develop political mechanisms to mediate their economic conflicts, usually provided that the Japanese make some concessions to American demands, rather than vice versa.

5. The term 'international public goods' is widely used in the IPE literature as a means of defining the objectives of G7 cooperation. While useful, this term presupposes the question: 'good for whom?' Even if one accepts the idea, for example, that the public good of monetary stability is good for all (although it may benefit creditors rather than debtors) the question still arises as to how a stable currency is to be achieved. Is the means to control the supply of a public good kept specifically in the hands of one class of the population (such as financiers and bankers)? Who controls the bankers if they are given independent status to guarantee the values of currencies, for example by raising interest rates to very high levels and provoking recession? What is the importance of a sound currency relative to other economic objectives, such as full employment or wider criteria, such as distributive justice?

6. For example, Cohen (1978).

7. Kindleberger (1973).

8. Such arguments were used to pressure Germany and Japan (as well as some of the Gulf states) into making contributions to US and UK military costs in them 1991 Gulf War, a process coordinated through the G7 finance ministers. Much more political economy research needs to be done on the degree to which international monetary and military questions are being integrated, in forums such as the G7 and the UN Security Council. This process may be likened to the institutionalization of a tributary system, akin to a form of global tax collection to pay for international security, with the USA at its centre following the collapse of the USSR.

9. Keohane (1984).

10. Walter (1991).

11. Gilpin (1987), Keohane (1984).

12. For example Van der Pijl (1984); Cox (1987); Gill (1990); Helleiner (1991); Walter (1991).

13. De Cecco (1974)

14. Polanyi (1944).

15. Emphasized by Carr (1945).

16. Cox (1987).

17. Gill and Law (1988); Gill (1990); Cox (1987); see also Gill and Law (1989).

18. See Gill (1991) for elaboration, and Gill (ed.) (Forthcoming, 1993).

19. Cox (1983, p. 169).

20. Gramsci (1971 edn).

21. Ruggie (1982).

22. Gill (1986; 1990).

23. De Cecco (1979).

24. Helleiner (1990).

25. As Helleiner (1991) and other revisionist historians have shown, this meant that US foreign aid, including Marshall aid, was used to balance European capital exports to the USA, and capital flight from Europe in the early postwar years.

26. De Cecco (1979, p. 60).

27. Ibid.

28. On the origins, see Strange (1986).

29. Ibid.; Frieden (1987).

30. Frieden (1987, p. 80).

31. Ibid., p. 81

32. Helleiner (1991).

33. Strange (1988, p. 105).
34. Strange (1988).
35. For example, Strange (1986); Frieden (1987); Law (1989).
36. Many of the key policy changes after the Second World War, such as the US decision to suspend the convertibility of the dollar into gold in August 1971, have simply been announced to the rest of the world without discussion or prior notification (in this case by telephone from the White House).
37. Triffin (1960).
38. Helleiner (1991).
39. Helleiner (1991) also emphasizes, along with Strange (1986) that at the time of the oil shock the authorities had a choice: they could have strengthened cooperation, for example via the IMF, and used international organizations to recycle the funds. That they did not do this reflected US veto power over any significant change in the international monetary and financial structures, as well as a reduction in the policy autonomy of the transnational supervisory and regulatory structure characteristic of postwar central bank cooperation, and a reduction of the collective power of the major capitalist states *vis-à-vis* the financial markets.
40. Strange (1986).
41. Helleiner (1991).
42. For example, Arrighi (1982); Gill (1986); Strange (1987).
43. Webb (1991).
44. Hawley (1987).
45. Gilpin (1976).
46. Calleo (1982).
47. Helleiner (1991).
48. Cerny (1990).
49. Also in 1976 the IMF Interim Committee met to abolish the official price of gold and the floating of exchange rates was legalized, although the IMF was given 'firm surveillance' over such rates, higher IMF quotas came into force, and the use of SDRs (special drawing rights) was widened. It may also be remembered that in 1976 there was a major change in UK economic policy and a seismic split in the ranks of the ruling Labour Party, occasioned by a major balance of payments crisis, and which caused the UK Labour Government to go to the IMF for a loan.
50. At the informal (though publicly announced) Plaza meeting only the five finance ministers were in attendance, plus a word-processor operator and a small simultaneous translation team for the French and the Japanese: all G7 meetings are conducted in English. Subsequent meetings of the G5 have been equally 'informal'.
51. Strange (1986).
52. Gill (1990).
53. Putnam and Bayne (1987).
54. Gilpin (1975).
55. Walter (1991, p. 224).
56. The G10 consisted of the G7 plus Netherlands, Belgium and Switzerland, although Switzerland was not an IMF member. It has traditionally met at the times of the IMF annual meetings and at the Spring IMF Interim Committee meeting, at both deputy and at ministerial level. This forum has been important in international monetary initiatives since its formation in 1962.
57. Group of Thirty (1984).

References

Arrighi, G. (1982), 'Crisis of hegemony', in S. Amin *et al.*, *Dynamics of Global Crisis*, London: Macmillan, pp. 55–108.

Calleo, D. (1982), *The Imperious Economy*, Cambridge, MA: Harvard University Press.

Carr, E.H. (1945), *The Twenty Years' Crisis*, New York: Harper.

Cerny, P. (1990), *The Changing Architecture of Politics: Structure, Agency and the Future of the State*, London: Sage Publications.

Cohen, B.J. (1978), *Organising the World's Money*, New York: Basic Books.

Cox, R.W. (1983), 'Gramsci, Hegemony and International Relations: An Essay in Method', *Millennium: Journal of International Studies*, **12**, 162–75.

Cox, R.W. (1987), *Power, Production and World Order: Social Forces in the Making of History*, New York: Columbia University Press.

De Cecco, M. (1974), *Money and Empire*, Oxford: Blackwell.

De Cecco, M. (1979), 'The Origins of the Postwar Payments System', *Cambridge Journal of Economics*, **3**, 49–61.

Destler I.M. and R. Henning (1990), *Dollar Politics*, Washington DC: Institute for International Economics.

Frieden, J. (1987), *Banking on the World*, New York: Harper & Row.

Funobashi, Y. (1988), *Managing the Dollar: From Plaza to the Louvre*, Washington, DC: Institute for International Economics.

Gill, S. (1986), 'American Hegemony: Its Limits and Prospects in the Reagan Era', *Millennium: Journal of International Studies*, **15**, 311–36.

Gill, S. (1990), *American Hegemony and the Trilateral Commission*, Cambridge: Cambridge University Press.

Gill, S. (1991), 'Historical Materialism, Gramsci and International Political Economy', in C. Murphy and R. Tooze (eds), *The New International Political Economy*, London: Macmillan, pp. 51–75.

Gill, S. (ed.) (forthcoming 1993), *Gramsci, Historical Materialism and International Relations*, Cambridge: Cambridge University Press.

Gill, S. and D. Law (1988), *The Global Political Economy: Perspectives, Problems and Policies*, Baltimore: Johns Hopkins Press.

Gill, S. and D. Law (1989), 'Global Hegemony and the Structural Power of Capital', *International Studies Quarterly*, **36**, 475–99.

Gilpin, R. (1975), *US Power and the Multinational Corporation*, New York: Basic Books.

Gilpin, R. (1987), *The Political Economy of International Relations*, Princeton: Princeton University Press.

Gramsci, A. (1971), *Selections from the Prison Notebooks of Antonio Gramsci*, ed. and trans. by Q. Hoare and G. Nowell Smith, New York: International Publishers.

Group of Thirty (1984), *Economic Cooperation from the Inside*, New York: Group of Thirty.

Hawley, J. (1987), *Dollars and Borders: US Government attempts to restrict capital flows, 1960–1980*, New York: M.E. Sharpe.

Helleiner, E. (1990 and 1991), 'American Hegemony and Global Economic Structure: From Closed to Open Financial Relations in the Postwar World', PhD thesis, draft and final version, London School of Economics.

Keohane, R.O. (1984), *After Hegemony: Cooperation and Discord in the World Political Economy*, Princeton: Princeton University Press.

Kindleberger, C. (1973), *The World In Depression, 1929–39*, Berkeley: University of California Press.

Law, D. (1989), 'Transatlantic Economic Co-operation: the Baker Initiatives and Beyond', in S. Gill (ed.) *Atlantic Relations: Beyond the Reagan Era*, Hemel Hempstead: Harvester Wheatsheaf, pp. 139–55.

Polanyi, K. (1944), *The Great Transformation: The Political and Economic Origins of our Times*, Boston: Beacon Press.

Putnam, R. and N. Bayne (1987), *Hanging Together: The Seven Power Summits*, Cambridge, MA: Harvard University Press.

Ruggie, J.G. (1982), 'International Regimes, Transactions and Change – Embedded Liberalism in the Post-war Economic Order', *International Organisation*, **36**, 379–415.

Strange, S. (1986), *Casino Capitalism*, Oxford: Basil Blackwell.

Strange, S. (1987), 'The Persistent Myth of Lost Hegemony', *International Organization*, **41**(4), Fall, 551–74.

Strange, S. (1988), *States and Markets*, London: Pinter.

Toffler, A. (1990), *Power Shift*, Toronto: Bantam Books.
Triffin, R. (1960), *Gold and the Dollar Crisis,* Princeton: Princeton University Press.
Van der Pijl, K. (1984), *The Making of an Atlantic Ruling Class*, London: Verso.
Walter, A. (1991), *World Power and World Money*, New York: St. Martin's Press.
Webb, M.C. (1991), 'International Economic Structures, Government Interests, and International Coordination of Macroeconomic Adjustment Policies', *International Organization*, **45**, 309–42.

5 Negotiating financial openness: the Uruguay Round and trade in financial services

Geoffrey R.D. Underhill

Two basic assumptions underpin, and are sustained by, the analysis in this chapter. First, that the internationalization of production, trade and finance in the postwar era represents a profound structural transformation of the economies of the OECD area and a significant departure from the national capitalist economic order envisaged at Bretton Woods. Second, that these structural changes are in turn transforming the politics of domestic states in the system. In this regard, the chapter will examine those crucial aspects of the Uruguay Round negotiations which are aimed at liberalizing trade in financial services. In particular, we will analyse the interaction between domestic and international levels of state decision-making concerning the emerging services trade regime, on the one hand, and the process of market change, on the other. This chapter, then, is about the relationship between politics and markets, the trade regime and the domain of money and finance. The Uruguay Round – the latest of several rounds of negotiation to extend the coverage of the General Agreement on Tariffs and Trade (GATT) with its expanded negotiating agenda, provides an opportunity to look at all these issues together in a case study context, whereas they have hitherto largely been treated separately in the literature despite widespread recognition that they are inextricably intertwined.

I Introduction

The chapter will argue four points. First, that the attempt in the Uruguay Round to liberalize trade in financial services is a significant political step by the international community with far-reaching consequences for the world economy and domestic economic management. The second point follows from the first: that there are considerable repercussions for state policy-making if an international cooperative agreement on trade in financial services is reached. Third, that this extension of GATT into new domains contradicts the predictions of the theory of hegemonic stability and negates the validity of the systemic-level theories of international relations generally known under the label of 'neo-realism'. Finally the study permits an examination of the two-way relationship between politics and markets, demonstrating how international cooperative agreements can initiate a structural transformation of economies, and how the resulting changes in market structure play back into the politics of domestic societies.

The argument

The first point is that the liberalization of trade in financial services will represent a major political decision by the international community with far-reaching consequences for domestic economic policies and the structure of the global economy. In the immediate postwar period, financial services industries and capital markets were essentially national in scope.[1] Until recently, a combination of exchange controls and complex systems of domestic regulation ensured that, in the domain of finance, the global economy remained segmented and subject to relatively efficient national political control. Although there have long been 'international' banking and securities markets,[2] whose impact on domestic sectors has increased in recent years, the Uruguay Round negotiations represent a new departure.[3] The talks aim to open up hitherto tightly regulated and protected domestic markets for financial services to foreign competition, a further step in the direction of internationalization, and to impose rules beyond the direct control of national authorities. As has occurred in the domain of manufacturing trade, a successful General Agreement on Trade in Services (GATS) will, over time, lead to the emergence of genuinely transnational markets for financial and other service sectors. As a result it will have a major impact on the stability and management of financial services sectors and on patterns of investment in the world economy. Competition for markets will be greatly intensified, leading to a period of difficult adjustment for financial institutions.[4] At the same time, a GATS will have a substantial impact on the abilities of states to manage the process of capital formation. Not surprisingly, the talks are raising controversy in domestic political systems.[5]

The further internationalization of the financial services sector through the GATS will represent an important change in the structure of economies in the OECD area. It has already been demonstrated in the domain of trade in goods that internationalization transforms the politics of economic policy-making in these economies.[6] Although there is a dearth of research into the question, it follows that similar changes are taking place in relation to the politics of money and finance. Governments are constrained by the need to maintain the confidence of international money markets in order to prevent capital flight and downward pressure on the national currency. Payments imbalances take on a new meaning as capital transfers dwarf the financial flows associated with international trade in goods. It certainly seems clear from available evidence that major financial institutions already active on international markets, along with their supporting interest groups in the USA and Europe, strongly favour the conclusion of a GATS which would submit

the financial sectors of these economies to international rules which governments could not challenge, and would open domestic markets up to international competition on this basis.[7] The control of capital flows would pass
largely to private market actors outside the control of any one nation-state
and, paradoxically, national government decisions in the context of the Round
negotiations will have yielded this result.

All in all, it seems certain that the proposed agreement will begin a period
of structural transformation of national economies. As has happened with
international trade in manufactures, liberalization and the establishment of
internationally agreed rules for services trade will presage the emergence of
a truly transnational market for financial services. The effects will undoubtedly differ, depending on the particular sector involved (primarily banking,
insurance or securities dealing) but they will be significant regardless.

The second point followed from the first. There are enormous repercussions for state policy-making if a GATS for financial services is negotiated.
A successful accord will represent a significant constraint on sovereign
policy-making prerogatives relating to the regulation of a crucial sector of
the economy and to the control of money. To this effect, GATT economists
clearly expect a services deal to accelerate the internationalization of economic decision-making in general. Drawing attention to the pivotal role of
service sectors in the expansion of international trade, they argue that

> the greater the availability and the lower the costs of the needed services, the
> faster the pace of globalization of markets. Thus, while there are many factors
> behind the growing emphasis on global markets and the declining importance of
> national boundaries for many production and investment decisions, it is clear
> that technological advances in services sectors are playing a pivotal role.[8]

The constraints on national policy-making prerogatives arise for a number of
reasons. To begin with, there is the linkage among policy domains. The
soundness and stability of financial institutions is a concern of prudential
supervisory policy. The rapid innovation and securitization of financial markets in recent years has already had implications for the soundness of the
banking sector.[9] A successful GATS will increase competitive pressures as
foreign institutions make inroads into the domestic preserves of financial
intermediaries. Furthermore liberalization would interfere with established
patterns of prudential supervision:

> 'marketisation', or asserting market discipline as the chief measure of the suc-
> cess or failure of an institution, alters the traditional, regulated pattern of risk-
> taking.... Yet an increase in private (i.e. market) risk control is a necessary
> complement of the extension of markets if distortions in competition are not to
> occur among various national industries.[10]

In this way, the GATS rules will eventually place some constraints on the structure of national prudential supervisory frameworks to the extent that these regulations may be seen as unfair trade practices. These constraints are likely to be minor at first, and there certainly will be provisions in the accord for national policy objectives relating to the stability of financial institutions,[11] but they will increase as liberalization gathers pace. This is likely to manifest itself through pressures from firms to harmonize domestic regulatory frameworks across boundaries with a view to levelling the competitive 'playing field'.

Another related policy domain concerns the broader regulatory framework for financial institutions. The GATS will necessarily involve a certain amount of domestic deregulation of financial services sectors. Governments which restrict national firms to certain activities, particularly the United States with its Glass–Steagall Act and state banking laws, are concerned about competition from foreign firms whose national legislation confers relative advantages in international competition.[12] The United States is clearly concerned about the potential pressure from European 'universal' banking institutions.[13] The fear of Japanese banking groups is never far from the surface.[14]

Another policy linkage is between financial services sectors and monetary policy.[15] Financial institutions are primarily concerned with providing credit and other forms of finance, which affects the money supply. National measures to control inflation and the growth of the money supply will be constrained by liberalization and multilateral rules, and their effectiveness limited further by the emergence of transnational financial services markets. Market discipline will increasingly be the order of the day for national monetary and related policies. The management of government debt will likewise be affected – the close relationships between central banks and private issuers of government paper constitute an unfair competitive advantage on official securities markets.

Indeed the internationalization of markets in banking has already struck at the heart of national systems of monetary control, sometimes impairing its very effectiveness unless there are accompanying measures of coordination among states.[16] A further implication for monetary policy is related to the principle of 'national treatment' which will underpin the emerging services trade regime. Because of the peculiar nature of services sectors, national treatment implies 'right of establishment'.[17] While technology permits the provision of some financial products without an establishment, other activities such as retail lending clearly require a physical presence if foreign institutions are meaningfully to perform their function as intermediaries. Once foreign firms begin to operate in a particular domestic environment, they will also require freedom to move the necessary factors of production across borders. In the case of financial services industries, this means capital; thus the national control of money is impaired.

The agreement implies, then, the more or less complete liberalization of capital flows. The freedom to supply credit or securities makes little sense if the money involved is to be excluded from a particular national economic space. This has repercussions for balance of payments policies as well as the money supply, to say nothing of the control of foreign investment.[18] Clearly the liberalization of financial services trade strikes at the core of national systems of economic management and state decision-making, and will be a source of constant pressure for the coordination of macroeconomic policies. The weaker economies may have little say in this situation, so the implications for the future of the international political economy could be considerable.

Finally, and most obviously, just as the GATT currently proscribes certain national trade policies, so an agreement imposing rules on trade in financial services and establishing a process of steady liberalization will hamper domestic policies to promote or protect the development of the financial sector. The opening of markets to foreign competition will lead to a period of adjustment. Not all financial institutions, nor indeed entire sectors, will benefit. There will be winners and losers, and this may generate demands for protectionism if the experience of manufacturing trade is at all relevant. However these domestic political pressures to manage the process of economic change to the advantage of national firms will conflict with the rules imposed by the agreement – rules establishing transparency, national treatment, reciprocity and non-discrimination as the principles governing trade in financial products. There may be disputes in which GATS panels come down on one side or another. State economic managers will have divested themselves of important policy tools at precisely the time when the internationalization of economic decision-making may have its most detrimental effects on domestic firms. The consequences will undoubtedly be different for the various financial services industries which will be affected by the agreement. Securities brokerage may be harder hit than, say, the life insurance sector. Much research remains to be done to assess the political and economic impact of the negotiations on the various forms of financial institutions in different national settings. All in all, a GATS in financial services represents a crucial step towards a transnationalization and indeed privatization of important policy domains through the creation of markets across borders.

The third point was that this extension of GATT into new domains contradicts the predictions of the theory of hegemonic stability and negates the validity of the systemic-level theories of international relations.

[T]he theory of hegemonic stability is perhaps the most prominent approach to explaining regime change in the various issue-areas of the contemporary international political economy. Its proponents essentially argue that, as stated by Robert Gilpin, 'the existence of a hegemonic or dominant liberal power is a necessary (albeit not sufficient) condition for the full development of a world market economy'. The dominant power must bear the 'cost' of providing the 'public good' of a liberal market economy and correspondingly strong, liberal international regimes. The dominant power must be able and willing to discipline others to prevent the problem of 'free-riding'.[19]

The theory of hegemonic stability is firmly rooted in the neo-realist tradition of international relations. Neo-realism insists on the primacy of international systemic factors in explanations of world politics,[20] hence the focus on hegemony and the economic power structure as the most important variable to explain the process of change in the international political economy.

The theory goes on to predict that the relative decline of American hegemony will lead to the fragmentation and erosion of the liberal character of the GATT trade regime, manifested in a rise in protectionism: 'The weakening hegemon will be less and less willing to bear the costs of openness...as the economic success of others in the system challenges the hegemon's capacity to do so while remaining competitive.'[21] Some have applied this approach to the mixed results of the Tokyo Round of multilateral trade negotiations, portraying the outcome of the Round as a major step towards the fragmentation of the liberal trading order, with dire predictions of worse to come.[22] The 1980s, with the constant threat of protectionism emanating from the US Congress and certain states within the EEC, can be held up as a confirmation of this trend.

The first remark to make in this regard is that the liberal order, far from collapsing, is being extended into new domains such as financial services through the Uruguay Round negotiations. As will be demonstrated, there is much debate over the issue of unconditional most-favoured-nation treatment (MFN) with respect to services trade and other issues in the Round. But openness is not in question – just the form the open regime is to take and the specific nature of the rules that are to apply to each sector. Despite the predictions of systemic approaches for regime development, then, the Uruguay Round represents an even more radical and ambitious step in the direction of liberalization than the earlier Tokyo Round. The agenda of the Uruguay Round implies expanding the scope of GATT to include rules governing a series of policy issues related to fair competition in international trade. Among these are state policies towards the control of foreign investment (Trade-Related Investment Measures, or TRIMS), Trade-Related Intellectual Property Rights (TRIPS), an enhanced dispute settling procedure, a revision of GATT opt-out clauses, and of course the vast services sectors of national economies. This constant extension of GATT rule-making into new domains hardly corresponds to a steady closure of the trade regime. Instead we see an attempt at an international cooperative agreement to introduce market decision-making processes into important areas of domestic policy-making. Nowhere is this extension of the GATT more dramatic than in the financial services industry, given the policy linkages described above. In view of these linkages, a successful financial services agreement will contribute to greater openness of the financial system as well as the trade regime. In fact 'openness' v. 'protectionism' turns out to be a false dichotomy set up by hegemonic stability theorists concerned with American power.[23]

A second remark is that this extension of markets across borders will lead to new patterns of interdependence among states and their societies through the new market structures. These new patterns of interdependence are likely significantly to alter the policy preferences of segments of domestic economies, on the one hand, and to affect policy processes, on the other. This points to the inadequacy of the systemic level of analysis developed by neo-realists in the context of the theory of hegemonic stability. We will understand little if we focus exclusively on the changing distribution of power in the global economy. We should focus instead on the *interaction* of the domestic and international domains. A successful financial services agreement in the Uruguay Round will constitute a political decision on the part of the GATT membership to change the structure of markets, accelerating the process of transnationalization of economic decision-making and conferring advantages upon some market actors and disadvantages upon others. This will in turn lead to a pattern of sectoral restructuring at the domestic and international levels of analysis. The new patterns of interdependence which develop in the context of the emerging market structure will shift the policy preferences of market actors in various domestic political systems as firms respond to the incentives of new market structures and regulatory frameworks. This is likely also to alter the balance of power among domestic market actors within political systems, with increased power for actors which are closely integrated into international markets, and big losses for firms which are too small or too limited in scope to avail themselves of this option.

A third remark is that this process of negotiations has not taken place in a political vacuum. Unlike the universe portrayed by rational choice perspectives associated with neo-realism, states are not searching for the most economically rational policy option in the light of some objectively defined national interest and process of market innovation. The systemic level of analysis again affords little understanding here. Instead some more powerful states in the system are responding to pressures from the segments of their domestic financial services sectors which are best placed to benefit from further marketization and transnationalization.[24] The role of Citicorp and American Express in pressing for the services negotiations is no secret in Washington, and the US was the driving force behind the services talks as shall be demonstrated. These firms continue to keep a close watch on the negotiations through lobby groups such as the Coalition of Service Industries, the Bankers Association for Foreign Trade, and the Financial Services Council.[25] Financial services, formerly a preserve of national control, are now the object of open political lobbying to alter the structure and regulatory framework of the sector in favour of marketization of the policy process and transnationalization of the markets themselves.

If the theory of hegemonic stability and the systemic level of analysis it applies is inadequate, there exists a more fruitful line of theoretical enquiry. This involves conceptualizing not only the linkages between domestic and international political processes, but also the relationship between structural economic change in the market and political processes at both levels of analysis. In the domain of finance, government decision-making (and non-decision-making) led to the emergence of international financial markets. Adjustment to internationalization in turn leads to changes in the perceived economic interests of market actors. Given that these powerful economic agents have considerable political resources, political pressures are created for a further restructuring of the regulatory framework governing money and finance.

The Uruguay Round negotiations to liberalize trade in financial services may be seen in this light. In this view, hegemony is of relatively little importance as a variable, and is neither a sufficient nor a necessary condition for explaining changes in the domain of trade, money or finance. The crucial factor would seem to be the emergence in the postwar period of a transnational market system which benefits some and imposes costs on others. The interests associated with the rise of this system seek to pry open protected markets and to extend the internationalization of economic decision-making to new sectors of activity, and they have the political resources to do so. Along the way there is considerable political conflict with those interests which benefit from a more segmented international economy based on the state as an economic unit, and the national capitalism associated with Keynesian economic policies and corresponding systems of domestic regulatory priorities. None the less, the changing patterns of domestic politics are likely to lead to greater levels of openness and liberalization in the face of US decline, not less, as predicted by the theory of hegemonic stability at the systemic level of analysis. The evidence presented in this case study will help us reformulate the ways in which we explain regime change in the international political economy.

The fourth and final point of the argument derives from the third: the study permits an examination of the two-way relationship between politics and markets. The role of the state and of political processes is often obscure in the domain of financial markets, where the state's capacity to direct capital flows in global markets without incurring substantial opportunity and political costs appears so limited.[26] However the Uruguay Round negotiations for the liberalization of trade in financial services may be seen as a highly political process to extend the scope of markets – a process which, as has been emphasized, is not happening in a political vacuum. It is also a response to structural change in international financial markets, change set in motion by prior political decisions. This refers to the decisions (and non-decisions) which led to the emergence of the unregulated Euromarkets themselves[27] and eventually to the national deregulation of financial institutions in the face of intensified competition and rapid innovation in the sector.[28] The success of the Round will in turn have a considerable impact on the choices of economic policy-makers; it will shape the conflicts of interest within and among states with respect to the distribution of economic resources and the direction of economic development.

Therefore an analysis of the Uruguay Round negotiations on trade in financial services offers an insight into the political conflicts, domestic and international, which surround the negotiation of international cooperative agreements that presage a structural transformation of economies. The state remains the seat of decision-making and the principal forum for political conflict. The analysis also shows how the earlier changes in the structure of financial markets (the rise of the Euromarkets and deregulation) play back into the politics of domestic societies. The Uruguay Round represents a process of political decision-making to de-segment national capital markets and marketize an important domain of the economy. International cooperative agreements to create transnational market structures provide the political underpinning for an increasingly global economy.

Points three and four suggest that there is an alternative framework to systemic explanations of the international political economy.[29] This approach emphasizes the linkages between domestic and international levels of analysis. The starting-point is an understanding of the emerging transnational economic structure and of the changing policy preferences of the economic actors involved.[30] The process of marketization through international negotiation can only be understood in terms of the changing interests of market actors and the political resources that they wield as articulated through the system of states. There is essentially one political process, with the state managing the constraints of the domestic and international domains through domestic policy-making, on the one hand, and intergovernmental bargaining, on the other. There is no clear division between the domestic and international environments, particularly as many economic interests now span borders – a situation a successful Round will enhance.

The case study which follows will be studied in the light of these arguments, but first a final remark to conclude this section: it is significant that the issue has been characterized as 'trade' in financial services. Despite the policy linkages outlined above, the negotiation has not been portrayed as a capital markets issue. Nor is it, as in the case of the EC Single Market in financial services, about the harmonization of domestic regulatory frameworks for the financial services sector, although this is one of the objectives. Sensitive issues such as foreign investment, prudential supervisory policy, balance of payments effects and monetary policy will only indirectly be on the agenda. It is easier to point to the benefits of liberalized 'trade', linked to prospects for renewed economic growth, than to demonstrate potential gains from a major restructuring of the regulatory framework for financial institutions.[31] It is a restructuring which grants them more independence and flexibility than in the past, on the one hand, but submits them to the greater risks of a market environment, on the other.

The end result will be to accelerate a trend which has been in evidence since the rise of the Euromarkets. The financial services industry is no longer the 'servant' of the production process – no longer part of a nationally controlled process of capital formation for industrial investment. Financial products are now largely created and traded for their own sake. Capital flows related to financial market transactions vastly overshadow those related to trade in manufactured goods. Further liberalization will give the traders themselves yet more control over much of the world's money.[32] In this sense, the liberalization of capital markets symbolizes the power of finance capital, with its interest in policies of sound money, strong key currencies and the harmonization of macroeconomic environments, whatever the cost in terms of lost employment or industrial decline.

This is not to say that the financial services industry and the manufacturing sector are irretrievably divorced. In fact, in its multinational variant, industry has become closely integrated with finance capital as major banks followed their customers abroad.[33] Each relies on the ability to move money: multinational corporations (MNCs) in order to take advantage of an international division of labour; international financial institutions in order to take advantage of the most favourable investment climate. Both therefore have an interest in open economic regimes, particularly in trade and finance. In the Uruguay Round, the conflict between these and more domestically oriented interests can clearly be seen.

II   The Uruguay Round and the liberalization of trade in financial services

The efforts of the major industrialized nations to regularize and liberalize trade in financial services through the GATT are still in their relative infancy.[34] Although it is expected that an agreement will indeed result from the current multilateral Round, and that it will include financial services, even the eventual accord will only set the framework for rules in the financial and indeed other services sectors:

> It will not be possible to build, within the period of the Uruguay Round negotiations, a complete set of rules.... For example, it seems dangerous and probably impractical to try to develop sweeping rules, such as a broad national treatment obligation, which would apply to all 'services', regardless of industry.[35]

The actual extent of liberalization, then, is likely to be limited at first, given the degree of controversy involved: 'Finance ministries and central banks are not likely to relinquish their grasp over monetary policy to accommodate free trade advocates'.[36]

The push for a GATS

There are two ways in which the impetus for a financial services agreement in the wider context of a GATT services trade deal may be discussed. The first is in terms of its basic economic rationale for respective national economies. The second is in terms of the interests of economic actors and their articulation in domestic political systems: that is, through organized pressure on government for liberalization in order to facilitate access to foreign services markets and to level the competitive 'playing field' to the extent possible. In both cases, the United States took the lead, but other countries, particularly the EC with the ambitious 1992 programme on the way, soon saw the benefits.

The economic rationale was fairly straightforward. One objective was an expansion of trade in services. National service sectors have traditionally been highly protected, and it is estimated that world trade in services would have grown faster but for the many barriers to transactions.[37] As European Commissioner Willy De Clercq asserted, 'the level of international trade in services stands at one quarter the level of trade in goods; services today constitute one of the most dynamic features of the world economy'.[38] Given that remaining barriers to trade in goods are difficult to dismantle, because of the contentious nature of the adjustment process, a consensus emerged among the industrialized nations on the desirability of developing markets in what had become the fastest-growing sector of most industrialized economies.[39]

The new round of multilateral trade negotiations was also motivated by the ongoing economic difficulties of the industrialized economies.[40] The extension of international markets into new areas through cooperative inter-governmental action, specifically trade in agriculture and services, was seen as a potential stimulant to growth.[41] GATT economists have also stressed that important links exist between the 'provision of services and merchandise trade', and that 'access to competitively-priced producer services is increasingly important in determining the ability of firms to compete at home or abroad'.[42] 'Services transactions are increasingly "commingled" with the production and trade of goods. Companies today rely on advanced communications systems...',[43] and of course financial services.

According to the standard economic rationale, then, countries with competitive advantages in services trade might be expected to pursue a GATS. It is therefore not surprising that the United States took the lead, with a number of the Washington 'think-tanks' pressing the Administration to accept the case in favour.[44] The US interest was clear: America possessed the largest service economy, with over 75 per cent of the workforce and 69 per cent of gross national product (GNP) dependent on service industries, and a spectacular record of job creation to accompany this fact. The services account of the balance of payments had typically been in substantial surplus, but US export performance in the sector was three times below the collective service exports of EEC countries.[45] The Reagan Administration, upon assuming office in 1981, was particularly anxious to deal with this issue, believing that the American economy had a comparative advantage, particularly in financial services,[46] in a context of declining US trade competitiveness in manufactures.[47] The Congressional Office of Technology Assessment (OTA) estimated in 1986 that the American government's balance of payments statistics understate US services exports by as much as half.[48] In particular, government services statistics did not take into account the enormous receipts of foreign US affiliates.

Not surprisingly, the report called for better analysis of services sectors, with financial services high among the priorities. Information on banking exports and imports was sufficiently vague for the OTA to exclude banking from aggregate services figures. There were virtually no data on the revenues of foreign banks operating in the United States (banking imports) or on foreign holders of US securities (securities exports).[49] However an estimate was provided: the overall impact of banking on the balance of payments from 1982–1984 was an annual surplus of between $16 and $21 billion.[50] '[A] clear conclusion can be drawn for this sector: the balance of gross banking receipts and payments represents a substantial, if declining, US surplus'.[51] The insurance sector had a mild deficit of about $1 billion annually over the same period,[52] and remaining financial services (brokerage and investment banking) were estimated at somewhere between a deficit of $0.4 billion in 1982 and a surplus of $0.9 billion in 1984.[53] All in all, then, financial services sectors made a positive contribution to the US balance of payments and this contribution may be considerably underestimated.

The enthusiasm of the US government meant that it accepted the economic logic in favour of liberalizing financial services trade, but this decision hardly took place in a vacuum. There was a second type of pressure to include services in the new Round: private groups and firms within the industry were perfectly clear about their interest in bringing the service sectors under the umbrella of the GATT, and no group was so unequivocal as the major US banks. At first the government was concerned to mobilize an internal constituency in the services area 'in order to give its demand that services be included in a new negotiation greater credibility'.[54] In financial services, this was not difficult. International banking and financial intermediation were already well established, but there were virtually no genuinely *transnational* markets for financial services. The US industry was concerned to develop such markets and open up foreign sectors. As mentioned in section I, the role of American Express, Citicorp and others is well known in this regard.

While the government was in little need of persuasion, pressure was needed on the increasingly protectionist Congress. One of the major groups promoting the negotiation was the Coalition of Service Industries (CSI), which made its choice clear, expressing its support for the Administration's efforts to introduce services into the GATT.[55] Listing the barriers to trade in financial services in foreign markets, and using banking as an example, a Coalition representative welcomed the progress made with some foreign governments on these issues: 'As serious problems persist, however, we would hope that they could be addressed under broader international understandings.'[56]

> So, we basically need help in this situation, and we don't have an organisation or structure to help the service industries deal with this rising tide of restrictions.
> ...We need to use the GATT. It is the best thing we have got. We don't know what we would do if it weren't there....We badly need to get going and we think the GATT initiative offers us the best opportunity.[57]

Furthermore improved access to foreign markets was linked to Administration and industry strategies to reinforce the stability of financial institutions in the USA and 're-evaluate restrictions on US financial institutions'.[58] Deregulation would help make US institutions competitive on global markets, and access to foreign markets through a GATS would strengthen the sector in turn. These policy linkages and the strategy were heartily endorsed by the 'Mayflower Group', a coalition of financial services industry organizations which in 1987 became the Financial Services Council.[59] Congressional representatives clearly recognized the connection as well:

> It is my hope that...we can soon begin to consider legislation covering financial services. It is an imperative for the purposes of competitiveness...that we address the problems that our financial services industries are experiencing in this nation, particularly as contrasted with the opportunities that some of our competitors have as a result of the different structures that they have for providing capital to their industries.[60]

The US government and private sector were, then, very much behind the effort to get services in general, and the financial sector in particular, on the GATT agenda. But the US position was always a potential double-edged sword, cutting two ways in the international community. The push by the Administration and private interests should be read in the light of broader developments in US trade policy, of which the 1988 Trade Act with its 'super 301' provisions is the most recent manifestation.[61] US financial service groups in favour of liberalization were at pains to emphasize market access as the primary goal of an agreement, with Japan and the EC as the frequent bugbears.[62] The ambivalent attitude of the US financial sector was summed up by the following statement by Harry L. Freeman, Executive Vice-President of American Express:

> [D]ifficulties notwithstanding, it is critical to work towards an effective multilateral agreement on financial services that demonstrates a commitment to open and vigorous trade in financial services. The alternative to such an agreement could well be a steady stream of contentious bilateral disputes.
> Make no mistake about it: American financial services companies with substantial international operations want a strong and comprehensive multilateral agreement that establishes global rules to govern trade in financial services....At the same time, however, financial-services firms in the United States are prepared to take an alternative *bilateral or regional* [original emphasis] approach if an effective GATT agreement is not reached....An agreement that does not, for example, promote effective market access and establish strong disciplines on discriminatory treatment will not be acceptable to the private sector.[63]

The United States was not the only country which developed an interest in services trade. The European Community was, in the mid-1980s, the largest exporter of services. European interest was heightened by the move to a Single Market in financial services under the 1992 initiative.[64] A number of EC member countries have implemented policies of deregulation of financial institutions, the best known of which was the City of London's 'Big Bang'. Some European countries, particularly Germany, also had a tradition of 'universal' banks which engage in all manner of financial intermediation. Furthermore it was realized that the 1992 programme within the EC was a much more radical step than the Uruguay Round. The adjustment associated with 1992 would be under way regardless, and would enhance the international competitive position of the EC financial sector in the event of more limited liberalization through the GATT talks. Of course the combination of the EC and the United States created almost irresistible pressure in the international community to pursue the services negotiation.

Setting up the negotiation

In sum, new initiatives in an international forum to expand the scope of the international market for financial services were seen as a way to relaunch the apparently moribund GATT and the world economy. The United States and the EC were quite resolute in the pursuit of this goal by the time of the 1986 Punta del Este declaration opening the new GATT Round. The goal was to

> establish a multilateral framework of principles and rules for trade in services, including elaboration of possible disciplines for individual sectors, with a view to expansion of such trade under conditions of transparency and progressive liberalisation and as a means of promoting economic growth of all trading partners and the development of developing countries.[65]

This would, however, be controversial. The intention was to apply the GATT principle of 'national treatment' of foreign goods on the national market to foreign suppliers of services: 'Such a definition would logically carry with it a foreigner's *right to establish* and *right to do business*'.[66] This is because the effective provision of services is linked to a presence in a market: they cannot be stored or shipped. The need for service suppliers to establish such a presence represents a challenge to immigration restrictions, foreign investment and financial control policies, and issues of international factor mobility.[67] The foreign investment issue in particular upset the less developed countries (LDCs); it is noteworthy that UNCTAD (United Nations Conference on Trade and Development) tended to emphasize the linkage between financial services trade, foreign direct investment and the control of the sector by major multinationals based in developed economies.[68]

Efforts to liberalize trade in financial services predated the Uruguay Round itself. The most important activities are banking, insurance and securities.[69] In addition to the 'prenegotiation' phase of the Round itself,[70] the OECD has paid considerable attention to these sectors in the past few years through its Committee on Financial Markets.[71] The emphasis has been on promoting liberalization of national policies, with respect to outside involvement in national financial services industries. Much of the effort was focused on studies to identify obstacles to trade in these sectors, where reliable data of any kind is notoriously scarce.[72] This OECD effort was in addition to national studies which were carried out on behalf of the GATT Secretariat.[73] Support for liberalization had been growing as the governments of the advanced economies began to realize the potential benefits for their economies. There developed a consensus of sorts among the EEC, Japan, and the US and Canada that the issue should be vigorously pursued in GATT.[74] In this way the issue was placed on the agenda of the Uruguay Round trade negotiations by the ministerial gathering in September 1986, despite fairly intense opposition from many of the developing countries.[75]

Opposition from the LDCs was not the only obstacle. There were genuine conflicts of interest among the more advanced nations, with potential winners and losers. The GATT negotiating countries all had quite different banking industry structures and degrees of openness to foreign institutions. The Japanese might be the target of aggressive demands for market access from the EC and the USA. For example, the Japanese Ministry of Finance showed its intention to resist the amendment of its policies in response to foreign concessions in trade talks.[76] In the case of the United States, foreign banks were often limited in their ability to establish full-scale banking operations across the country, although seldom more so than US banks themselves.[77] Traditionally, and this has been upheld consistently by acts of the Federal Congress, it is the state authorities which have controlled the geographic location of banks in the USA.[78] Individual states do have the constitutional power to prohibit foreign banks from setting up establishments within their jurisdiction,[79] although only a handful of states actually do so.[80] None the less liberalization is likely to upset the balance of political power between the levels of government in this regulatory domain, something which the states could be unwilling to countenance.[81] State governors[82] openly voiced their disapproval in this regard in later stages of the talks;[83] state banking supervisors have lobbied hard to preserve state freedom of choice on important regulatory issues. By and large, federal trade negotiators are respecting state limitations in this regard.[84]

Liberalization would also interfere with established patterns of prudential supervision in national banking industries. As the OECD put it,

> A fundamental issue…is the extent to which market responses to signs of strains developing in an institution can be expected to develop in a way congruent with the overriding public policy objective of preserving the integrity of the financial system…. Indeed, concern has frequently been expressed that over-reliance on public disclosure and market discipline might lead to further instability in the financial system as a result of over-reactions by the market to actual or perceived changes in a bank's situation.[85]

In other words, 'marketization', or the assertion of market discipline as the chief measure of the success or failure of an institution (a consequence of liberalization), alters the traditional, regulated pattern of risk-taking. It may impose significant costs on some historically solid institutions which based their stability on a particular prudential regulatory framework, now torn asunder. Yet an increase in private (that is, market) risk control is a necessary complement of the extension of markets if distortions in competition are not to occur among various national industries. Indeed the extension of markets in banking has already struck at the heart of national systems of monetary control, sometimes impairing its very effectiveness unless there are accompanying measures of coordination among states.[86] These are only a few of the issues surrounding the negotiations over liberalization, and it is likely that initial efforts will be limited as a result. The threat to the infant financial sectors of Third World countries is commensurately greater.

As far as trade in securities is concerned, most markets have been national in dimension and, consequently, the almost exclusive preserve of national firms.[87] Inadequate capitalization and expertise have, in many cases, rendered these firms inappropriate for international competition on the expanding global markets. The frenzied pace of merger and joint-venture activity associated with the City of London's 'Big Bang' (27 October 1986) is an example of the sort of adjustment which liberalization may bring to most markets. In the City, the doors were thrown open to all for membership of the Stock Exchange,[88] and market-makers faced intensified competition and smaller returns on capital, with consequent downward pressure on profit margins.[89] Foreign dealers, especially the Japanese, moved into new positions of prominence, and old and venerated City institutions were merged or gone forever. Even newcomers suffered: the investment dealing operations of both the Midland Bank and Lloyds Bank, set up to profit from the Big Bang, had to beat a hasty retreat in 1987.[90] There is little reason to suspect that accelerated liberalization will not bring similar upheavals in other markets in addition to the pressures it imposes on national supervisors of financial institutions.

The Round begins
If these were the very serious political and economic conflicts of interest which may be linked to the extension of markets in the financial services sector, what has been accomplished by the Uruguay Round? There were, in fact, five main elements to the negotiations: (a) definitional issues (what constitutes trade in services?);[91] (b) statistical issues and the development of a comprehensive data base (statistics-gathering in trade in services is severely underdeveloped compared with trade in goods); (c) a conceptual framework on which rules and procedures in trading relations might be based; (d) what specific service sectors the agreement would cover; and (e)

which measures and practices limit or encourage the expansion of trade in the sector.[92]

At Punta del Este controversy had centred on the inclusion of services in the GATT talks. This was essentially a developed country–LDC confrontation, with India and Brazil taking the hard line against the United States. The issue was resolved by a last minute deal: 'it was agreed between the Americans and the Indians that the session would launch a negotiation on services, but that it would be undertaken in a separate structure from that on goods, which presumably would lessen the prospects for trade-offs between these two areas'.[93] In this way, there was a Group of Negotiations on Goods (GNG) and a Group of Negotiations on Services (GNS).[94] At early meetings (23–5 February 1987) and subsequently, the very principle of liberalization of trade in the services sector was the subject of a wide-ranging debate.[95] Apart from disagreement over the very principle of international regulations for trade in the sector, there was initially no consensus on either a definition of trade in services or the development of a comprehensive data base.[96] The negotiations also sought to deal with the inherent tension between the objective of liberalization and the commitment, in the original Punta del Este declaration,[97] to accommodating the policy objectives of national laws and regulations applying to service sectors.[98] This was particularly important to the European Community and conflicted somewhat with the more far-reaching American proposals.[99] Likewise the developing countries were concerned about the status of their emerging service sectors and their role in national economic development.

The third point, concerning the conceptual framework, proved to be the most controversial, and stalled progress on the last two points. It had already been established that fundamental GATT rules and procedures would apply to the negotiations. In particular, 'national treatment' would obtain, which meant that the regulatory and fiscal treatment of imported services would have to be broadly equivalent to those produced domestically.[100] So would the principle of transparency.[101] There were, however, many outstanding issues when it came to applying this general framework to individual service sectors.[102] Of considerable concern was the question as to how far the principle of reciprocity, the original basis of GATT rules on trade in goods, should be extended in the domain of trade in services. This issue would dog the negotiations all the way through. The American proposal called for the extension of this principle as far as possible,[103] but a Swiss proposal which received considerable attention, floated the idea of 'optional most-favoured-nation-treatment'.[104]

There still remained the underlying issue of the very principle of international rules for trade in services. The GATT ministerial gathering in Montreal in December 1988 did achieve some form of progress. The report to the ministers by the services negotiating group was initially torn up and a decision made to start afresh.[105] This strategy apparently helped unblock the situation, for there followed an agreement in principle to bring trade in services under international rules and regulations. However this agreement was left in abeyance until agreement was reached on four outstanding issues in the parallel talks on trade in goods.[106]

The Montreal Agreement, formally adopted in April 1989 in Geneva, was accepted by the developed countries and, grudgingly, by the LDCs. It was agreed that 'negotiations on the elaboration of a multilateral framework of principles and rules for trade should proceed expeditiously'.[107] Clearly the details of the agreement remain to be worked out, but a number of principles were agreed upon as a framework for the negotiations. As expected, 'transparency' of national laws and regulations concerning the services sector was to be provided for, along with 'progressive' liberalization on the basis of 'national treatment'. This last meant that foreign service suppliers would enjoy access to national markets under conditions 'no less favourable' than those applicable to national or other suppliers, and that this provision would apply to the cross-border movement of services, consumers and, crucially, factors of production 'where such movement is essential to suppliers'.[108] National treatment was to work in conjunction with the traditional GATT principle of non-discrimination or 'most-favoured nation'.

There were some general undertakings to look to the needs of the developing countries, helping them with the problems of market access and a vague commitment to assisting them with the development of their service sectors (seen as the *sine qua non* of effective liberalization). 'Particular account' was to be taken of the poorest LDCs, with all their attendant problems.[109] More important for the agreement as a whole were the provisions for safeguards and national regulation of service sectors. This had been a controversial area from the beginning, with the European Community insisting on the respecting of national policy objectives and regulatory purposes from the end of 1987.[110] This of course included national regulatory frameworks for banking and financial sectors, and by implication the more general macroeconomic policy objectives of the negotiating states. The actual agreement, under 'Safeguards and Exceptions', specifically mentioned balance of payments reasons as requiring special provisions for national policy intervention.[111] The 'asymmetries' in services regulation were formally recognized, as well as their relationship to important national policy objectives such as the 'pursuance of macroeconomic policies'.[112] An important part of future work would concern the application of the agreed principles to specific sectors, of which financial services was one.

Negotiations on financial services and the changing national positions
The Montreal Agreement was an important watershed. It marked agreement
in principle, on the one hand, and the beginning of serious detailed negotiations on the other. Trade policy-making establishments and national financial institutions' supervisors and regulators were beginning to reflect on the
enormous implications for the individual sectors involved of the whole
notion of a GATS. The more information they gathered on the matter the
more complex the issues became, and thus the more delicate the negotiations. The serious horse-trading would begin, not only with the GATT negotiating forum, but also on the domestic front. As domestic coalitions of
interests became aware of the direct implications for individual sectors,
national positions began to shift, subtly at first, but in important ways. The
issue of market access and the nature of reciprocity commitments became of
primary importance in financial services, and this was underpinned by the
stalemate of the entire Round over the issue of agricultural subsidies.

This will become clear as the negotiations are followed. In particular the
American position began to change. Nowhere was this more dramatic than
in the domain of financial services. The US government had consistently
been the champion of a far-reaching and broadly applicable agreement based
on a perceived competitive advantage in financial services. As negotiations
progressed, the general mood of the US private sector on trade policy began
to assert itself and the Administration had to tread carefully as Congressional leaders reflected on whether to continue to allow the Administration a
free hand in defining American policy preferences. The question of access to
foreign markets became central against a background of concern about the
competitiveness of the American financial services sector, as powerful interests, well organized into lobby groups inside the USA, kept a close watch
over the progress of the negotiations.[113] US firms were unwilling to sanction
unlimited reciprocity/MFN if foreign governments were to limit the extent
of liberalization.[114] Their point was quite simple (and not without justification): foreign institutions already had access to US financial services markets on a national treatment basis. In some states of the union, foreign
financial institutions had fewer restrictions than their domestic US counterparts.[115] If other countries did not make commitments on liberalization now,
the Round would simply institutionalize this unequal situation and leave
other countries no incentive to liberalize at a later date, given their acquired
advantages on the US market which American governments would be pow-
erless to alter under the agreement. It was all rather reminiscent of 1948–50
and the failure of the International Trade Organization (ITO) when the
American business community argued (rather disingenuously in view of US
trading practices at the time) that the agreement reached did not sufficiently
limit the scope for discriminatory treatment in foreign markets.[116] According

to confidential interview sources, the EC was slowly moving in the US direction, given the substance of EC talks on financial services with respect to the 1992 Single Market programme.

Financial services were discussed in sectoral group meetings on 18–22 September 1989.[117] Securities and banking services would have to be considered in relation to both cross-border financial flows and establishment/commercial presence. These sectors would prove to be problematic, it was recognized, because of their high degree of regulation and their close relationship to national and international economic management. Problem policy areas would be monetary policies, debt management and fiscal policies. Some countries clearly wished to maintain the integrity of national systems of regulation, while others stressed that there were many overly restrictive regulations which could be subjected to multilateral rules and disciplines. The problem areas were identified as rules affecting establishment, the operation of foreign-owned banks and securities houses, and the acquisition of domestic firms. Insurance services likewise presented considerable scope for liberalization. It was recognized that there had already been substantial progress on the liberalization of capital flows associated with trade in financial services.[118]

The United States presented the first complete draft legal agreement on trade in services at the negotiating group's meetings of 23–5 October 1989. All service sectors were to be included, with provisions for market access and right of establishment. The proposal called for a dispute-settling mechanism under the auspices of a Committee on Trade in Services.[119] The draft was surprisingly indulgent as far as exceptions to the proposed rules were concerned. Although non-discrimination, transparency and national treatment were the guiding principles, there were provisions for short-term balance of payments problems, domestic regulation of services, reservations and outright exceptions; countries would be able to exclude certain services in national schedules, and 'in situations where signatories have determined that a particular sector should not be included in the agreement, interested countries may enter into special accords among themselves whose provisions would not be legally binding on the other signatories'.[120]

In this way, the United States effectively turned its back on the idea of unconditional reciprocity/MFN. At the meeting during which the draft was presented, some countries expressed concern in this regard, pointing out that there was too much room for exceptions and reservations.[121] The LDCs were upset that there was no reference to the problems peculiar to their service sectors under the proposal, and India, Singapore and Korea presented papers of their own on issues of concern to themselves and other LDCs. The EC sought to elaborate on the notion of non-discrimination as it applied to services. The EC paper envisaged minimum levels of mutual obligations, which would lead in the process of liberalization to unconditional non-discrimination among signatories. Liberalization commitments would work on the basis of unconditional MFN among signatories.[122] This was significant: while the EC appeared to be comfortable with the idea of unconditional reciprocity, the USA was moving in the opposite direction, if slowly. The extensive provisions contained in the US draft agreement for exceptions, and the emphasis on special protocols between bilateral partners or small groups of nations, seemed to indicate this. In the meeting of 20–24 December, Japan not surprisingly expressed reservations about the application of a 'reciprocal market access approach',[123] presumably that implied by the US draft, and preferred an agreement based on unconditional MFN while allowing for reservations.[124]

By the time the GNS chairman had put forward a draft to provide a basis for the final stretch of the negotiations and to sum up the state of consensus within the group, on 18 December 1989, time was getting short for the negotiation of detailed sectoral provisions. This was reflected in the tight timetable established for the services negotiations at the first meeting of 1990, 16–19 January, to culminate in a complete draft framework agreement by the following July.[125] The entire Uruguay Round was scheduled for completion in December of the same year. By the summer, the situation looked ominous as the US position on a number of service sectors began to shift. GATT officials were wont to emphasize the considerable consensus which had emerged on the underlying principles to govern the agreement, but the specifics were causing problems. Six sectoral working groups had been established in May 1990 to explore the prospects for detailed sectoral annotations which 'would spell out in greater detail the [agreement's] application in particular sectors',[126] of which financial services was one. The status of the financial sector needed clarification, largely because of the many macroeconomic policy implications of an agreement on liberalization. The US Treasury became concerned about policy linkages and pressed to have financial services treated outside the services trade negotiations. According to the US Treasury's Undersecretary for International Affairs,

> It is not yet settled whether financial services...should be handled as a separate agreement or as an annex to the general services framework... some people argue that [they should be treated separately], and I'm one of them, because I think financial services needs to be negotiated by financial experts and it needs to reflect the prudential and regulatory aspects. Others argue that financial services should be part of services and come under the overall umbrella agreement for services...and so they have a different point of view about how you negotiate.[127]

The American position on financial services began to change in a context of increasing concern within the United States for the competitiveness of the services sector, for the soundness of American financial institutions, and a long-standing feeling that, unless concrete achievements on access to foreign markets were to be forthcoming, the US should look outside the multilateral framework for success. According to US trade officials: 'There is one thing I want to stress...and that is, we would, of course, press for the bilateral resolution to services-created problems using, among other things, the threat of section 301 of the Trade Act which was amended in the 1988 Trade Act.'[128]

What lay behind this dramatic change in US policy, which threatened the breakdown of the talks, no less? On the issue of competitiveness, the House Committee on Foreign Affairs had held hearings in November 1989 entitled *America's Services Trade Deficit*, alleging a $176 million gap in the current account.[129] Although witnesses emphasized that financial services still made a substantial positive contribution to the services trade balance,[130] and related the red ink essentially to the budget deficit,[131] there was alarm that in 'one of the last economic sectors in which the United States remains a world leader: the services sector',[132] the competitive edge might be slipping. Administration officials tried to counter by strongly emphasizing the competitiveness of the US economy in the domain of services, particularly financial services.[133] None the less it was pointed out during the hearings that 'in 1986...Japan for the first time surpassed the United States in the share of international banking business held'.[134]

Concern about Japanese financial institutions and access to Japanese markets had been around for some time.[135] Administration officials tried to combat Congressional alarmism,[136] but the issue would not go away. There was even concern that the European Community's 1992 project might be detrimental to the access of US financial institutions to the enlarged EC marketplace.[137] Extensive hearings were held on the issue of 'national treatment' by the House Task Force on the International Competitiveness of United States Financial Institutions.[138] In January of 1990, the chairman of the Senate Banking Committee, Senator Donald Riegle, introduced the Fair Trade in Financial Services Act (in British terms, a 'bill') to Congress. The act essentially extended to the financial services sector the changes in US trade policy which had been introduced in the 1980s, notably the concern with market access ('super 301' and the 1988 Trade Act). US regulators would be able to deny access by foreign institutions to the US market if it was determined that US firms did not have 'effective market access' in the home country.[139] Industry groups would be sceptical about the idea, as would the Administration, but the pressure was on in the light of the multilateral services trade negotiations.

However perhaps the biggest worry of US policy-makers and of Congress related to the parlous state of the American financial sector. Firstly the fragility of US financial institutions undermined their competitiveness. Only internationally competitive firms would benefit from liberalization:

> At our hearings last week on the deposit insurance fund we heard that the United States banking industry may not be doing as well as we once thought. Some have claimed that as much as one third of the assets of US banks are in banks that have inadequate capital. Many large money centre banks have enormous LDC debt liabilities which constrain their activities.[140]

The problems were immense: it was recently announced in the press that Citicorp, the largest American bank, had to pay junk bond-style yields on a $100 million issue of preferred stock in order to prevent the issue from collapsing![141] Chase-Manhattan has set aside between $500 million and $1 billion of loan loss reserves and proposed lay-offs of between 3500 and 4500 employees.[142] Standard and Poor downgraded the credit ratings of over 35 US banks in the first 11 months of 1990, and some more than once. Only J.P. Morgan maintained a rating of better than AA.[143] Many major US banks were therefore pulling back from foreign markets because they were not as competitive as they thought. The US Treasury realized this to its horror.[144]

Secondly the restrictive regulatory framework within the United States was seen by many as a major problem,[145] especially as far as the money centre banks (the large, internationalized US banks based in the 'money centres' of New York, San Francisco, Chicago and Miami) who viewed themselves as far more restricted by American banking laws than their foreign competitors operating in the same US market,[146] were concerned. Without some sort of reform of Glass–Steagall and of the other regulatory measures restricting the activities of American institutions, US firms would always be competing at a disadvantage.[147] Not all segments of the American financial sector wanted far-reaching deregulation of US banks unless it extended to other parts of the financial services industry – the securities firms were worried about banks encroaching upon their territory[148] – but the balance of opinion seemed to be in favour of a major restructuring of the regulatory framework.

In sum, market access at the international level might be an important concern, but many of the difficulties had to be resolved in the USA itself. This is a clear example of the way in which the linkages between the domestic and international political processes are crucial to understanding intergovernmental bargaining processes such as the Uruguay Round, as was argued in section I concerning the weaknesses of the hegemonic stability approach. The following samples of testimony in hearings before the International Competitiveness of United States Financial Institutions Task Force set the tone:

> We have problems overseas. Other countries have inappropriate laws and inad-
> equate market access. But our primary problem is here at home. Our primary
> problems are made in the United States, and we should spend most of our time
> talking about what we can do.[149]

> It is clear that we have a lot of weaknesses in our financial sector, most of them
> domestic in origin and self-inflicted through both our macroeconomic policies
> and our regulatory systems at both the federal and state level.[150]

All these interrelated concerns combined to produce a shift in the US position on services trade in general and the financial services sector in particular. The first services sector to come under pressure of US domestic interests
has been the transport industry, particularly maritime shipping.[151] The Administration decided to exclude shipping entirely from the prospective GATS.
There was a threat to do the same with aviation, despite contrary domestic
pressures for universal coverage.[152] Telecommunications were later added to
the list of exclusions,[153] and the US position became a major stumbling-
block in the negotiations.[154] Protectionist forces and groups favouring an
accord began to square up to one another.[155] The eventual failure of the
American banking reform bill in Congress in 1991, aimed at enhancing
competitiveness, contributed to the toughened stance of the Administration,
which highlights once again the link between domestic and international
policy processes.[156]

The US position on trade in financial services began to undergo a number
of gyrations. The Americans were floating the idea that the sector should be
separated from main GATS agreement and dealt with in a separate appendix.[157] The jurisdictional dispute between the Treasury and the US Trade
Representative seemed to be contributing to this change in position, despite
a claim by the latter that the problem had been resolved.[158] Most significant,
however, was whether MFN should apply to the sector on an unconditional
basis, or only in the case of reciprocal commitments on market access. The
USA preferred the latter position. The American banking industry, it seemed,
did not want to be tied down by limits built into a GATS.[159] They wanted to
pursue the aim of market access unencumbered by the niceties of a multilateral framework. A group of developed nations led by the Americans attempted to spin off financial services from the main agreement, presenting
their position on 22 October.[160] This approach was rejected by the LDCs,
who claimed that, now they had accepted the painful idea of a GATS for
financial services, it must come under the main framework agreement.[161]
The American Administration was in a tight position, with Congressional
leaders pushing the Riegle 'Fair Trade' bill and generally breathing down
their necks. At the GNS meeting of 22 November 1990, the USA dropped
the bombshell: automatic MFN would essentially be eliminated from the

draft services agreement, and a sector-by-sector approach would have to be adopted, or the USA would not sign.[162] The talks appeared doomed.

The beginnings of a breakthrough came on 6 December. The USA agreed that, in the framework agreement, unconditional MFN would have to apply, as long as signatories made binding market-access commitments by the end of the Round.[163] Reluctantly the USA backed a plan put forward by Canada, among others (which also received EC support) to resolve differences on financial services.[164] Under a general services framework agreement based on unconditional reciprocity, there would be an annex on financial services. The annex would provide for a two-track approach to liberalizing trade in the sector, permitting a certain flexibility. The first track would provide for binding commitments, including a dispute-settling procedure, on uninhibited access for foreign firms to national markets. The second track would provide for specified commitments on liberalization, allowing countries to take on obligations to the extent that they could. The key to the proposal's success, Canadian officials stated, was whether enough countries with important markets would take the first approach.[165]

None the less US officials remained firm in insisting: 'The real test of any services agreement will be the extent to which it provides market liberalisation.'[166] Congress kept up the pressure following a Treasury report that there was a lack of progress on market access/national treatment in overseas financial markets, especially with respect to Japan[167] (in January of 1991, the Treasury even announced that it was much more sympathetic to the Riegle 'Fair Trade in Financial Services' bill in the light of the report, setting the scene for the final stage of negotiations[168]). At this point the deadline for the Uruguay Round ran out, foundering on the question of trade in agricultural products, and had to be extended. There was insufficient time to complete negotiations on services in any event. There had been substantial agreement on a framework text, but the details of sectoral annexes, particularly on financial services, remained to be worked out. None the less prospects for an accord looked reasonable. There was sufficient consensus among the industrialized countries that some sort of internationally regulated progress towards liberalization is desirable, and the LDCs had come round to sharing the industrialized countries' basic approach.

Furthermore, since the suspension of the overall Round in December 1990, there has been extraordinary pressure from private interests to complete a services accord. The Coalition of Service Industries in the United States and counterparts in four countries urged this in mid-January 1991.[169] At a conference in Washington on 24–5 January 1991, manufacturing and services groups appealed to governments to come to terms with the agricultural issue.[170] The International Chamber of Commerce issued a similar call on 8 February.[171]

Since early 1991, the overall Round has essentially remained stalled on the question of agricultural trade. The breakthrough in the EC agricultural policy reform process in the spring of 1992 considerably improved prospects for a slow movement towards an overall conclusion to the Round, although a breakdown in agricultural negotiations in November 1992, on the eve of the US presidential elections (at the time of writing), has once again put the whole Round in possible jeopardy. Negotiations following the initial suspension of talks in fact resumed in March 1991, including the talks on financial services. Despite the two-track solution which had been accepted, the sticking-point as far as financial services was concerned remained the same as before: the USA wanted firm commitments from other countries that they would open up their financial sectors to US institutions as part of the GATS sectoral annex commitments. In fact the intensity of the disagreements appeared to increase as 1991 wore on and 1992 began. It is worth taking a look at the situation, for it is instructive of changes taking place within the GATT and helps reinforce the criticisms of the hegemonic stability approach raised above.

By late 1991, the main rule-making exercise had been completed, establishing the general principles of the GATS which would govern the sectoral annexes, although the question of exemptions from MFN provisions continued to pose problems.[172] Final agreement in the Round was not reached by the second December (1991) deadline, and the GATT chairman Arthur Dunkel was obliged to present a compromise *Draft Final Act* in an attempt to bring the talks to a conclusion on all fronts.[173]

What was needed in financial services was some progress on liberalization: otherwise a paradoxical situation would emerge which requires some explanation. Here the different structural positions and policy frameworks in the international economy of the various domestic financial sectors began to assert themselves and to call into question the workability of the overall framework of rules. The traditional GATT principles have been reciprocity and non-discrimination (unconditional MFN). Contracting parties which do not wish to apply these principles can only do so on certain conditions. Applied to the GATS, one country could opt out of the entire GATS agreement with respect to another (global non-application) or not at all. There was no provision for *sectoral* non-application directed at any one party which refused access to its markets. The only other form of exemption under traditional GATT rules concerned the MFN clause, but here too there was an awkward dilemma. Contracting parties would be permitted to violate MFN provisions (non-discrimination principle) for particular sectors, but not against one particular country, only against all parties at once.

The United States began to question these long-standing GATT norms in view of the virtual absence of liberalization commitments in the GATS sectoral annex for financial services.[174] Risking vilification from other GATT parties, the Americans had attempted to argue that *sectoral non-application* (conditional reciprocity) should be permitted under GATS. Otherwise, they pointed out, the GATS in financial services would be a retrograde step: the USA and other relatively open markets for financial services such as Canada and the EC, would be permanently committed to allowing access to their markets to firms from ASEAN or Korea, but would have no access to these markets and there would be no way of retaliating against them. The only GATS rule which would really bind these countries would be the transparency provisions, nothing to do with market access. To compensate the USA could only invoke non-application of the entire GATS against these countries, a ham-fisted instrument. Worse still, these countries would not have any incentive to move towards liberalization in the future because they would have institutionalized access to those US or EC financial services sectors and institutionalized protection of their own. Once the Round was over, the USA would no longer be able to make linkages between financial services and other issues in the Round which were vital to these countries. In short, this was a classic 'free-rider' problem.

The USA lost this battle despite attempts to persuade the EC and Canada to support the sectoral non-application position, and the Dunkel document of December 1991 stuck with the global non-application provisions. In early 1992, the USA therefore began to seek another way out of the free-rider problem with respect to liberalization commitments, this time through the MFN clause. But, as already stated above, a contracting party cannot refuse MFN in a specific sector, in this case financial services, to a particular country; MFN in any one sector must be refused to all contracting parties or none at all. American MFN exemption papers for the financial services sector were filed in March 1992, dumbfounding the other negotiating parties. Much political capital was made by other countries over this move. The American negotiators held firm, letting it be known that, if clear liberalization commitments from appropriate countries were forthcoming, the MFN exemptions would be withdrawn. The American delegation is clearly unhappy with the exemption procedure, but awaits a change of mood in Geneva which would permit another look at sectoral non-application.[175]

The EC and Canada, of course, faced precisely the same problem as the USA. Their markets were relatively open and yet there were few commitments on liberalization from non-OECD countries.[176] There was greater reluctance, however, to resort to the US tactics, despite the evident concern of the EC private sector;[177] hence they had not supported the USA on sectoral non-application. None the less there was a subtle shift in the EC strategy as they grappled with this dilemma. The EC approach was to table some very limited exemptions while advancing a specific threat that, in the absence of market access commitments, a blanket exemption in line with the US move would be considered. It was perfectly clear that the EC had no intention of allowing the reciprocity commitments enshrined in the GATS to be undermined and would insist on a certain level of mutual liberalization obligations for all parties.[178] Since December 1991, the EC business community has certainly been waking up to the problem at hand, so some movement is on the cards.

It becomes clear, then, that the different domestic regulatory and market structures of respective financial services sectors, and their interaction with the international political and economic domains, are crucial to our understanding of changes in the trade regime and money and finance. The systemic level of analysis alone would tell us little of the situation in the Round. At the very least, agreement on the core GATS principles would appear likely in the event of a breakthrough on agriculture, with the USA claiming a financial services exemption pending further market access talks with the appropriate countries. Even if this prediction of eventual success proves overoptimistic, less formal cooperation among the advanced countries of the OECD is likely to lead in the same direction. None the less there is no real interest in a 'mini-GATT' for services, even financial services, among the OECD nations in the event of a failure of the Round. The OECD area is already relatively open – it is not where the problem lies. European and US firms want access to markets which hitherto have been closed. The hope remains for a global package deal, in keeping with the original strategy of the Round: a focus on so many sectors that there would be substantial benefits for everyone, LDCs, NICs (newly industrialized countries) and industrialized countries alike. A services deal on its own might have little benefit for non-OECD countries, but the prospect of success on textiles and agriculture alters the picture. The Round provided sufficient carrots and sticks for all; if the issues had been dealt with separately the negotiators faced almost certain failure.[179]

III   Conclusion

This chapter has argued that an eventual agreement on financial services will have far-reaching consequences for the structure of the world's economy and for state policies in the domain. The American insistence on market access is a deliberate move to alter the policy framework of service sectors in a number of target countries. If, as is still expected, the Round comes agonizingly to a close in the coming months, a political agreement based on international cooperation will likely be reached which will open some of the best protected economic activities to market-based international competition for the first time.

The chapter has also demonstrated that hegemony as an explanatory variable is relatively unimportant for understanding current developments in the international trade regime or money and finance. Instead we have pointed to the importance of understanding the relationship of politics and markets at both the domestic and international levels of analysis. The issue was one of reaching political agreement on the extent to which transnational market processes should form the basis of economic decision-making in sectors closely related to the macroeconomic control of domestic economies. The United States pressed the international community for an agreement on services, with special emphasis on the financial sector, but the Administration had to retreat on this issue when it came into contact with the reality of domestic interests profoundly unsure of their international competitiveness in a rapidly changing industry. A more important constraint on the US negotiators was that the structure and openness of their financial services markets meant that a GATS could constitute a trap for the American sector in the absence of access to hitherto closed overseas markets.

At the same time the LDCs moved from a position of outright rejection to embracing the idea of an agreement, and the European Community woke up to the opportunities such a deal might offer in the light of the 1992 project. The power of the United States was important – the Americans, among others, could consistently frustrate the talks – but the need to move beyond the systemic level of analysis and notions of declining hegemony was clear.

An eventual agreement will only be a starting-point. All delegations to the talks came to recognize the need for special treatment of financial services, especially where investment, balance of payments and macro policy issues were involved. It will be up to future negotiations to decide the ultimate level of liberalization and financial integration to result from the accord. Political conflict over the internationalization of markets in financial services will therefore continue, and there is much to be lost and much to be gained, depending on the outcome. The politics of negotiation will change, however, as liberalization begins to transform domestic sectors and their policy preferences.

Notes

1. Eric Helleiner, 'American Hegemony and Global Economic Structure: From Closed to Open Financial Relations in the Postwar World', unpublished PhD thesis, London School of Economics and Political Science, 1991, p. 10 and *passim*.
2. Eugene Versluysen, *The Political Economy of International Finance*, Farnborough: Gower 1981; Ralph C. Bryant, *International Financial Intermediation*, Washington, DC: Brookings Institution, 1987.
3. The Uruguay Round is a new departure, along with other developments such as international prudential supervisory agreements for banking in the context of the BIS (Bank for International Settlements) and international securities markets regulation through IOSCO (International Organisation of Securities Commissions).

4. The process of adjustment which both preceded and followed London's 'Big Bang' is instructive in this regard.
5. The US Congress has been quite exercised about these issues for some time. See, for example, US Congress, House of Representatives, Task Force on the International Competitiveness of US Financial Institutions, Subcommittee on Financial Institutions Supervision of the Committee on Banking, Finance, and Urban Affairs, *Role of the Financial Services Sector*, Hearings, 24 April 1990, Washington: US GPO, 1990.
6. See Helen V. Milner, *Resisting Protectionism: Global Industries and the Politics of International Trade*, Princeton: Princeton University Press, 1988; I.M. Destler and John S. Odell, *Anti-Protection: Changing Forces in United States Trade Politics*, Washington, DC: Institute for International Economics, 1987.
7. See below, section II.
8. GATT, *International Trade 1988/89*, annual report, overview of services trade, as cited in GATT *Press Release* 1463, 5 September 1989, p. 2.
9. See OECD, *Prudential Supervision in Banking*, Paris: OECD, 1987.
10. Geoffrey R.D. Underhill, 'Markets beyond Politics? the State and the Internationalisation of Financial Markets', *European Journal of Political Research*, **19**, (2 & 3), March/April 1991, pp. 197–225.
11. This was established by the agreement resulting from the mid-term review in Montreal, 5–9 December 1988. For terms of the mid-term agreement on services, see GATT, *News of the Uruguay Round*, no. 27, 24 April 1989, pp. 38–40. The agreement is covered below.
12. See United States House of Representatives, Subcommittee on Financial Institutions Supervision…Committee on Banking, Finance, and Urban Affairs, *Oversight Hearings on the European Community's 1992 Program*, Hearings, 26–8 September 1989, Washington: GPO, 1989.
13. Ibid., p. 2.
14. See United States Senate, Committee on the Budget, *United States Access to Japanese Financial Markets*, Hearings, 6 May 1987, Washington: GPO, 1987.
15. See OECD, *Banking and Monetary Policy*, Paris: OECD 1985.
16. See ibid., p. 4.
17. Janette Mark and Gerald Helleiner, *Trade in Services; the Negotiating Concerns of the Developing Countries*, Ottawa: the North–South Institute, 1988, p. 21.
18. It is worth noting that the Uruguay Round is pursuing the issue of state regulation of foreign investment flows in separate but parallel negotiations on Trade-Related Investment Measures or TRIMS.
19. Geoffrey R.D. Underhill, 'Industrial Crisis and International Regimes: France, the EEC, and International Trade in Textiles 1974–1984', in *Millennium: Journal of International Studies*, **19**, (2), Summer 1990, p. 186. Passages from Gilpin are from *The Political Economy of International Relations*, Princeton: Princeton University Press, 1987, p. 86 and pp. 72–3, respectively.
20. See Robert Keohane's introduction to Robert O. Keohane (ed.), *Neo-Realism and its Critics*, New York: Columbia University Press, 1986, pp. 14–15.
21. Underhill, 'Industrial Crisis and International Regimes', p. 186.
22. Stephen D. Krasner, 'The Tokyo Round: Particularistic Interests and the Prospects for Stability in the Global Trading System', *International Studies Quarterly*, **23**, December 1979, pp. 491–531.
23. See argument of Isabelle Grunberg, 'Exploring the "Myth" of Hegemonic Stability', *International Organisation*, **44**, (4), Autumn 1990, pp. 431–77.
24. Particularly, and not surprisingly, the USA. It is not difficult to understand why this might be so. The long-standing role of MNCs in the US economy, especially in the banking and securities industries, means that important economic actors with political resources in the American political system stand to benefit substantially from increased access to other markets.
25. Confidential interviews in Washington, 20 March–4 April 1992, confirmed the role of Citicorp and American Express, as well as that of these organizations. The Chairmen

and other senior executive officers of both these corporations, among others, continue to sit on the elaborate system of government–private sector consultative committees which oversee the US negotiators in the Round.

26. The relationship of politics to markets in the domain of international finance has been argued extensively in G.R.D. Underhill, 'Markets beyond Politics?'. The article refutes the traditional economic liberal position which attributes internationalization to the actions of individual market actors.

27. See Marcello de Cecco, 'International Financial Markets and US Domestic Policy since 1945', *International Affairs*, **52**, (3), July 1986, pp. 381–99.

28. See OECD, *Prudential Supervision in Banking*.

29. See Underhill, 'Industrial Crisis and International Regimes', pp. 190–92.

30. This point was highlighted in a work on the shifting policy preferences of manufacturing sectors in an increasingly internationalized world economy by Helen Milner, *Resisting Protectionism*.

31. However US Congressional and Administration policy-makers have been drawing the very clear linkages between the Uruguay Round, the competitiveness of the American financial services sector and deregulation. The Congress has been holding hearings on the subject, having formed a task force on the Competitiveness of US Financial Institutions under the umbrella of the House Committee on Banking, Finance and Urban Affairs. The Treasury recently came out with somewhat radical reform proposals which would effectively repeal Glass–Steagall (*New York Times*, 8 November 1990, p. C1). These ideas were developed in the Treasury's February 1991 'Green Book', *Modernising the Financial System: Recommendations for Safer, more Competitive Banks*, Washington: Department of the Treasury/GPO, 1991. The European Community is of course involved in an elaborate programme to complete the Single Market in financial services, which raises all these issues directly (see Underhill, 'Markets beyond Politics?', pp. 9–17).

32. Susan Strange has discussed the problems associated with the growth of international financial markets at length in *Casino Capitalism*, Oxford: Basil Blackwell, 1986; see also the discussion of supranational money in Wachtel, *The Money Mandarins*, New York: Pantheon, 1986.

33. Wachtel, *Money Mandarins*, pp. 97–9.

34. Less formal agreements concerning trade in services, particularly banking and securities, have, however, been under negotiation for the last 30 years or so under the auspices of the OECD. In recent years these efforts have been accelerated (see, for example, the account in OECD, *Prudential Supervision in Banking*, pp. 47–51), a phenomenon which should be seen as part of the general context of the Uruguay Round negotiations on trade in services.

35. John H. Jackson, 'A Constitution for Trade in Services', in *The World Economy*, **11**, (2) June 1988, p. 188. It is significant that even Jackson argues for a limited agreement, including special dispensations for 'foot-draggers'. He is associated with the American Enterprise Institute (author of *International Competition in Services*, Washington: American Enterprise Institute, 1988), one of the Washington 'think-tanks' most closely linked to pressing the US government to pursue a GATS.

36. Jonathan Davis Aronson and Peter F. Cowhey, *Trade in Services: a Case for Open Markets*, Washington: American Enterprise Institute, 1984, p. 36.

37. GATT, Task Force on Trade in Services, 'Communication from Canada pursuant to the Ministerial Declaration on Services, 18 January', *Background Report*, Geneva; GATT, 1984, p. 18.

38. This was part of a speech by De Clercq, European Community representative to the GATT ministerial gathering at Punta del Este, Uruguay, 16 September 1986, reprinted in *Bulletin of the European Communities* (*EC Bulletin*), 19 September 1986, p. 15.

39. Ronald K. Shelp, 'Trade in Services', *Foreign Policy*, **65**, winter 1986–7, pp. 76, 79–80.

40. One work advocating a new round of multilateral negotiations even referred to growth in its title: see Gary Clyde Hufbauer and Jeffrey J. Schott, *Trading for Growth: the*

Next Round of Trade Negotiations, Washington: Institute for International Economics, 1985.

41. GATT, 'Ministerial Declaration', *EC Bulletin*, pp. 17, 21; GATT, *News of the Uruguay Round (NUR)* 003, 16 March 1987, p. 5.
42. GATT, *Press Release* 1463, 5 September 1989, p. 1.
43. Hufbauer and Schott, *Trading for Growth*, p. 67.
44. See, for example, Aronson and Cowhey, *Trade in Services*.
45. Shelp, 'Trade in Services', pp. 76–9.
46. Gilpin, *The Political Economy of International Relations*, p. 333; GATT, *Background Report*, p. 5.
47. Although ominously, North America showed the fastest growth in services imports in 1987: about 9 per cent per year (GATT, *Press Release* 1463, 5 September 1989, p. 2).
48. United States Congress, Office of Technology Assessment, *Trade in Services: Exports and Foreign Revenues (OTA Report)*, Special Report, September 1986, Washington: GPO, 1987, p. 3.
49. Ibid., pp. 8–9.
50. Ibid., p. 57.
51. Ibid., p. 58.
52. Ibid., p. 76.
53. Ibid., p. 79.
54. Gilbert Winham, 'The Prenegotiation Phase of the Uruguay Round', *International Journal*, **XLIV**, (2), p. 293.
55. United States Senate, Committee on Finance, *Possible New Round of Trade Negotiations*, Hearings, 23 July 1986, Washington: GPO, 1986, written submission of George J. Clark, Executive Vice President, Citibank, on behalf of the Coalition of Service Industries Inc., p. 9; numerous interviews in Washington, 20 March–4 April 1992.
56. *Possible New Round*, written submission of George J. Clark, p. 13.
57. Ibid., statement of George J. Clark, p. 7.
58. United States Senate, Committee on Banking, Housing, and Urban Affairs, *Strengthening the Safety and Soundness of the Financial Services Industry*, Hearings, 21, 22 and 23 January 1987, Washington: GPO, 1987, written statement by George D. Gould, Undersecretary for Finance at the US Treasury, p. 14.
59. Ibid., written testimony of George D. Gould, p. 16.
60. United States House of Representatives, *Deregulation of Financial Services*, Hearings, of Subcommittee on Commerce, Consumer Protection...of the Committee on Energy and Commerce, 12 May 1988, Washington: GPO, 1988, opening statement by subcommittee chairman Rep. Florio, p. 2.
61. For the new departures in US trade policy in the 1980s, see Jagdish N. Bhagwati, 'United States Trade Policy at the Crossroads', in *The World Economy*, **12**, (4) December 1989, pp. 439–80.
62. This was emphasized in a number of Congressional hearings. See, for example, United States Senate, Committee on the Budget, *United States Access to Japanese Financial Markets*, Hearings, 6 May 1987, Washington: GPO, 1987: 'Japanese financial institutions are now the largest and the strongest in the world....Major security firms in Japan are giants compared to ours, and Japanese financial institutions are now top players in our markets....How are American financial concerns doing in the Japanese markets?....[There is] some progress. For example, four American firms have been allowed to buy seats on the Tokyo stock exchange....I think more can be done and more should be done to open up access to Japanese financial markets. In our own country, we have not denied access to our allies who wish to participate in our financial markets' (opening statement of Chairman of the Committee Chiles, pp. 1–2); also United States House of Representatives, Subcommittee on Financial Institutions Supervision... Committee on Banking, Finance, and Urban Affairs, *Oversight Hearings on the European Community's 1992 Program*, Hearings 26, 27 and 28 September 1989, Washington: GPO, 1990. As the situation in Japan improved, over time the

attention shifted to NICs such as Korea, Taiwan and the ASEAN states (confidential interviews, Washington, DC, 20 March–4 April 1992).

63. Harry L. Freeman (Executive Vice-President, American Express), 'Bilateralism versus Multilateralism in Trade in Financial Services', *The World Economy* (Matters of Opinion section), **12**, (4) December 1989, pp. 557–8.

64. Phedon Nicolaides, 'The Emerging International Regime for Services', *The World Today*, **46**, (1), January 1990, p. 11.

65. GATT, 'Ministerial Declaration', *EC Bulletin*, p. 21.

66. Mark and Helleiner, *Trade in Services*, p. 21; original emphasis.

67. Ibid., pp. 20–21; see also OECD, *Elements of a Conceptual Framework for Trade in Services*, Paris: OECD Mimeo 3318, 1987, pp. 3–6, 9–11, 16–18.

68. See United Nations, Centre on Transnational Corporations, *Transnational Corporations, Services, and the Uruguay Round*, New York: UN 1990, pp. 111, 123–7, 128–35.

69. OECD, *Elements of a Conceptual Framework*, p. 6.

70. See Gilbert R. Winham, 'The Prenegotiation Phase of the Uruguay Round', esp. pp. 291–4.

71. See, for example, the OECD studies on trade in services, especially on banking and securities, respectively (OECD, *International Trade in Services: Banking*, Paris: OECD, 1984; OECD, *Prudential Supervision in Banking*). The OECD has also attempted to draw up a conceptual framework covering the issues involved in trade in services (OECD, *Elements of a Conceptual Framework*). For some time the OECD has had codes of liberalization for capital movements and invisible transactions, and a National Treatment Instrument, all of which concern the several aspects of trade in financial services, including the right of establishment. A joint working group of the Committee on Financial Markets and the Committee on Capital Movements and Invisible Transactions is currently updating these arrangements (OECD, *Prudential Supervision in Banking*, p. 49).

72. For example, *OTA Report*; Shelp, 'Trade in Services', pp. 66–7; 76–9.

73. Of which GATT, *Background Report* (1984) is one.

74. Shelp, 'Trade in Services', pp. 80–81. The OECD Trade Committee had even developed a conceptual framework for trade in services similar to that which underpins GATT rules for trade in goods. This fitted in with OECD codes of practice on liberalization of capital movements and trade in invisibles (ibid., pp. 70–71).

75. Shelp, 'Trade in Services', p. 64.

76. Phedon Nicolaides, 'The Emerging International Regime for Services', p. 11.

77. US prohibitions on interstate branching apply as much on the whole to US institutions as to foreign ones, and do not therefore constitute a violation of national treatment as such – just a nuisance. In fact, it appears that foreign banks in the USA, most (over 90 per cent) of which are state-chartered, enjoy greater freedom to carry on parallel banking and securities activities than most US institutions. At the urging of the money centre banks, which had no such flexibility of their own, the federal International Banking Act (1978) put a stop to this (existing arrangements at the time were 'grandfathered'). The US Treasury eventually came to conclude, then, that foreign banks had it too easy in the USA. It was made clear to this author that restrictions on foreign banks were far more likely to emanate from the US Treasury than from state bank regulators, who want as much banking business for their respective states as they can get.

   This helps to explain why, as will be seen later, the USA became so concerned in the financial services negotiations about unconditional MFN. Foreign banks in US markets already had a more liberal regime than their competitor US-owned institutions. What was needed was better market access for American institutions in those foreign markets which remained essentially closed (confidential interviews, 20 March–4 April 1992, Washington, DC).

78. Interview with Mr Robert Richard (Regulatory Affairs), Conference of State Bank Supervisors, Washington, DC, 1 April 1992. Some states even prevented banks from *intra*-state branching, let alone *interstate* branching. The last of these regulations

preventing banks from having more than a single office in that state disappeared as recently as 1991.

79.   GATT, *Background Report*, p. 49.
80.   Interview with Robert Richard, as cited above.
81.   Shelp, 'Trade in Services', p. 78.
82.   To say nothing of the representative organization of the small banks, the Independent Bankers' Association of America (IBAA): interview with IBAA officials, Washington, DC, 3 April 1992.
83.   *Inside US Trade*, **9**, (6), 8 February 1991, p. 10.
84.   Interview with Robert Richard, as cited above.
85.   OECD, 'Prudential Supervision in Banking', *Financial Market Trends*, (35), November 1986, p. 22.
86.   OECD, *Banking and Monetary Policy*, Paris: OECD, 1985, p. 4.
87.   OECD, 'International Trade in Services: Securities', *Financial Market Trends*, (35), May 1987, pp. 16–17; interview with Paul Guy, Secretary General of the International Organization of Securities Commissions (IOSCO), Montreal, 10 December 1991.
88.   Paul Stonham, 'Big Bang: Short- and Long-Term Effects in the UK', in *Big Bang un anno doppo: Esperienze estere e proposte per la riforma dei mercati mobiliari Italiani*, Incontri di Rocca Salimbeni, Siena, 27–8 November 1987, p. 8.
89.   Ibid., p. 15.
90.   Ibid., p. 16.
91.   On the difficulties of coming up with a definition, see Shelp, 'Trade in Services', pp. 66–9.
92.   It should be noted at this stage that, as the Round proceeded, it became extremely difficult to separate the various strands of the negotiations: services, tariffs, agriculture and so on. Each set of the negotiations came to be seen as part of a larger package, which helps explain how capitalizing on progress in some areas came to be contingent on successfully unblocking talks in other areas, most notably agriculture.
93.   Winham, 'The Prenegotiation Phase of the Uruguay Round', p. 299.
94.   GATT, 'Ministerial Declaration', p. 21. The Group Negotiating Services is part of the Uruguay Round, but in a formal sense it is not part of GATT activities. This was at the insistence of the developing countries. Many LDCs in fact argued that UNCTAD would be a more appropriate forum for the negotiation of the trade-related aspects of services. This was because trade in services is closely connected with such issues, sensitive for the LDCs, as inward investment, technology transfers and the control of multinational corporations (Mark and Helleiner, *Trade in Services*, pp. 1–3, 19).
95.   GATT, *NUR* 001, 16 March 1987, p. 4.
96.   GATT, *NUR* 006, 8 July 1987, pp. 2–3.
97.   *EC Bulletin*, 19 June 1986, p. 21.
98.   GATT, *NUR* 014, 24 February 1988, p. 4.
99.   For a summary of US Proposals, see GATT, *NUR* 012, 10 December 1987, p. 5.
100. It would also mean, as noted above, that foreign suppliers of services requiring a presence in local markets in order to 'export' their services would have a right of establishment.
101. Shelp, 'Trade in Services', p. 76.
102. GATT, *NUR* 006, 8 July 1987, pp. 2–3.
103. GATT, *NUR* 012, 10 December 1987, p. 5. The US was eventually to retreat substantially from this position.
104. GATT, *NUR* 013, 21 December 1987, p. 5; GATT, *NUR* 014, 24 February 1988, p. 3. This idea was later echoed in a submission by Mexico as 'relative' reciprocity: GATT, *NUR* 018, 2 August 1988, p. 12.
105. *Globe and Mail*, (Toronto), 7 December 1988.
106. GATT, *Focus*, (59), 01/89, pp. 1–2.
107. GATT, *Focus*, (61), 05/89, p. 15.
108. Ibid.
109. Ibid.

110. Sidney Golt, *The GATT Negotiations 1986–1990: Origins, Issues and Prospects*, Washington, DC: the British North America Committee, 1988, pp. 46–7.
111. Of course, the capital transfers associated with the sale of banking and other financial services, as well as some other sectors where large capital transfers are involved, dwarf the actual amounts of value added gained from service provision itself.
112. GATT, *Focus*, (61), 05/89, p. 16.
113. Confidential interviews, Washington, DC, 20 March–4 April 1992.
114. The ambivalence of the US position on liberalization and reciprocity was given expression by Harry L. Freeman, Executive Vice-President of American Express, as noted in footnote 63 above.
115. Interview with Robert Richard.
116. Richard N. Gardner, *Sterling–Dollar Diplomacy in Current Perspective*, New York: Columbia University Press, 1980, pp. 372–8. The major difference between 1948 and the financial services negotiations was that in 1948 US trade policy was anything but liberal, so they had something to trade off in future negotiations. US negotiators concluded (with considerable justice) that in financial services they really had no further concessions to make as far as liberalization of the US sector was concerned. If other countries such as Japan and Korea did not open up now, the USA would fall into a permanent trap wherein others would have no incentive to grant further concessions to US financial institutions, preferring to remain 'free-riders' with access to the American market.
117. GATT, *NUR* 031, 16 October 1989, p. 12.
118. Ibid., p. 13.
119. This appeared to follow the recommendations of John H. Jackson, who did a study for the American Enterprise Institute. See his article, based on that study: 'Constructing a Constitution for Trade in Services', pp. 192–4.
120. United States, *Global Trade Issues: US Policies and Proposals,* Washington: US Information Agency, June 1990, p. 20.
121. GATT, *Focus*, (67), December 1989, p. 7.
122. Above account from *NUR* 032, 21 November 1989, pp. 12–14.
123. GATT *Focus*, (68), February 1990, p. 12.
124. Ibid.
125. GATT, *Focus*, (69), March 1990, p. 8.
126. GATT, *Focus*, (71), May–June 1990, p. 7.
127. United States House of Representatives, Subcommittee on Financial Institutions Supervision...International Competitiveness of US Financial Institutions, Task Force of the Committee on Banking, Finance and Urban Affairs, *National Treatment in Policy and Practice In the United States and Abroad*, Hearings, 28 February 1990, Washington: GPO, 1990, testimony of Robert Mulford, Undersecretary for International Affairs, Department of the Treasury, p. 24.
128. United States House of Representatives, Subcommittee on International Economic Policy...Committee on Foreign Affairs, *America's Services Trade Deficit*, Hearings, 2 November 1989, Washington: GPO, 1990, testimony of Richard Self, Deputy Assistant US Trade Representative for Services, Insurance, and Banking, p. 42.
129. Ibid., p. 1.
130. See ibid., for example testimony of C. Fred Bergsten, Institute for International Economics, p. 5.
131. Ibid., statement of committee Chairman Rep. Gejdenson, pp. 1–2.
132. Ibid., written statement of Hon. Toby Roth, p. 21.
133. Ibid., testimony of Linda F. Powers, Deputy Assistant Secretary for Services, US Dept. of Commerce, p. 24; testimony of Richard Self, Deputy Assistant US Trade Representative for Services, Insurance, and Banking, pp. 40–41, 43.
134. Ibid., testimony of Toby Roth, p. 22.
135. See United States Senate, *United States Access to Japanese Financial Markets*; United States Senate, Subcommittee on International Economic Policy...Committee on Foreign Relations, *United States–Japan Services Trade*, Hearings, 28 September 1988,

Washington: GPO, 1989. The latter was the fourth series of hearings on the subject in a three-year period (p. 4).

136. See *United States Access to Japanese Financial Markets*, testimony of E. Gerald Corrigan, Federal Reserve Bank of New York, pp. 2–10.

137. United States House of Representatives, *Oversight Hearings on the European Community's 1992 Program*, pp. 4–11, 31; and testimony of John R. Price of Manufacturers Hanover Trust on behalf of the Bankers Association for Foreign Trade, pp. 97–9.

138. *National Treatment in Policy and Practice in the United States and Abroad.*

139. *Wall Street Journal*, 30 January 1990, p.B2.

140. *Oversight Hearings on the European Community's 1992 Project*, p. 2.

141. *Globe and Mail* (Toronto), 25 October 1990.

142. *Financial Post* (Toronto), 21 September 1990, p. 6.

143. *The Economist*, 3 November 1990, pp. 87–8.

144. Confidential interview, Washington, DC, 20 March–4 April 1992.

145. Roger Taillon, the managing director of Standard and Poor, reflected that it was 'ironic' that the difficulties of many US banks were due to developments linked to internationalization and liberalization (*Globe and Mail* (Toronto), 7 March 1991, p.B8).

146. Confidential interviews.

147. There is an enormous amount of testimony in Congressional hearings to the effect that the regulatory restrictions on the activities of US financial institutions, at both the state and federal levels, handicap these firms in international competition, and that this handicap becomes greater as more and more countries adopt deregulation. See *United States Access to Japanese Financial Markets*, p. 4; *Deregulation of Financial Services*, p. 2; *Oversight Hearings on the European Community's 1992 Program*, pp. 2–3; *National Treatment in Policy and Practice in the United States and Abroad*, pp. 12, 14.

148. *Strengthening the Safety and Soundness of the Financial Services Industry*, op. cit., testimony of Robert A. Gerard, Managing Director, Morgan Stanley Inc. on behalf of the Securities Industry Association (1987), pp. 486–7: "The major securities firms of this country are thoroughly competitive, internationally. The major commercial banks in this country are thoroughly competitive, internationally....We consider ourselves and a number of our major securities firm competitors to be very strong in London and Tokyo....If our ability to compete with the commercial banks, domestically, goes down, I don't know whether we can retain that strength.'

149. *National Treatment in Policy and Practice in the United States and Abroad*, Subcommittee Chairman LaFalce, p. 32.

150. *Role of the Financial Services Sector*, testimony of C. Fred Bergsten, p. 4.

151. *Inside US Trade*, **8** (31), 3 August 1990.

152. Ibid., p. 13.

153. *International Trade Reporter*, **7**, (42), 24 October 1990, p. 1614.

154. *Inside US Trade*, **8**, (45), 9 November 1990, pp. 5–6.

155. *Inside US Trade*, **8**, (42), 19 October 1990, pp. 1, 5–6.

156. See P. G. Cerny, 'Global Finance and Governmental Gridlock: Political Entropy and the Decline of American Financial Power', in Richard Maidment and James A. Thurber (eds), *The Politics of Relative Decline: The United States at the End of the Twentieth Century*, Oxford and New York: Polity Press and Basil Blackwell, forthcoming 1993.

157. *International Trade Reporter*, **7**, (37), 19 September 1990, p. 1428.

158. Ibid.

159. *International Trade Reporter*, **7**, (37), 19 September 1990, p. 1428.

160. *International Trade Reporter*, **7**, (42), 24 October 1990, p. 1615.

161. Ibid., pp. 1614–16.

162. *International Trade Reporter*, **7**, (47), 28 November 1990, pp. 1801–2.

163. *Inside US Trade*, **8**, (49), 7 December 1990, p. 3.

164. *International Trade Reporter*, **7**, (48), 5 December 1990, pp. 1821–2.

165. Above account from *Inside US Trade*, **8**, (49), 7 December 1990, pp. 1 and 7.

166. *International Trade Reporter*, **7**, (48), 5 December 1990, p. 1822.

167. *International Trade Reporter*, **7**, (50), 19 December 1990, pp. 1928–9.

168.   *Inside US Trade*, **9**, (2), 11 January 1991, p. 12.

169.   *Inside US Trade*, **9**, (3), 18 January 1991, pp. 1, 21–2.

170.   *Inside US Trade*, **9**, (5), 1 February 1991, pp. 1, 18–20.

171.   *Inside US Trade*, **9**, (6), 8 February 1991, p. 22.

172.   GATT, *Focus*, (86), November–December 1991, p. 8.

173.   GATT, *Focus*, (87), January–February 1992.

174.   This account relies largely on evidence from confidential interviews, Washington, DC, 20 March–4 April 1992.

175.   Part of the problem here seems to be that the US negotiators were initially divided on the question. The Treasury always saw sectoral non-application as the way forward; the trade negotiators (Department of Commerce and the US Trade Representative) were not surprisingly more attached to traditional GATT norms. Until this dispute was resolved, it was difficult for the USA to work on bringing the EC and the Canadians along. Hence the whole issue blew up rather late in the day to threaten the talks.

176.   The EC had voiced its concern in this regard in December 1991, upon publication of the Dunkel Draft: GATT, *Focus*, (87), January–February 1992, p. 3.

177.   It has been pointed out that in the EC the private sector has much less access to the negotiators. By contrast, in the USA, the Chairman and other directors of Citicorp and American Express sat on an elaborate system of consultative committees advising the US negotiators in Geneva and asserting their particularistic interests.

178.   Especially given the reciprocity provisions of the EC's 1992 legislation with regard to financial services, which refers specifically to mutual reciprocity.

179.   Confidential interviews, Washington, DC, 20 March–4 April 1992.

PART III

STATES, REGIONS AND THE INTERNATIONAL FINANCIAL ORDER

6 American decline and the emergence of embedded financial orthodoxy

Philip G. Cerny

I Introduction: the infrastructure of the infrastructure

Finance has often been thought of as the 'life blood' of the physical economy. Indeed today, with the coming of the information revolution and what the French call the 'dematerialization' of financial instruments – the shift from physical share and bond certificates and so on to entries in a centralized computer system – it might be seen to have the characteristics of the nervous system as well. Finance, which is based more and more on the comprehensive abstraction of processes of exchange, incarnates the very fungibility of capital. It is, in the last analysis, the very embodiment of capital accumulation, and the fundamental, indispensable process of exchange which enables markets to exist in the first place and to function in the real world. It is 'the infrastructure of the infrastructure', and in the contemporary world this is more true than ever. An international financial system of some kind has always been a necessary and critical precondition of the development and expansion of the capitalist economic system *per se*, and the globalization of finance carries with it the prospect of a genuinely international capitalist economy, with all of its problems and prospects.

But, as Karl Polanyi pointed out in the 1940s,[1] the establishment of a capitalist market economy, and of the kind of financial system which is needed to create and sustain it, does not happen by itself. It is a political act, in two complementary ways. In the first place, the capitalist market is only one concrete dimension or potential form of social organization, and its predominance over other dimensions and forms requires that the necessary norms and structural conditions be authoritatively imposed or collectively adopted. In the second place, a range of critical and necessary *preconditions* for the organization and operation of a stable and efficient market require the backing of the state. These include the establishment within a circumscribed territory of clearly defined and enforceable property rights, common standards of value such as weights and measures, a currency for exchange and accumulation, a system of contracts, a legal system to enforce the above, and a coercive state apparatus to sanction predators.

In the past, of course, these attributes have been the attributes of states; international law has been customary and weak in its application to specific cases, unless backed by a powerful (hegemonic?) state or supported by a group of states acting in concert. The result has been that international markets have often either been only sporadically efficient and limited to attending to the utilities of small sub-groups of society, on the one hand, or else they have themselves been the creations of states, on the other.[2] Now the establishment of the conditions for a modern transnational capitalist market system in the 19th and 20th centuries has been primarily enabled through the financial hegemony of one power, first Britain and later the United States. In both cases, however, the limitations of such a hegemonic system have been manifested in the very tension between the nation-state and the international arena. In other words, some combination of the hegemon's national decline and the growing conflicts of interest between the national interests of the hegemonic state and the requirements for market stability and efficiency have undermined first the financial stability and, in turn, the wider economic efficiency of the international marketplace.[3]

The validity of this broad neo-realist picture, however, depends upon the continuing predominance of the role of the state and, conversely, upon the lack of a supra-state, transnational financial structure which can perform at the international level the same kind of political functions which the state has traditionally performed through its Janus-faced domestic and interstate structural centrality.[4] Now there does indeed exist a transnational financial structure, as Susan Strange has argued.[5] But to what extent does it possess structural *autonomy*? In other words, to what extent do the actors operating within the transnational financial structure have the capacity to act independently of constraints from other structures – especially states – and to use the resources available to them to pursue autonomous organizational goals, bypassing the constraints embedded in the state and/or the states system?

Analysts like Robert Cox and Stephen Gill,[6] who stress the structural autonomy of capital, see the emergence of a world production and/or financial structure as creating a new Gramscian global hegemony which transcends and controls state action, in the same way that national capital dominated in an earlier era and created the conditions for the cultural hegemony of the nation-state. Free-market economists like McKenzie and Lee[7] regard the retreat of the state in the Reagan–Thatcher era as the harbinger of a more efficient allocation of resources at the global level, a market system with a higher equilibrium, free from the distortions of state intervention. Globally aware social democrats/liberals such as Robert Reich[8] also see a fundamental shift coming in the role of the state, with much greater limitations on the scope of its interventions. The present writer's own argument[9] is that *the concept of the national interest itself is expanding* to embrace the international dimension in new ways; that is, that the 'competition state' (which has come to replace the welfare state) is itself forced by the imperatives of international competition into *reinforcing transnational structures*. Right across the ideological and analytical spectrum, therefore, there is a realization that globalization is a new phase, which in some ways replaces or transcends the nation-state, and in other ways absorbs or assimilates the state itself as a *proactive* reinforcing element in the globalization process. Only the neo-realists hold out by using the catch-all concept of 'regimes' to keep the state in the driver's seat at the transnational level. But what has been remarkable in the financial arena since 1971 and the breakdown of the Bretton Woods system has been the lack of a stable state-based 'regime' except in the vaguest sense of the virtual abdication of state power via the floating exchange rate mechanism.[10]

What is controversial about financial globalization, however, is (a) the extent, (b) the evenness/homogeneity, and (c) the impact on the world economy of the process. Has globalization, firstly, become irreversible? Are we in a situation where states can no longer, as in the 1930s, effectively pursue an alternative, domestically oriented path? If autarchy (introversive self-sufficiency) is dead, whether in terms of import substitution industrialization in the Third World[11] or of effective exchange rate manipulation in the First, then what is the scope for governments to manipulate the economy for domestic and, in particular, democratic ends? It is argued that financial globalization has severely restricted state economic policy, and will do so in increasingly complex ways; the scope for a new Keynesian/Polanyian humanization of markets is distinctly limited.

The second debate concerns the extent to which globalization is a homogeneous phenomenon, or whether there are growing contradictions and tensions between financial globalization, rooted in the increasing abstractness and fungibility of financial transactions and power in the information technology age, and the requirements of production and trade. Even within the financial arena, is there a tension between different sorts of financial market? It will be argued below that tensions of both of these kinds will characterize the international political economy for the foreseeable future, and that the most abstract financial markets will predominate.

Finally what will this mean for the 'real' economy and for the political structure of financial power? It may mean, as McKenzie and Lee argue in *Quicksilver Capital*, a renewed surge of stable growth in the world economy, or it may mean, as is argued below, a new *embedded financial orthodoxy*. Embedded financial orthodoxy, as was seen in the 1920s, is prone to unstable cycles of boom and slump, characterized by the use of blunt instruments like interest rates rather than fine-tuning, and dominated by calls for financial stability before all else (including, but not limited to, the permanent prioritization of anti-inflationary policy). Keynes warned that financial markets drain resources from the real economy and Eric Helleiner has argued that the strength of the postwar world economy (under American hegemony) stemmed, not from financial openness and the liberalization of financial markets, but from the strict *control* of international finance under the Bretton Woods system.[12]

In the current context, trends indicate that transnational-level financial regulation has yet to develop in any effective way, as Stephen Gill and Geoffrey Underhill argue.[13] Interstate cooperation was seen as a solution in the 1980s, but such regimes have not been particularly effective, except in certain limited areas such as the 1988 Basle Agreement on bank capital adequacy, which has had its own unsettling effects, as we shall see below. The recent abdication of G7 in the face of Soviet/Russian chaos is undoubtedly significant here. And although a move to separate trading zones has been widely canvassed, it seems likely to be a piecemeal affair, despite the failure so far of the Uruguay Round, and is not likely to provide a serious countervailing power structure to globalizing finance. A new state-based hegemony also seems unlikely, although Michael Prowse has recently argued in the *Financial Times*[14] that genuine European monetary union might well create an effective ECU standard for the world as the United States declines and the Japanese financial bubble bursts. It is unlikely, however, that a situation will emerge in which the *politics* of global finance are sufficiently coherent to ensure either financial market stability or a positive synergy with the wider growth of the 'real economy'. Whether this is the beginning of an epoch of crisis, a transition to some more closely structured world politico-financial order, or just an extended phase of 'muddling through', it is impossible to say at this stage. It will be argued below that the latter is the most likely outcome of the new age of 'embedded financial orthodoxy' in 'the infrastructure of the infrastructure'.

II   Finance and American hegemony

We have already dealt in detail in Chapter 3 with the changing relationship between the international financial system and state-based systems of regulating and promoting financial institutions and services. However the globalization of finance does not merely constrain the policy-making role of the nation-state. Finance is at the very heart of the issue of the hegemony and decline of states in the international system. It lies at the intersection of the inner power structure of the state, on the one hand, and the web of transnational linkages – those complex interactions which systematically cut across both markets and political systems and weave them together – on the other.[15] Finance is the tie which binds economic resources, military power and political capacity into a structured system of resource allocation. The power to shape the international financial system gives a state (or, indeed, any structured power nexus[16]) the capacity to manipulate the world's purse strings. America's 'rise to globalism'[17] was as much a question of its ability at a particular historical point to stabilize and shape the structure of the international financial system as it was a question of military superiority or economic power resources – if not more so.

In terms of American power in the postwar era, this can be seen at two levels. At one level the United States, during and after the Second World War, virtually controlled the 'power of the purse' in the capitalist world (and could deny its financial blessings to the non-capitalist world). But at another level it was not merely the 'cash' itself that America controlled which counted. Rather it was the very way that money was created, traded, protected and put to work in an increasingly interdependent (and American-guaranteed) world capitalist economy. Because American elites since the war had generally come to accept the view that the national interests of the United States included underwriting the health of the world economy, it had become a fundamental task of American foreign policy to supply the strategic blueprint for, and maintain the day-to-day organizational framework and operation of, the international financial system.

At the same time, however, the growing complexity of the international financial system and the proliferation of competing claims from other states (as well as from a range of non-state actors) made that task increasingly difficult and, in the view of many American policy-makers, increasingly unrewarding. Furthermore, since the 1960s, the erosion of US financial hegemony, and the growing complexity of international finance itself in a more interpenetrated world economy, have cut directly across domestic issues of financial market structure and the politics of stock market and banking regulation (as well as, more indirectly, across monetary policy, trade policy and industrial policy, among others). This complex interaction of domestic economic and sub-state structures with global economic and inter-state structures – known to international relations analysts as 'second structuralism' or 'neo-structuralism' – has increasingly made the politics of financial regulation crucial to America's position as an international financial 'great power'.[18]

For example, the process of financial 'deregulation' in the 1970s and 1980s was meant to strengthen the position of American financial institutions and markets in a new, more interdependent global setting, as well as to make for more efficient allocation of financial resources at home, as earlier chapters have emphasized. But this was not to be, as the crisis in the Savings and Loans industry so clearly demonstrates. Several interrelated issues have therefore come to a head recently, as the executive branch proposed and Congress disposed – or, in the event, disposed of – the most important attempt to reform the system of banking regulation since the New Deal regulatory system was put in place in the early 1930s in order to help prevent another Great Depression. The various bills submitted to Congress in the course of 1990 and 1991, particularly the Bush Administration's own proposals, were ultimately defeated in virtually all of their specific recommendations for reforming the regulatory process itself. Congressional politics came to the fore, and the result has been an outcome desired by very few.[19]

In an earlier article[20] the present writer attempted to develop an analysis of the way the fragmented and 'entropic' character of the American political system in general has been closely related to the 'relative decline' of the United States in terms of its hegemonic power in the international system. At the same time, a longer-term project on financial market deregulation (and re-regulation) in advanced industrial states has been undertaken. The broader work will examine how different states with diverse institutional structures (especially, of course, distinct financial regulatory systems) have attempted to adapt to and to benefit from changes in the international environment. These changes have been summed up, as discussed in Chapter 3, in the popular notion of the so-called 'integrated, 24-hour global financial market-place' of the 1980s and 1990s. Adaptation has been seen to be necessary in order (a) to improve the competitiveness of various states' home-based financial services industries and (b) to enable their domestic economies to profit from wider transnational changes. It may be, of course, that transnational changes have fundamentally altered or even undermined the capacity of states and policy-makers to pursue these kinds of goals at all. Indeed the capacity of states to adapt to the 'globalization' of finance may (and often does) involve attempting to change the structure and rationale of regulatory systems themselves.

Taking these two research strands together, it is suggested that we can identify three phases of change in the way that American financial power has evolved (and latterly declined). In the first place, the very fact that the US regulatory system itself was internally divided created *permissive conditions* in which forces for change at the international level fed into a cycle of deregulation at home. The dynamic of 'regulatory arbitrage', which plays divided regulators off against each other (particularly American regulators, but increasingly those of other countries as well), has been a major route to financial market liberalization.[21] Once the United States had itself been pushed into deregulation in the 1970s, therefore, its regulators and, later, legislators were for a time able to set the pace of change both at home and abroad.[22] Secondly, however, other countries have in more recent years been able to use their more centralized and streamlined domestic regulatory systems to catch up, and even to create new forms of competitive advantage both globally and within the USA. Finally, in a third phase, the policy-making process in the United States has reached an impasse over further steps to be taken. It is impossible to move back to earlier kinds of regulation – the genie is out of the bottle – but the barriers to effective *re*-regulation are also too high. The cracks in the US regulatory system have been exposed, and this in a period of greater financial volatility (since the October 1987 stock market crash), banking crisis (especially the Savings and Loans crisis) and lengthening economic recession. From all of this it is concluded that the entropic or 'gridlock' character of the American political system has significant implications, potentially quite negative, for American financial competitiveness and, consequently, for the wider issue of declining American hegemony in the international system.

Financial power – and the capacity and will of both state and private sector actors to use that power – has been at the core of the problematic of international hegemony ever since the emergence of the modern states system in the 19th century. It has often been asserted, particularly by the 'realist' school of international relations theory, that the lack of a common governing structure in the international arena analogous to the state in domestic politics – referred to as the 'anarchical' character of international society[23] – means that order in the international system must come, not from a higher or wider authority, but from the configuration of states themselves. These states are sovereign and autonomous, but, as with individuals in Thomas Hobbes's 'state of nature', their overriding primary objective – virtually the 'categorical imperative' of states, the 'bottom line' for state policy-makers – is their survival and security as states *per se* in a fundamentally hostile world. Given that states possess different resources, and therefore different power potentials, as well as different political systems, cultures and images of the 'national interest', the structure of the international system can be seen as an historically evolving configuration of power relationships, a set of ideal-type 'balances of power' located in the real world. These power configurations have often been depicted in ways which are reminiscent of the arrangement of molecules in biological or chemical science or the configuration of balls in a game of billiards.

A condition of 'hegemony', in this context, denotes a particular configuration of power relations. In it, one predominant power exists, by way of its resource potential and its decision-makers' political capacity to use that potential. Furthermore that state's continuing predominance requires that its own security – its capacity to survive, prosper and pursue its 'national interests'[24] – depends upon the stability and utility of the wider configuration or balance of power within which it is located. The 'hegemon', paradoxically, relies for its *own* security and 'national interest' on the stabilization and maintenance of the *wider* world order. In the language of collective action theory, the problem of 'free-riding' is, in effect, obviated or transcended. It is in the very interests of the hegemonic power itself to contribute sufficient resources and political will to ensure the continued provision of certain 'public goods' which are essential for sustaining the system as a whole.[25] The resulting condition is referred to in realist language as one of 'hegemonic stability'.[26] Although some authors see the condition of hegemonic stability as fragile and transient, given the ultimately anarchical nature of the international system, others see it not only as realistic in the longer term but also as probably the most feasible stable power configuration securable in a potentially explosive world.

Indeed the concept of 'hegemony' itself, and particularly the definition presented in the realist account paraphrased above, is widely contested.[27] Most conceptions of hegemony have in common, however, the criterion that the leading state (or states) in the international system is not simply the strongest, but also has the capacity to set *and enforce* the international rules of the game. This, however, is effectively a far more complex requirement than mere location in a unidimensional configuration of power. It requires economic power: the hegemon must be the 'leading economy'[28] and be able to shape international structures of trade, production, consumption and so on. It requires cultural power, in which there is a widely accepted identification of national interests with universal or supranational goals (and the acceptance by 'follower' states that *their* own national interests are furthered by following the leader). It requires military power: the capacity to use force to sustain the system when economic or cultural discipline fails or when external challenges arise. Crucially, too, it requires the decisional capacity of the hegemon to coordinate the above three types of power in order to establish and maintain a coherent set of rules and sanctions, and to enforce those rules in a transnational or even supranational fashion.

However each of these categories of power is also a complicating factor, which may, potentially at least, qualify, and may even undermine, the realist notion of hegemony. Economic power, especially in a capitalist society, is usually diffused to some extent among competing economic actors, actors often linked into transnational networks, thus hedging around the state's capacity to 'act' as a *de facto* power unit, both at home and in the international arena. Cultural power comes up not only against competing ideologies, ethnic and religious cleavages, nationalism and so on, but also against the diffusion of knowledge characteristic of the 'transnational knowledge structure'.[29] Decisional capacity is undermined by domestic political cleavages, turf battles between policy-makers and the structural division and diffusion of power characteristic of any state when analysed as a 'structured field of action'[30] – as well as by 'second structural' linkages between domestic structures and global structures. In this context, it might seem that the bottom line of the problematic of hegemony is military power – for, as Buzan writes, in the last analysis, 'military means can dominate outcomes in all other sectors'.[31] But in an epoch when transnational interpenetration is increasing and 'low politics' is in the ascendancy over 'high politics',[32] military means are often ineffective, counterproductive or simply unusable, as has been demonstrated, in very different ways, with regard to both the nuclear 'balance of terror' and the Vietnam war.

The main basis for the plausibility of the hegemonic stability approach, in fact, does not come so much from the theory of collective action *per se* – this would posit the potential existence of a somewhat wider range of stable alternatives[33] – nor from whether states actually act in real situations as holistic units or 'billiard balls', but from the observance of history. Since the consolidation of the major European nation-states from the 17th to the 19th centuries, the most apparently stable epochs have been those of the *pax britannica* of the mid-19th century and the *pax americana* of the mid-20th. Whether either Britain or the United States actually played the theoretically prescribed role of 'hegemon' and fulfilled all of the criteria discussed above is, of course, a matter of judgement and can be contested.[34] But while the relative significance of each dimension will always be a matter for historical debate, all of the above elements can be seen to have contributed in one way or another to both British hegemony in the 19th century and American hegemony in the 20th.[35]

If we look at the history of the British and American hegemonies, however, and at the decline and *failure* of those hegemonies, including the long interregnum during much of the first half of the 20th century, what we see is a situation in which the most crucial factor is not so much broad economic power, nor cultural dominance, nor military power (as important as those are), but *financial* power. And the crucial element of financial power is a stable and guaranteed international payments system. Without such a guaranteed international payments system, trade decays into mercantilism and protectionism; as a result, culture and knowledge become inward-looking and suspicious of the foreign; and military power becomes zero-sum and predatory rather than balancing or stabilizing. The key to British hegemony was not British balance of power diplomacy on the European Continent (*pace* Henry Kissinger[36]) expansion of the Empire, the navy, nor even the Industrial Revolution, but the maintenance of the gold standard. Furthermore this was, it must be emphasized, not because it constituted a central policy aim of the British *state* as such. The gold standard emerged from and developed through deeply embedded networks linking the Treasury, the Bank of England and the City of London, that small section of London which houses the centre of Britain's financial services industry (London's Wall Street, commonly referred to simply as 'the City' or, copying American parlance, 'the street'). British financial institutions were concerned primarily with financing trade (as well, of course, as financing the state itself). During the 19th century this increasingly meant financing trade between third (that is, non-British) parties. The other main role of the City was to direct British investment capital abroad, mainly to the Empire and to the United States.[37]

Now the British state was not only laissez-faire in terms of economic policy, but also, in Badie and Birnbaum's terms, a 'civil society' state (or 'weak state') based on the dominance of socioeconomic interests rather than an autonomous politico-bureaucratic elite.[38] The flag followed trade – and investment – rather than the other way around. Indeed this was a crucial characteristic of Britain as a new kind of polity, based on the objective of strengthening *self-regulating market mechanisms* rather than either a feudal or a command economy.[39] If there was any hegemonic 'power nexus' in the 19th century international system, it can be argued that this manifested itself, not in the British state *per se*, but in a transnational network of *haute finance* with the City of London at its core.[40] Of course, the British state also played a necessary and critical supporting role, until the gold standard system was fatally weakened in the First World War, thereby putting an end to an already declining British hegemony.[41] Finance, not force, was the core of the *pax britannica*. Its final collapse was consummated in war, but its fate had already been sealed by the rise of a new, mercantilist and autarchic form of 'finance capital' which became dominant among late industrializing nations towards the end of the 19th century – Germany, Russia and Japan. Britain began her relative economic decline around 1870,[42] and the system which she guaranteed and ran soon became inimical to her other political and economic national interests. This would become fatal after the First World War was over.

Perhaps the most influential work in the development of the hegemonic stability school deals, in fact, with the interregnum between the *pax britannica* and the *pax americana*, the period between the two world wars. Economic historian Charles P. Kindleberger argues that the root cause of the economic overheating of the 1920s and the Great Depression of the 1930s, which in turn reinforced the global trend towards more virulent and totalitarian forms of autarchy, was the lack, not of a military or diplomatic hegemon in the world system, but of a *financial* hegemon.[43] In the 1920s, several closely intertwined factors – the volatility of financial flows between Europe and the United States, the lack of an international consensus on a range of structurally significant financial issues (especially German reparations) and the political inability of the United States to go beyond undermining the economic and social health of the major powers – were all symptomatic of a wider disease of the epoch.

Britain's role was fatally undermined by her shift from being the world's creditor to becoming a debtor nation. She could no longer guarantee the stability of the system, no longer having the financial capacity to be the 'lender of last resort' when adjustments were required. Other countries such as France and Germany were still in the throes of postwar crisis or decline, and in the United States a combination of political isolationism, on the one hand, and the belief of bankers and bureaucrats in the necessity of restoring the gold standard,[44] on the other, prevented both state actors and private sector actors from considering anything so unthinkable as structural reform of the international financial system itself. With the Great Depression, of course, came the collapse of world trade and the final demise of the gold standard. It took the Roosevelt Administration in the 1930s several years to shift fully from domestic planning and corporatism to free trade. By the outbreak of the Second World War, however, and the subsequent formulation of American economic war aims, that shift would be virtually complete.[45]

Indeed there arose a consensus among American elites[46] that a new world order was required, one in which American structural leadership, hegemony, would be necessary to guarantee free trade. And the key to that new world order had to be, first and foremost, a new international financial system to replace the defunct gold standard. Since the mid-1930s, and the tying of the dollar to gold, the slow recovery of prewar world trade had come to depend on a *de facto* dollar standard. This would be the lynchpin of the new system agreed at Bretton Woods in 1944.[47] By fixing to the dollar the exchange rates of the member states of the International Monetary Fund – the new (American-backed) international lender of last resort – the world would once again have a stable and guaranteed financial system. This was to be a free trade system, but not, therefore, a free market system *in toto*. Indeed the mechanisms of the Bretton Woods system, as Eric Helleiner has argued, rested on an apparent paradox: in order to promote the liberalization of trade, finance would have to be controlled.[48] American hegemony in the postwar period may have been made possible by its military victory over the Axis; but it was the world's dollar shortage after the war which gave the USA the leverage to impose a new financial system which would stabilize the Western economies and guarantee the peace.

The Bretton Woods system fulfilled this role through most of the years of the Long Boom. But it, like the gold standard before it, had built-in tensions which would eventually undermine it. Those tensions came to the fore in the 1960s. A first apparent paradox was that the very success of the free-trading system underpinned by Bretton Woods (reinforced in 1947 by the General Agreement on Tariffs and Trade and the Marshall Plan) had encouraged the recovery and growing international competitiveness of Europe and Japan. A second apparent paradox lay in that, within the United States itself, Bretton Woods was coming to be seen as less useful, and less in America's national interest, than it had been after the war. Chronic balance of payments deficits, followed by chronic balance of trade deficits, highlighted America's decreasing competitiveness. Outflows of American capital abroad, further-more, were not being repatriated in turn; they made their way, for example, to the newly expanding Euromarkets in London, where they could escape domestic regulatory controls. The 'dollar shortage' had turned into a 'dollar overhang'.[49]

The 'dollar overhang' had drawbacks for both the United States and the European states. Although many US multinationals benefited by expanding their European and other overseas investment, this merely served to sharpen the contrast between America's growing internal economic stagnation and the apparent dynamism of Europe and Japan. On the one hand, these coun-tries put the United States under pressure to devalue the dollar against gold in order to counteract the USA's own external deficits. The privileged posi-tion of the dollar as the lynchpin of the system, they argued, allowed the USA simply to 'print money', whether to pay for the Vietnam war or to finance its external deficits. In both cases the effect was to infuse the interna-tional system with expatriate dollars, raising the money supply in an infla-tionary fashion. On the other hand, of course, this pressure from outside seemed to American policy-makers to threaten the Bretton Woods system as a whole by undermining the dollar's guarantee of stability, as well as under-mining the ability of the United States to conduct an autonomous economic policy. They resisted by demanding the revaluation of competitors' curren-cies instead (ignoring the potentially deflationary effects of this approach for the wider international economy).

The resulting political stalemate between the Nixon Administration and America's major trading partners led to an outcome which was politically preferred by very few (except for the not yet predominant group of monetar-ist economists led by Milton Friedman and their then relatively small band of political adherents) the abandonment of the Bretton Woods system itself and the move to a system of floating exchange rates. In effect the interna-tional financial system was transformed by the back door. The former finan-cial hegemon was no longer able to guarantee the system by itself; neither could it exploit its eroded political capital to persuade its partners and rivals to restructure the system around its preferred options.[50] International finance had been based since the Second World War on the attempt to restrict and control financial markets in order (paradoxically) to liberalize trade. What would the sudden liberalization (Cohen calls it 'privatization'[51]) of the cor-nerstone of this system, the foreign exchange market, mean, in turn, for the role that finance would come to play in the future? What would be its impact on trade? And how would this new role for finance intersect with the wider power structure of the international system?

III Globalization, deregulation and the decline of American financial hegemony

The development of the international financial system since 1971, and its impact on the wider world order, has been interpreted in three contrasting ways. In the first of these, American hegemony still exists; however it is of a much more complex and subtle kind. From this perspective, the floating exchange rate system was not merely adopted by default, but was in fact imposed on the world by the USA through the back door, whether by conscious intent or inadvertently through a 'non-decision'.[52] Indeed America's key (and structurally irreplaceable) position in the world financial system, despite its ostensible withdrawal, could thus be seen to continue to confer on the USA a Gramscian type of hegemony, based on American 'structural power', even if it no longer possessed the realist kind (based on 'relational power').[53] But was this a *usable* form of power, one which would contribute to developing a more efficient, market-based system, or was it just the power to cause disorder by default?[54]

From a second perspective, however, the move to floating exchange rates marked the end of real US hegemony and signalled the advent of a more volatile and potentially dangerous world order. In this emerging order (or latent disorder) stability would have to be continually negotiated between several major economic powers, especially Japan and Germany, in addition to the United States. The form which this new disorder would be likely to take is, as might be expected, contentious. To some of those taking this view, escalating neo-mercantilism in trade – new forms of protectionism, especially of the non-tariff kind – is likely to mirror an analogous trend in finance, reinforcing the tendency for the multilateral liberal system to be undermined at its heart, in the monetary sphere. For others, however, partial agreements to avoid crises, such as the Plaza and Louvre Accords in the mid-1980s, could lead to more cooperative habits of interstate behaviour in the longer term.

A third interpretation, however, has been simply that the dramatic expansion of financial flows, as a result, directly and indirectly, of the floating exchange rate regime, would make international financial markets into autonomous, transnational structures. In the future, the '24-hour, integrated global financial market-place' would increasingly constrain and shape state behaviour, imposing upon monetary policy, fiscal policy and trade policy a much greater 'market discipline' than before.[55] Proponents of this perspective, too, are divided. Would this new market discipline lead to future economic growth and a more efficient allocation of resources as, variously, monetarist and supply-side economists would contend? Or, conversely, would it impose a new 'embedded financial orthodoxy' on states, producing either greater long-term rigidity and stagnation, or more volatile 'boom and bust' cycles? The focus of that debate in empirical terms, as we will see in more detail below, has been the problem of deregulation and the implications of deregulation for the state – in this case, the American state.

The issue of deregulation, then, has raised questions which go beyond both neo-realist hegemonic stability theory and the Gramscian notion of hegemony, to raise once again the question of the nature of collective action. Both of these versions of hegemony, in different ways, see *interstate* competition and cooperation as the dominant mode of international interaction and system structuring, even if in the second case this interstate competition and cooperation is the consequence of the dominance of a transnational financial class mediating its interests through state apparatuses.[56] However such an interstate system must ultimately depend for its effective operation upon what was earlier called the 'decisional capacity' of state apparatuses. States are not merely hierarchical objects which behave like solid, billiard ball-type units. They are real historical entities, composed of complex patterns of conflict and coalition-building, mediated through institutional structures, sociopolitical cleavages and the competition of economic interests. At the same time, of course, the international system is not merely a configuration of unitary states, but a complex congeries of states and other cross-cutting structures.[57]

Within this context, it has been argued that finance has always been both a cross-cutting, transnational structure, and one of the crucial elements of state-building and state power. To the extent that particular powers have been internationally hegemonic in the modern era, their hegemony has been inextricably intertwined with the dominance of structured coalitions of state actors and private sector actors which have been able to marshal both financial and other power resources in order to stabilize and to shape the world financial order. The gold standard and the Bretton Woods system, then, were not merely the instruments of a hegemonic state apparatus. They represented the *intersection* of private financial power, the power of state actors and apparatuses (internally as well as externally) and the state or condition of the transnational financial structure.

Holding together this complex hegemonic 'crossroads' in each case, however, was a decision-making network mediated through the Janus-faced state. State elites provided crucial linkages between different groups of domestic and international private, as well as state, actors. At one level, provisions of the law, a key attribute of 'state-ness', provided both the operational rules for this complex process and the basis for its legitimacy. At the same time, the good faith and credit of the state, and the influence of its financial apparatuses, such as treasuries, central banks and so on, provided more tangible guarantees of its material solidity. Furthermore the state's diplomatic apparatus coordinated international political negotiations. Also the state's military power was always present, in both the background and the foreground of the *pax britannica* and the *pax americana*.

In essence, therefore, what held this complex system of finance and hegemony together – the glue of the system – was not the state as a supreme hierarchical unit *per se*, but the complex character of the state's structure, including the decision-making processes which the state embraced. The key independent variable was in effect the *decisional capacity* of the state, that is to say, the capacity of state actors to organize their own efforts, marshal the state's resources and coordinate them with private resources, and manipulate the international environment in a coherent, consistent and goal-directed fashion. At this point in the analysis, two quite distinct but cross-cutting factors come to the fore. On the one hand, the process of financial deregulation becomes a critical focus of both the substance and the process of policy-making. On the other, the problematic character of decision-making in the American state itself – what we have called its tendency to Madisonian 'entropy' – re-emerges as a critical element in foreign economic policy for virtually the first time since America's entry into the Second World War.

The first factor to consider is deregulation. This became crucial because a policy based on deregulation is compatible with certain key constraints present in (a) the domestic political process and (b) the anarchic character of the international system. The breakdown of the postwar financial hegemony of the American state, represented by the shift from the Bretton Woods system to the floating exchange rate regime, has been, as we have seen, described as the result of a 'non-decision' (or a series of non-decisions) in the context of the decreasing competitiveness of the domestic US public and private financial structure (faced with the rise of Europe and Japan). But the shift to a floating rate regime did also have a wider political and economic rationale, that of deregulation. It was proactively supported, as we have already noted, by monetarist economists as well as some politicians, for the very reason that it was supposed to obviate state control of the foreign exchange markets.

Now such financial deregulation can be seen as either (a) a (positive) transfer of responsibility for the allocation of financial resources to the (supposedly more efficient) financial markets, or (b) the (negative) abandonment of responsibility for managing the international financial system. The strength of deregulation as a policy option, however, is that it can be both of these things at the same time. On the one hand, deregulation, both in the financial arena and in more general terms, can appear to be a *non-policy*. It involves, ostensibly at least, the *removal* of regulations.[58] On the domestic level as well as on the international level, it can attract an alliance of strange bedfellows, because it does not appear to require agreement on the direct, authoritative distribution or redistribution of resources; this is, in theory at least, left to the market. On the other hand, unlike the multilateral decision-making processes embodied in the IMF or the GATT, the decision to deregulate can be – and generally is – a *unilateral* one. This was a crucial advantage in an international system where consensus, in this case, hegemonic consensus around the Bretton Woods system, was breaking down. Deregulation, then, is a policy option which it is possible to pursue in an anarchical international system when there exists what public choice theorists call an 'empty core': the systematic lack of sufficient shared preferences for there to emerge a collectively agreed outcome. These twin facets of deregulation, the apparent absence of the necessity for actors' agreement on substantive alternatives and the fact that it can be decided upon unilaterally, are crucial for understanding the development of the post-Bretton Woods international financial system.

One of the most important issues in the study of the international financial system (as with, for example, trade) is the 'collective action problem'. In the trade arena, multilateral action has been seen as necessary and vital for the maintenance of an open, liberal world trading order. Unilateral action, in contrast, has been seen as having by its very nature a neo-mercantilist 'closure' effect. However, in the financial arena, as Helleiner[59] has pointed out, the converse is the rule. Multilateral action, exemplified by Bretton Woods (which, despite US hegemony, was still a multilateral regime), is necessary in order to control – essentially to restrict – financial flows in an open trading world where abstract money would simply flow around and through most national-level controls. Furthermore it is central to the Keynesian approach, which lay behind the Bretton Woods system, that open and unregulated international financial markets (a) have an inherent tendency to be volatile and destabilizing (as manifested in his analysis of the 1920s) and (b) drain funds from industrial investment and trade, thereby both undermining the virtuous circle of open trade and crowding out production.

Therefore multilateral control of financial flows, achieved mainly through fixed exchange rates, would be an *a priori* necessity in order to maintain a virtuous circle of free trade and the growth of production. In other words, world-wide economic growth via free trade requires a closed, not an open, international financial regime. *Unilateral action, in contrast, has the effect of 'opening' the world financial system even further.* What might be called the 'widening circle of deregulation', then, reflects an interactive series of unilateral choices by states to deregulate at first limited, but later more sweeping, categories of financial transactions, markets and institutions. Therefore the collective action problem, as presented by trade-oriented analysts in international political economy – and they represent a much higher proportion of active researchers than do finance-oriented analysts – must be stood on its head in the financial field.

Such a deregulated international market-place, freed from postwar controls, was supposed to become a far more efficient allocator of capital than the Bretton Woods regime had ever been or, more importantly, could ever be. But the corollary is that the very mechanism of deregulation is supposed to remove the state from the financial decision-making process: its very *raison d'être* is to reduce the state's decisional capacity! Furthermore the widening circle (whether virtuous or vicious) of deregulation touched off by the collapse of Bretton Woods[60] has been seen as undermining the decisional capacity of far more unitary, 'strategic' states than the USA.[61] Deregulation, then, was the reaction of the American state to the problems it was experiencing in maintaining its financial – and therefore its political – hegemony, but deregulation, by its very nature, entailed the next turn of the screw. For deregulation is meant to transfer decision-making responsibility from the state to the market. From now on, the American state would be increasingly unable to act in a (realist) 'state-like' fashion, because the parameters of state decision-making would be increasingly set by transnational financial markets.

At the same time, the second factor mentioned above comes into play – the complex decisional structure of the American state. It might be argued that the decisional capacity of the American state has always been inherently fragile. This is the consequence of its institutional structure, the system of 'checks and balances' embodied in the separation of powers and federalism. In a series of issue areas either directly concerned with, or otherwise relevant to, foreign policy and America's role in world affairs, the American 'state' is divided, stalemated, entropic. Entropic states are peculiarly vulnerable in international affairs; the weakness of French foreign policy under the Third Republic has in large measure been attributed to what has been called France's 'stalemate society' of the epoch.[62] Furthermore the analysis which we have presented elsewhere of the consequences for international relations of America's 'political entropy' is analogous – and, indeed, complementary – to other analyses of US politics which have focused on the lack of positive policy-making power in the American political system on a range of domestic issues.[63]

A wide variety of relevant structural trends has been observed by analysts of American politics: the increasing isolation of the 'imperial presidency' from other levels of government; the 'incumbency factor' and the growing predominance of local affairs in non-presidential electoral politics; the strengthening and expansion of the committee system in Congress; a range of crucial trends in the US political party system, including phases of party dealignment and the long-term trend towards 'divided government' (different parties in control of the different branches of national government);[64] the increasing predominance of 'iron triangles', issue networks and policy communities as the crucial arenas for policy-making, dominating and even re-placing formal constitutional processes; the duplication of bureaucratic struc-tures, tasks and personnel across different branches and levels of govern-ment; and so on.[65] Probably the most salient issue area representing the failure of decisional capacity in the American national state is the entrenched conflict since the early 1980s between the President and Congress on budg-etary matters, leading to continuing structural deficits;[66] indeed this is likely to continue through the Clinton Administration.

In this context, what is surprising is not that the United States has lost financial hegemony, but that it ever gained it in the first place. That it did so, that the American state had sufficient decisional capacity to act in a hegemonic fashion in establishing and maintaining the postwar international monetary regime for so long, was the result of the convergence of several factors. One was the general growth of state intervention in the economy and the con-comitant growth of presidential power and of the federal (and presidential) bureaucracy, which stemmed from the Great Depression and the politics of the New Deal. This was extremely significant for foreign affairs as well, as a strong presidency in peacetime was not only an institutional innovation – something new in American political life – but also increased the capacity of the United States to act in a more centralized, 'state-like' fashion on the world stage.[67] A second element was the coming of the Second World War, which permitted the newly-consolidated national political–economic elite with its internationalist disposition to extend its predominance to a centrally controlled war economy as well as to the leadership of the political–military wartime alliance. This 'internationalist' elite continued to exert control over both domestic and foreign economic policy after the end of the war. A third factor was the lack, in the postwar period, of countervailing forces in the capitalist world: the other main capitalist powers, and indeed the forces of international *haute finance*, were on their economic knees, relatively speak-ing. And a fourth and final ingredient was the Cold War and the unifying dynamic which this imposed both on domestic political forces and on other countries within the US sphere of influence.

The intersection of these factors, along with traditional (if fragile) execu-tive prerogatives in foreign affairs and national security matters, created permissive conditions for bypassing the checks and balances of the Ameri-can constitutional system. The shorthand term for this phenomenon, its unifying, if mundane, symbol, was the 'bipartisanship' of postwar American foreign policy. By the late 1960s and early 1970s, however, those conditions no longer prevailed. A new set of circumstances – external deficits, a re-newed conservatism in domestic economic policy, the Vietnam war, detente with the Soviet Union, the competitive economic challenge from America's political allies (soon to be exacerbated by the slump of the mid-1970s, with its realignment of domestic as well as transnational sociopolitical forces) and (critically for American financial hegemony) the collapse of Bretton Woods – together led to a search for alternatives to a foreign economic policy which had lost its central rationale. In this situation, the USA was no longer in *political* control of the capitalist world economy, but American state and private sector actors – bureaucrats and businessmen – still had the *de facto* structural power to impose, by the back door, an approach which quickly became the core of a new domestic consensus, deregulation.

The momentum for deregulation came from the floating exchange rate system, but its impact was much wider. It cut across issue areas and across party lines.[68] Right and Left to some extent shared a diagnosis of the slump and its symptom of 'stagflation' which emphasized the failure of Keynesianism and the 'fiscal crisis of the state'.[69] In this context, the end of Bretton Woods led to the revival of calls by internationally oriented sectors of the American financial community for the deregulation of financial markets and banking. Subsequent deregulatory decisions (and non-decisions) were spread across four different Administrations – those of Nixon, Ford, Carter and Reagan – and cut across the executive branch, Congress, and a range of regulatory bodies. They concerned not only finance, of course, but also, and in a much more politically salient fashion, road haulage, airlines, communications and, eventually, under the Reagan Administration, a range of social policies too.

In finance they included not only the end of Bretton Woods and the move to floating exchange rates, but also the abolition of minimum commissions for securities trading (known as 'May Day' 1975), the lifting of a range of interest rate controls, the deregulation of the money markets (the Depository Institutions Deregulation and Monetary Control Act, 1980), the deregulation of Savings and Loan institutions (the Garn-St. Germain Act, 1982) and a variety of other measures, including measures designed to attract foreign funds (and also increasingly footloose American funds) which had previously preferred, for example, the unregulated Euromarkets. Together these measures had the effect of removing traditional barriers between distinct kinds of financial markets, primarily barriers erected in the New Deal period. This permitted banks, brokers and market-makers to engage in 'arbitrage' between different financial markets at home and abroad in order to get the highest rate of return on their capital. This in turn led to a wave of financial innovation which is still continuing. The structural changes in financial markets which resulted are the focus of intense debate as to whether deregulation is leading, as its supporters claim, to a more efficient allocation of capital in the world capitalist system generally, or whether it will lead, as its detractors claim, to more October 1987-style stock market crashes, more banking failures and the rest.[70] Indeed current debate focuses on the role of international financial deregulation in provoking the long recession, dating back to 1989 and still with us, and on the austerity policies with which it has been associated.

IV   The dilemmas of re-regulation

In this environment the substance of the political and economic debate has shifted from deregulation *per se* to 're-regulation'. Now the term 're-regulation' can mean several different things. We distinguished above (see Chapter 3) between two types of re-regulation. The first type is inextricably intertwined with deregulation itself, that is, the drafting and implementation of new 'deregulating regulations'. These new regulations are intended precisely to *promote and reinforce market-oriented behaviour itself*, as distinct from the traditional conception of regulation as controlling or constraining markets according to authoritative non-market criteria. The second type, in contrast, involves new authoritative – market-*constraining* – measures to prevent both old and new kinds of market failure: that is, to control and counteract various perverse unintended consequences (latent or manifest) which may have been caused by the original deregulation itself.

Now neither of these types of re-regulation is wholly incompatible with deregulation. Indeed 'Type I' re-regulation is, by definition, necessary for deregulation itself to proceed; and 'Type II', furthermore, usually involves not so much a wholesale return to previous authoritative, market-constraining regulatory patterns, but rather a mix of linked proposals: (a) further specific deregulatory measures (accompanied, of course, by 'Type I' re-regulation); and (b) a range of 'Type II' re-regulatory measures designed, it is hoped, to prevent the kinds of unintended consequences which earlier experience with deregulation had revealed, as well as to anticipate further drawbacks.

The deregulation of financial markets, unlike some other kinds of deregulation, *has* had the intended effect of at least partially permitting and speeding up the further integration of American financial markets into what Strange has called the 'transnational financial structure', as all of the authors in this book agree.[71] To that extent, therefore, further national-level re-regulation has become much more difficult. The genie is out of the bottle, so to speak. This situation could be described as one of 'level shift', which has two kinds of possible consequences for the process of deregulation/re-regulation. In the first place, the level of the *problem* itself has shifted. American banks and financial markets, on the one hand, and the banks and financial markets of other countries, on the other, are not only 'interdependent', but, much more importantly, 'interpenetrated'. There are direct linkages between international financial markets – markets for securities of various kinds[72] and, of course, for banking services – and domestic markets. Arbitrage between these markets can in theory, if the players are determined and knowledge-able enough (as well as having the necessary resources), take place in a variety of different centres in a range of different countries, in effect, on a 24-hour basis.

In this context, the most effective form of re-regulation might seem to be to evolve new multilateral mechanisms (or breathe new life into old ones). This might, in theory, be done in two main ways, either by developing more effective forms of *intergovernmental* cooperation, or by establishing (and/or strengthening) more autonomous *transnational* regimes.[73] In other words, the very process of regulatory change itself, whether defined as deregulation or re-regulation (or some combination of the two), must, to some extent, become internationalized (or transnationalized). The problem here, however, is that transnational regimes are easy to prescribe but are hard to establish – as Underhill demonstrates in Chapter 5, above – and to make work effec-tively. This is, above all, for the simple reason that, as realist theory has emphasized, there is no overall transnational or supranational state, nor even any latent equivalent – the existence of a highly interdependent and inter-penetrated international system notwithstanding.

In effect, then, unless there is a *cumulative and simultaneous mobilization of different states' perceptions of their national interests*, in an essentially additive process, rather than a hierarchically organized one, even well-estab-lished transnational regimes are likely not only to lack authority but also to be rudderless and fragile in practice. Although some progress has been made in managing exchange rates (for example, the Plaza and Louvre Accords of 1985–6, as discussed by Gill in Chapter 4, above) and agreeing common capital adequacy standards for banks – and probably soon for securities firms as well[74] – these mechanisms are still very limited. They are circum-scribed in at least two ways: in terms of their specific technical content (for example, capital adequacy standards, as important as they are, are only one regulatory tool with limited application) and in terms of their operational feasibility (attempts by central banks to manage exchange rates are highly dependent upon market conditions, as shown in the sterling crisis of Septem-ber 1992).

One critical ramification of 'level shift', then, is that, although interna-tional-level regulatory solutions may be potentially the most effective re-sponse to the problems of volatility, market failure, and so on in internation-alized financial markets, such solutions are not likely to be forthcoming, especially in the short or medium term, to anything like the extent necessary to deal with the legacy of deregulation. Therefore, although successive Ameri-can Administrations seem to have been quite capable, in certain international negotiations at least, of overcoming the sort of bureaucratic and legislative turf battles which have paralysed domestic re-regulatory politics, the impact of the most important resulting agreement, the 1988 Basle Accord on bank capital adequacy standards, represents only a limited success. The element of success, of course, lies in the fact that an apparently workable intergovernmental agreement was reached on a significant aspect of prudential regulation, and that it is actually being implemented, despite some setbacks.[75]

The limitations, however, are twofold. In the first place, capital adequacy is just one ingredient in effective prudential regulation, the effects of which are disputed. Indeed some would argue that agreement on capital adequacy ratios, however important they might be in themselves, might prove merely to be a substitute for wider and more effective regulatory action. In the second place, the adoption of strict capital adequacy standards may be having perverse consequences by causing banks to retrench, reducing their lending in order to bolster their capital ratios. In this way they are sometimes said to be contributing to the 'credit crunch' which has characterized the recent recession. In the event, the process of adjustment has been a problematic one, and may be in danger of partially breaking down. Thus the Basle Accord may well demonstrate just how far the deregulation and internationalization of financial markets in fact circumscribe the action of even the most effective and strategically placed state policy-makers. Indeed further multilateral regulatory steps are proving somewhat more difficult to achieve. The lesson of the agreement on capital adequacy does demonstrate, however, that such steps are not impossible. But it also indicates that future projects are likely to require certain conditions to be successful.

Four such conditions can be identified from a look at the Basle case. The first is, of course, that an effective *international* coalition must be formed, in such a way that no major state can impose a blocking veto.[76] The second is that the subject-matter of any agreement must be sufficiently limited in scope for it to be treated as a technical issue and dealt with by experts away from the political limelight. Politicization, whether at an intranational or at an international level, would probably prove to be an insuperable barrier, if not always to the conclusion of any specific agreement, then to its effective implementation. The third condition – in fact a corollary of the second – is that the state actors charged with undertaking (a) the negotiation and (b) the implementation of such a regulatory agreement need to have the legal and political autonomy and discretion to carry out these tasks without having to engage in turf battles or competitive politicking at a party or interest group level.[77] In effect, the open and competitive American political system has to behave as if it were an autonomous, cohesive, 'state-like'[78] bureaucratic apparatus both internally and externally – a tall order in the normal run of events. The fourth and final condition translates the first three onto the economic plane. This is quite simply that the form of regulation agreed upon must be effectively enforceable: that is, it must not be overly vulnerable to being undermined by normal market activities or by the standard avoidance tactics which the private sector will inevitably apply.

The success of the negotiations which led to the Basle Accord, in the last analysis, then, depended upon the capacity of the Federal Reserve to take an effective lead role, the deference with which the Fed was treated by American bureaucrats and politicians on this issue, and the still problematic ability of national regulators to ensure the compliance of the private sector.[79] Paradoxically, however, when compared, say, with the Bretton Woods Agreement or even the shift to floating exchange rates, the Basle episode may be the exception that proves the rule. What it reflects may be the limits of American financial power, not the continuation or resurrection of US financial hegemony.

In effect the problem is no longer one of 'American' financial hegemony, or, indeed, the financial 'hegemony' of any state as such. The problem is one of the 'transnational financial structure', in which the actions of bureaucrats and politicians are located within a much more complex setting than that of the state, or even of the 'states system'. Their 'second structural' linkages, not those of the state, constitute the major part of the 'structured field of action' within which they are located and the parameters of which define their possibilities. With regard to the issue of developing common capital adequacy standards for securities firms, for example,[80] it is not the relationship of the US Securities and Exchange Commission with the American 'state' *per se* which is the crucial structural dimension, but the SEC's relationship with both a range of domestic and transnational financial institutions and markets, and the relevant regulatory agencies and financial state apparatuses in *other* countries (and the European Commission too), which is the real locus of decision-making – and non-decision-making. The shift of the *problem* to the transnational level, then, does not hold out the promise of broadly-based transnational *solutions*.[81]

These developments, in turn, highlight the second principal set of consequences of the 'level shift' entailed by financial deregulation and internationalization, those which effect the domestic political process as such. This can be characterized as a 'whipsawing' of the state between increasing system entropy, on the one hand, and growing demand for political action, on the other. That demand takes two forms. In the first place, liberal democratic political systems are based on the assumption that political officials are accountable for the outcomes of policy decisions made by and through the state. Politicians are, in turn, expected to pursue policies which prevent financial crises, market failure and so on. When crisis and market failure occur, in an open political system with widespread access for individuals and interest groups to a range of state actors at different governmental levels (a feature which is particularly prevalent in the United States), re-regulation *at the domestic level* becomes a salient political issue. Politicians must at least address the issue, and may attempt to seize the opportunity to propose domestic-level solutions, even if such solutions are unlikely to be effective, or even operationally feasible, because of international constraints.[82]

In the second place, whatever the possibilities for preventive action, the state in any case must deal with the domestic *consequences* of financial deregulation, international constraints notwithstanding. This may mean pursuing unpopular monetary policies in order to maintain exchange rates in a floating system (as with Britain's membership of the European Exchange Rate Mechanism between 1989 and 1992) or it may mean bailing out failing banks and S&Ls – the latter leading to a Hobson's choice of either raising taxes[83] or increasing the already intractable federal budget deficit. This is sometimes referred to by its critics as the 'creeping socialization of the financial system'.

In effect, then, just as 'level shift' imposes new demands for autonomous, cohesive, 'state-like' policy action upon the political process, that process itself becomes less capable of operating in the transnationally required way. Given these constraints, the most likely outcome, principally for the United States, but increasingly for other countries too, will be to exacerbate the vicious circle of political entropy. The more political activity of a re-regulatory kind is generated, the less will the political system be capable of even processing those demands, much less converting them into effective policies and implementing them efficiently. Indeed the search for cures can speed the spread of the disease. In this context, whatever decisional capacity the state may have previously possessed is further eroded.

This, it is argued, is what has happened with regard to the decline of America's postwar financial hegemony. The process of financial deregulation which really took off with the end of Bretton Woods in 1971 may have indicated that the USA still possessed considerable 'structural power' at that time, even if it had already eroded considerably since 1944. But the consequences of that financial deregulation, especially given the unusually fragmented nature of the American state, has led to the rapid erosion of what remained of US financial hegemony, whether structural or relational. Indeed, when combined with the fiscal and monetary policies of the Reagan era, it has made the American state dependent on foreign capital: first by way of inflows of foreign capital (mainly from Japan) to finance the federal budget deficit; then in terms of America's slide in the mid-1980s from being the world's largest creditor nation into being the world's largest debtor; and finally with the USA going cap in hand to Germany, Saudi Arabia and Japan in order to finance American participation in the Gulf war.

The erosion of financial hegemony has had significant consequences which go beyond the financial arena *per se*. On the one hand, US influence in non-financial issue areas at the international level has been undermined; and on the other, the capacity of the American state to control its domestic economy has been dramatically reduced. The same can, of course, be said for other countries as well – even for Japan, as the recent bursting of the Japanese 'financial bubble' and the slowdown in growth there demonstrates. However, with the erosion of American financial hegemony, the call for transnational re-regulation has become stronger at the very same time as the limits prevailing at that level have become more evident. Also at the same time, the constraints on domestic re-regulation have become more obvious as that process has begun to run into the sand. Together these trends highlight and exacerbate the entropic nature of the American system. This is even more striking when viewed in an international context, for the growing interpenetration of the international political economy demands that states play a more coherent role in organizing and manipulating their manifest and potential 'competitive advantages'.[84] This is what we have elsewhere called the advent of the 'competition state', and it poses questions for the American political system itself.[85]

V Conclusions

As was argued in Chapter 3, financial market deregulation and re-regulation, in their various guises, have come to constitute a major developmental trend, not only in the world economy, but also in world politics. Processes of regulatory arbitrage, market expansion and the development of the competition state in a more open world, among other factors, have led to a range of intertwined structural changes which have had different impacts upon different states. The role of the United States is especially problematic in this context. Its incapacity to act as a competition state, combined with the remnants of structural power which it possessed at the end of the 1960s, paradoxically opened the door to embedded financial orthodoxy by setting off a vicious circle of unilateral deregulatory decisions. One result is that it is not capable of taking action domestically to counteract the competitive advantages which more strategic competition states enjoy and to re-regulate its own financial regulatory system in a competitive direction. Neither, at the same time, is it capable of real action to push for re-regulation at a transnational level.

The United States may still be the largest single market in the world (although it was losing that title to the European Community at the end of 1992) and it may still house the largest and most liquid capital markets, but it is no longer the financial hegemon. It lacks the decisional capacity to give and exercise leadership. Its state apparatuses, as well as its financial institutions and markets, are truly caught up in transnational 'second structural' webs, but this is increasingly true, as we have already said, of all states. In this context the international system lacks a financial control mechanism. The revival of the state which characterized Polanyi's 'Great Transformation' is over. The neo-realist 'states system' can no longer be a surrogate for international institutions which do not exist, and international regimes and mechanisms such as the Bank for International Settlements, the G7, or even a post-Uruguay Round GATS are not strong enough to counteract the widening circle of deregulation. Piecemeal, unilateral deregulatory choices, unlike the situation in trade, will continue to feed further regulatory arbitrage and lead to *de facto* openness, whatever its benefits and drawbacks for the global political economy as a whole.

Of course American institutions, politicians and bureaucrats will still play a highly significant role, but the real core of the process will be a new *haute finance*, not so much one of conspiracy and greed (as the late 19th-century image would have it) as a self-sustaining structural web or pattern of financial decision-making. This pattern will privilege the financial economy over the real economy and constrain the domestic capacity of governments to 'promote the general welfare', as the Preamble to the Constitution of the United States would have it. Whether the new political economics of the Clinton Administration, with its emphasis on 'reinventing government', on 'steering, not rowing', and on focusing economic policy on the more immobile factors of capital such as infrastructure and human capital (rather than on mobile factors such as money or the direct promotion of industry), will be a feasible substitute for the Keynesian welfare state in this context remains to be seen. But even if it does, it will not lead to a new American hegemony, nor even to the old-style hegemony of any single state. The transnational financial system, partly thanks to the United States in the first place, now marches to its own tune. In the words of singer/songwriter Nanci Griffith, 'I am a back-seat driver from America, and I am not at the wheel of control.'

Notes

An abridged version of this chapter will be published in Barry Gills and Ronen Palan (eds), *Transcending the State-Global Divide: The Neostructuralist Agenda in International Relations*, Boulder, CO: Lynne Reinner, 1993.

1. Karl Polanyi, *The Great Transformation*, New York: Rinehart, 1944.
2. For an argument along these lines, see Geoffrey R.D. Underhill, 'Markets Beyond Politics? The State and the Internationalization of Financial Markets', in P. G. Cerny (ed.), *The Politics of Transnational Regulation: Deregulation or Reregulation?*, special issue of the *European Journal of Political Research*, **19**, (2 and 3), March/April 1991, pp. 197–226.
3. See Michael Mann and John Hobson (eds), *States, International Markets and Hegemonic Regimes*, Aldershot and Brookfield, VT: Edward Elgar, forthcoming.
4. See Cerny, *The Changing Architecture of Politics: Structure, Agency, and the Future of the State*, London and Newbury Park, CA: Sage Publications, 1990.
5. Susan Strange, *States and Markets: An Introduction to International Political Economy*, London: Pinter, 1988, ch. 5.

6. See Stephen Gill and David Law, *The Global Political Economy*, Hemel Hempstead and New York: Harvester Wheatsheaf and Simon & Schuster, 1988.

7. Richard B. McKenzie and Dwight R. Lee, *Quicksilver Capital: How the Rapid Movement of Wealth Has Changed the World*, New York: Free Press, 1991.

8. Robert B. Reich, *The Work of Nations: Preparing Ourselves for 21st–Century Capitalism*, New York: Alfred A. Knopf, 1991.

9. *The Changing Architecture of Politics*, ch. 8.

10. Strange argues elsewhere the useful view that American power in the financial arena derives from its structural strength *in spite of* its effective abdication of decision-making in key areas of international finance: *Casino Capitalism*, Oxford: Basil Blackwell, 1986.

11. See Nigel Harris, *The End of the Third World*, Harmondsworth: Penguin, 1985.

12. Eric N. Helleiner, 'American Hegemony and Global Economic Structure: From Closed to Open Financial Relations in the Postwar World', unpublished PhD dissertation, London School of Economics and Political Science, 1991; see Chapter 2, above.

13. See Chapters 4 and 5 of this volume.

14. 14 October 1991.

15. For a persuasive description of the 'transnational financial structure', both in terms of the distinctive character of specifically *financial* webs and linkages and in its relation to the structuring of international power in the wider sense, see Susan Strange, *States and Markets*, especially pp. 88–114.

16. Whether a state, a 'concert' of states, a 'regime', a global elite network or a transnational market structure and so on.

17. Stephen E. Ambrose, *Rise to Globalism: American Foreign Policy 1938–1970*, Baltimore and Hardmondsworth: Penguin, 1971.

18. See Barry Gills and Ronen Palan (eds), *Transcending the State–Global Divide: The Neostructuralist Agenda in International Relations*, Boulder, CO: Lynne Reinner, 1993.

19. P. G. Cerny, 'Global Finance and Governmental Gridlock: Political Entropy and the Decline of American Financial Power', in Richard Maidment and James A. Thurber (eds), *The Politics of Relative Decline: The United States at the End of the Twentieth Century*, Oxford and New York: Polity Press and Basil Blackwell, forthcoming 1993.

20. P. G. Cerny, 'Political Entropy and American Decline', *Millennium: Journal of International Studies*, **88**, (1), Spring 1989, pp. 47–63.

21. Most of the literature derives from economic journalists and financial analysts, whose perspective is often quite unsophisticated in terms of political analysis. The main exception that I have found so far, although by a practising banker rather than an academic political scientist, is Soichi Enkyo, 'Financial Innovation and International Safeguards: Causes and Consequences of "Structural Innovation" in the US and Global Financial System, 1973–1986', unpublished PhD dissertation, London School of Economics, 1989. See also Chapter 3, above.

22. The knock-on effects of US decisions (and, significantly, non-decisions) on the international financial structure in this period is dealt with in detail by Susan Strange in *Casino Capitalism*.

23. Cf. Hedley Bull, *The Anarchical Society: A Study of Order in World Politics*, London: Macmillan, 1977; Kenneth Waltz, *Theory of International Politics*, Reading, MA: Addison-Wesley, 1979.

24. The language of realism often effectively 'reifies' the state. When such language is used here, I am referring not to some anthropomorphic, holistic state which can 'act' by and through itself, but to the outcomes of some structured process of decision-making. For a consideration of these issues, see P. G. Cerny, *The Changing Architecture of Politics*, especially ch. 4.

25. The problem of maintaining public goods in the face of individual actors' tendencies to 'free-ride', and the particular conditions in which it may be in the interest of one predominant actor to provide those public goods himself or herself, are examined in Mancur Olson, *The Logic of Collective Action*, Cambridge, MA: Harvard University Press, 1971.

26. See also discussions in Chapters 4 and 5, above.
27. One important alternative is the Gramscian conception of hegemony: see Stephen Gill, 'American Hegemony: Its Limits and Prospects in the Reagan Era', *Millennium: Journal of International Studies*, **15**, (3), Winter 1986, pp. 311–36. A broader critique, based on a more general analysis of the weaknesses of realism, is Helen Milner, 'The Assumption of Anarchy in International Relations Theory: A Critique', *Review of International Studies*, **17**, (1), January 1991, pp. 67–85.
28. See Angus Maddison, *Phases of Capitalist Development*, Oxford: Oxford University Press, 1982.
29. Strange, *States and Markets*, pp. 115–34.
30. Cerny, *The Changing Architecture of Politics*.
31. Barry Buzan, 'Is International Security Possible?', in Ken Booth (ed.), *New Thinking About Strategy and International Security*, London: Harper Collins Academic, 1991, p. 35. Furthermore, of course, the military is traditionally the most hierarchically organized of all sub-state structures, constituting, at least in times of war, a sort of sociological backbone which other sub-structures of the political system usually lack.
32. The distinction between 'high' and 'low' politics (and the increasing relative significance of the latter) is a central theme of a leading International Relations textbook: Charles W. Kegley, Jr. and Eugene R. Wittkopf, *World Politics: Trend and Transformation*, London and New York: Macmillan and St Martin's Press, 3rd edn, 1989.
33. See Robert O. Keohane, *After Hegemony: Cooperation and Discord in the World Political Economy*, Princeton: Princeton University Press, 1984.
34. See Mann and Hobson (eds), *States, International Markets and Hegemonic Regimes*.
35. Indeed I have argued that American 'decisional capacity', in particular, was a transient phenomenon and therefore that its decline has been a major element in the overall relative decline of the USA in the late 20th century: Cerny, 'Political Entropy and American Decline'.
36. Kissinger is in the mainstream of international historians, however, when he attributes the relative stability of post-Napoleonic international politics to Britain's role as a military and political 'balancer of power' in Europe: *A World Restored: Metternich, Castlereagh, and the Problems of Peace 1812–22*, Boston: Houghton Mifflin, 1957.
37. See Geoffrey Ingham, *Capitalism Divided? The City and Industry in British Social History*, London: Macmillan, 1985.
38. Bertrand Badie and Pierre Birnbaum, *The Sociology of the State*, Chicago: University of Chicago Press, 1983.
39. The seminal work to develop this perspective is Karl Polanyi, *The Great Transformation*.
40. This argument is presented in compelling if polemical fashion in ibid., ch. 1.
41. See Dan P. Silverman, *Reconstructing Europe After the Great War*, Cambridge, MA: Harvard University Press, 1982.
42. Cf. Tom Kemp, *Industrialization in Nineteenth Century Europe*, London: Longman, 1969; E.J. Hobsbawm, *Industry and Empire*, Harmondsworth: Penguin, 1969.
43. Charles P. Kindleberger, *The World in Depression 1929–1939*, London: Allen Lane, The Penguin Press, 1973. While it might be argued that Kindleberger is looking (analytically speaking) for an *economic* hegemon in the wider sense, his analysis seems to me to define the bottom line of hegemony in *financial* terms.
44. 'The American Morgan partners were instrumental in putting England back on gold. It was their holy cause. ... Like Monty Norman [Governor of the Bank of England], the Morgan partners feared that if exchange rates weren't tied to gold, they would be managed by politicians ..., giving a bias toward inflation and paper money. ... For Jack [J.P. Morgan, Jr.], the return to gold was gospel. Hadn't his father saved America's gold standard in 1895? ... The House of Morgan insisted on high British interest rates as the answer. Instead, ... Ben Strong [Governor of the Federal Reserve Bank of New York, an ally of both Morgan and Norman], depressed American interest rates. This was no small technical matter: it would be blamed by some for causing the 1929 crash on Wall Street'

(Ron Chernow, *The House of Morgan: An American Banking Dynasty and the Rise of Modern Finance*, New York: Touchstone, 1990, pp. 274–5).

45. Cf. Lloyd C. Gardner, *Economic Aspects of New Deal Diplomacy*, Boston, MA: Beacon Press, 1971; E.F. Penrose, *Economic Planning for the Peace*, Princeton: Princeton University Press, 1953.

46. See G. John Ikenberry, 'A World Economy Restored: Expert Consensus and the Anglo-American Postwar Settlement', *International Organization*, **46**, (1), Winter 1992, pp. 289–321.

47. Still the standard work on this process is Richard N. Gardner, *Sterling–Dollar Diplomacy in Current Perspective*, New York: Columbia University Press, rev. edn, 1980.

48. Helleiner, 'American Hegemony and Global Economic Structure', and Chapter 2 in this volume.

49. See Robert Triffin, *Gold and the Dollar Crisis*, Princeton: Princeton University Press, 1960.

50. The first of these was the establishment of 'special drawing rights' backed by the International Monetary Fund (although a limited version of SDRs was set up); the second was the Smithsonian System, based on a moveable 'basket' of currencies rather than gold. (The latter, agreed in 1971, collapsed almost immediately; however an analogous system has been adopted as the basis of the Exchange Rate Mechanism of the European Monetary System.)

51. Benjamin J. Cohen, *In Whose Interest? International Banking and American Foreign Policy*, New Haven, Conn.: Yale University Press for the Council on Foreign Relations, 1986, p. 70.

52. The significant 'non-decision', that is with systematic structural consequences, is the explanation put forward by Strange in *Casino Capitalism*.

53. As argued in Gill, 'American Hegemony'.

54. Fred L. Block, *The Origins of International Economic Disorder: A Study of United States International Monetary Policy from World War II to the Present*, Berkeley and Los Angeles: University of California Press, 1977.

55. 'Simply put, ... a country can have at most two of the following three conditions: a fixed exchange rate, monetary policy autonomy, and capital mobility' (Jeffry A. Frieden, 'Invested Interests: The Politics of National Economic Policies in a World of Global Finance', *International Organization*, **45**, (4), Autumn 1991, pp. 425–51.

56. The Gramscian approach has, in effect, two levels of operation. On the one hand, the heart of the analysis lies in the crystallization of a transnational capitalist ruling class. On the other hand, however, the *political* action of this class – the way that it develops and sustains its hegemony – must still be carried out through the existing mechanisms of the states system (in the absence of a supranational authority) although this in turn puts emphasis on a more subtle structural, rather than a simple relational, conception of the way state power actually manifests itself in practice. See Gill, Chapter 4, above.

57. Milner, 'The Assumption of Anarchy in International Relations: A Critique'. See also P. G. Cerny, 'Plurilateralism: Structural Differentiation and Functional Conflict in the Post-Cold War World Order', *Millennium: Journal of International Studies*, **22**, (1), Spring 1993.

58. This is, of course, a contested view of what deregulation actually entails. For a critique of the notion that deregulation is a simple removal of regulations, see Cerny, 'The Limits of Deregulation' in Cerny (ed.), *The Politics of Transnational Regulation*.

59. Helleiner, 'American Hegemony and Global Economic Structure'.

60. It is often argued, of course, that the collapse of Bretton Woods was not the beginning of the process; that is usually attributed to the chronic US balance of payments deficits in the 1960s and the rapid expansion of the unregulated Euromarkets to recycle exiled dollars. The shift to floating exchange rates is none the less usually thought to have led to a crucial acceleration and expansion of the deregulation process by removing the main regulatory obstacle to market-induced international capital flows.

61. See P. G. Cerny, 'The "Little Big Bang" in Paris: Financial Market Deregulation in a *dirigiste* System', *European Journal of Political Research*, **17**, (2), March 1989, pp.

169–92. The concept of the 'strategic state' is developed in John Zysman, *Governments, Markets, and Growth*, Ithaca, NY: Cornell University Press, 1983.

62. For the wider concept of the 'stalemate society', see Stanley Hoffman, 'Paradoxes of the French Political Community', in Hoffmann, *et al.*, *In Search of France*, Cambridge, MA: Harvard University Press, 1963, pp. 1–117; for foreign policy in particular, see Jean-Baptiste Duroselle, 'Changes in French Foreign Policy Since 1958', in ibid., pp. 310–17.

63. See, especially, Theodore J. Lowi, *The End of Liberalism: Ideology, Polity, and the Crisis of Public Authority*, New York: Norton, 1969; Cf. Cerny, 'Political Entropy and American Decline'.

64. Although it is widely believed that the election of President Clinton in November 1992 has closed the era of 'divided government', at least for the time being, divided *party* control is only one element of the 'gridlock' syndrome, as President Carter found out to his cost in the late 1970s.

65. The best recent summary of these themes is Hedrick Smith, *The Power Game: How Washington Works*, New York: Random House, 1988.

66. Interest payments on the national debt each year are now higher than the defence budget.

67. L.C. Gardner, *Economic Aspects of New Deal Diplomacy*.

68. See Martha Derthick and Paul Quirk, *The Politics of Deregulation*, Washington, DC: Brookings Institution, 1985.

69. James O'Connor, *The Fiscal Crisis of the State*, New York: St Martin's Press, 1973.

70. For details of the process of financial deregulation and innovation in various comparative and international perspectives, cf. Strange, *Casino Capitalism;* Adrian Hamilton, *The Financial Revolution*, London and New York: Viking Penguin, 1986; Martin Mayer, *Markets: Who Plays..., Who Risks..., Who Gains..., Who loses...*, New York: Simon & Schuster, 1988; Sarkis J. Khoury, *The Deregulation of the World Financial Markets: Myths, Realities, and Impact*, London: Pinter, 1990; and Michael Moran, *The Politics of the Financial Services Revolution: The USA, UK and Japan*, London: Macmillan, 1991.

71. Strange, *States and Markets*, ch. 5.

72. Although it is widely accepted that, for example, government debt markets (especially secondary markets for shorter-term treasury bills) are the most integrated, and equity markets the least; probably the most rapidly integrating markets are those for financial derivatives such as stock market index futures, while insurance markets may be the next major deregulatory battleground. See Chapter 3, above.

73. 'Intergovernmental cooperation' is defined as involving *states* and *state actors* as the main participants; this is the most viable process dealing with issues at an international level according to realist interpretations. The notion of 'transnational regimes' brings into the game – without necessarily leaving out state actors – a range of other significant actors, primarily those holding positions in bodies which have some level of structural autonomy (in terms of independent rules and resources) from states. These bodies range from public international organizations themselves – especially so-called 'supranational' institutions – to private entities such as large firms, financial markets, cross-national pressure groups and so on.

74. Richard Waters, 'Preliminary Agreement on Capital Adequacy for Securities Markets', *Financial Times – Financial Regulation Report*, February 1992, pp. 8–10. The distance which remains to be travelled to reach any real international consensus on capital adequacy standards for securities firms, however, has been strongly underlined by the very negative reaction by Richard C. Breeden, Chairman of the US Securities and Exchange Commission, to the capital standards recently proposed by the International Organization of Securities Commissions (IOSCO) and enshrined in the European Community's 1992 Capital Adequacy Directive (CAD). 'The levels of capital under the CAD are highly unsafe', Breeden said in October 1992: 'I am not sure the public understands that', *Financial Times*, 28 October 1992.

75. This is widely regarded to have been the case with the Basle Accord, in the negotiation of which the Federal Reserve under the chairmanship of Paul Volcker took a strong

lead: conversation with Dr Wolfgang Reinecke of the Brookings Institution, September 1991; cf. Ethan Barnaby Kapstein, 'Between Power and Purpose: Central Bankers and the Politics of Regulatory Convergence', *International Organization*, **46**, (1), Winter 1992, pp. 265–87.

76. Kapstein argues that the alliance between the Fed and the Bank of England was strong enough to impose its approach on a somewhat divided group of central bankers from other states: 'Between Power and Purpose'.

77. What Cohen calls 'policy coherence asymmetry' can be even more negative in its effects at an international level than at the domestic level: *In Whose Interest?*, pp. 248ff.

78. I use this in the sense conveyed by, for example, Badie and Birnbaum's conception of the 'true state' (*Sociology of the State*) or Eric Nordlinger's notion of the autonomous state: Nordlinger, *On the Autonomy of the Democratic State*, Cambridge, MA: Harvard University Press, 1981.

79. Kapstein, 'Between Power and Purpose'.

80. See above, note 74.

81. For example, the current crisis in the Uruguay Round talks over reforming the General Agreement on Tariffs and Trade has shown the limits of attempts to react to global trade problems through formal international cooperation, although the consequences of international cooperation in general are mixed. On the 'positive' side of the balance sheet, in addition to the Basle Accord discussed above, there have been partial successes such as the Plaza and Louvre Accords on exchange rate control, regional experiments such as the European Exchange Rate Mechanism, and informal cooperation such as the support provided to the financial system in several advanced industrial countries at the time of the October 1987 crash.

82. Such political reactions were extremely salient in the debate on the Bush Administration's 1991 abortive banking regulatory reform bill, especially in the key roles played by politicians such as Representative John Dingell, Chairman of the House Energy and Commerce Committee, which 'oversees' the regulatory bodies which supervise the securities markets (particularly the SEC). Dingell's successful attempts to include highly constraining 'firewalls' in the bill – partially undermining the bill's intention to repeal the Glass–Steagall Act – led to the abandonment of the final version by the Bush Administration itself and its heavy defeat in the House of Representatives. It was replaced by a much more narrow act to strengthen the faltering deposit insurance system, the Federal Deposit Insurance Corporation Improvement Act of 1991 (FDICIA). See Cerny, 'Global Finance and Governmental Gridlock'.

83. As is well known, the cost to 'the American taxpayer' of bailing out failed Savings and Loans institutions alone has been estimated at $300–500 billion over several years.

84. For the concept of 'competitive advantage' – and the contrast between it and the more traditional notion of 'comparative advantage' – see John Zysman and Laura Tyson (eds), *American Industry in International Competition: Government Policies and Corporate Strategies*, Ithaca, NY: Cornell University Press, 1983, chs 1 and 9.

85. See Cerny, 'Global Finance and Governmental Gridlock'.

7 The European Financial Area in the 1990s: Europe and the transnationalization of finance

Peter A. Vipond

I Introduction

Transnationalization of finance is a reality in the modern European economy, both internally and in its interconnections with the international economy. It is part of a general trend which affects manufacturing sectors of the economy as well, and has been documented in a spirited way by those who advise companies on corporate strategy.[1] The process as it specifically affects the financial sector has been analysed by corporate sector economists, and one recent study argued that the fungible nature of money allowed transnationalization to proceed most quickly in this sector.[2] Like most realities, however, closer inspection reveals a more complex situation than initial generalization allows.

The process of transnationalization whereby economic markets cease to be fully coextensive with the domain of sovereign states is undoubtedly under way. However it has progressed in some financial services markets, such as securities, far faster than others, such as retail banking. Equally there have been European markets in bonds since the early 1960s and wholesale global markets already exist for financial products such as reinsurance, foreign exchange and large standard loans. Even if the theory of finance teaches that there is only really one market for capital, the political economic reality in Europe points to the need to differentiate by product amongst other variables.

This chapter will argue that transnationalization of finance in a European context does not imply the atrophying of governance in the market-place. Whether through the continuing role of nation-states or through the emerging polity of the European Community, substantive policies have been developed which determine financial markets and services. This determination is only partial because the autonomous behaviour of financial services firms and the existence of exogenous shocks both preclude the possibility of complete control over financial markets through any form of governance.

There is also an important distinction between the state's (national or EC) capacity to determine some aspect of the operation of a market, such as the use of interest rates to affect the exchange rate, and the state's capacity to determine the *design* of the market by making rules, such as the requirement to have investment banking in separate subsidiaries, or to prohibit interest-bearing chequing accounts. Whilst the first is an *operational capacity* and is often well known, as when states seek to control monetary growth or interest rates or exchange rates, the second is a *design capacity* which affects the structure of the market. The distinction is important in the context of the transnationalization of finance because this process greatly weakens the operational capacity of states in financial markets. The declining operational capacity of states in financial markets can also be theorized through the related concept of 'embedded financial orthodoxy' which examines the same phenomenon in terms of the conditions imposed on nation-states by the need to maintain credibility in the financial markets for such products as currencies and bonds (see Chapter 6, above). Whereas nation-states are highly constrained in terms of their operational capacity to control interest rates, exchange rates and the like autonomously, they are able to maintain at least some influence over finance by retaining a design capacity. An interesting question to consider is how far this design capacity is a proactive attempt to plan markets for the future, and how far it is a reactive attempt to adapt to the company-led development of the financial marketplace. In this latter case the design capacity – the ability to determine market structure – would be rather more limited than in the former.

European integration in the late 1980s gathered momentum in the economic field in general and in finance in particular. After a number of years of failure, especially during the late 1970s when there was much talk of 'Eurosclerosis', it is now widely agreed that the situation has changed.[3] There is far less agreement on which factors were dominant in bringing change about or what that change has actually resulted in as regards the creation of a European market for capital. And there is even less agreement on what the creation of such a European Financial Area (EFA) may mean for the role of Europe and European financial markets in a more open international financial system.

It is clear that steps already taken towards such an area have been at the heart of the Single Market programme ('1992') and these will be set out in more detail below. These developments are, of course, part of a wider process of transnationalization of the global financial system. But it is far too early to tell whether the nature of European financial integration will be such as to give European financial markets and institutions strong competitive advantages in the developing international context. And it is unlikely, given the complex political arrangements in the European Community, that Europe will be in any position to challenge the United States (or perhaps Japan) for the increasingly unattainable title of global 'financial hegemon'. Nevertheless the transnationalization of European finance will give Europe's financial institutions and markets a key role to play in and between a range of different financial markets at the wider international level. European actors will be at the heart of any new international *haute finance*, and the development of the EFA, even if it does not lead to monetary union, will be increasingly important in the way those actors develop significant competitive advantages.

This chapter examines these issues by drawing on regulatory policy and by analysing the commercial decisions of financial firms. The aim is certainly not to produce a general theory of European financial integration but rather to contribute to an understanding of the way markets evolve and are redesigned over time. As already stated, it is argued that this process of market evolution is not under the full control of states or companies participating in the market. It is open-ended, with significant gaps in information at each stage. Hence, as both traditional policy analysis[4] and more recent policy analysis[5] have acknowledged, there are various constraints – technical, institutional and analytic amongst others – which mean that policymakers, whether in the European Commission or national central banks or national governments, do not possess the capacity to design the European Single Market exactly as they would wish. This in turn has implications for the understanding of political processes, as Majone argues.

> Learning to appreciate the pervasiveness of constraints is a good antidote to a common tendency of lay persons and social scientists alike to see power everywhere and to explain policy outcomes exclusively as the result of deliberate actions of powerful groups and individuals. In reality policy-makers are often less powerful than they are supposed to be.[6]

The argument of the chapter can be summarized as follows. In the first place, government has a major role in the transnationalization process, particularly through its capacity to determine certain aspects of market structure, in other words to design markets. This capacity is limited because of the open-ended nature of the policy process as regards financial markets, because of exogenous shocks and because the actions of financial companies (especially their strategic choices) are not simply the outcome of responses to government regulation. Although the EC is not a federal power and its ability to make executive decisions or create new rules for markets is circumscribed by the continuing power of national states, there are areas where it does have limited powers as a corporate actor. To the extent this is so, the powers of government are exercised at the national and at the EC level.

Secondly the creation of a single market for financial services in the EC is part of the process of the transnationalization of finance. This process is complex, however, and needs to be *differentiated* by an analysis of a range of different financial products and markets. The result within the EFA will not be the same market conditions, or the same cost of capital, for a number of reasons. This means further that, while Europe may develop a central role in key sectors of wider international markets, this is unlikely to lead to any general dominance of Europe as such in these markets.

Finally the single market for financial services is evolving through the interaction of governmental attempts proactively to *redesign* the market and thereby to realign the parameters within which the strategic choices of financial services companies are made in the market. Some financial companies are autonomous of government; others, such as state-owned firms, are not. Either way all need to develop strategies for the Single Market, and such strategies are not simply responses to shifting demand and supply curves for financial services. Rather they must take into account the matrix of rewards and penalties embedded in the new design of the marketplace itself. The way that transnationalization intersects with particular institutions and markets is still shaped by patterns of state intervention in the form of market design and regulation.

What this approach leads to is an appreciation of the interaction of governments, markets and companies in the political economy of financial markets. Further it leads to an awareness of the dynamic of change within financial markets and of the fact that this is an open-ended process, under the full control of neither policy-makers nor financial firms. If this is accepted, then, given the risks of contagion from the collapse of any significant financial firm within the EC, it is possible to grasp some of the dangers and difficulties facing policy-makers in their quest for market-oriented re-regulation within Europe and internationally.

In what follows this argument will be expanded. The next section will consider some recent research on institutions and policy-making in order to explain the role of governance in market design further. The third section will review the progress by analysing the emergence of the Single Market of the European Community (EC) out of the original common market of the European Economic Community (EEC). Related issues of EC mergers and the concentration of industry will be examined in the fourth section because of its clear implications for the design of markets via the control of market structure. The fifth section places the argument about the role of government in context by considering the strategic choices facing financial services firms in the EC market.

II Institutions and policy-making

There has been renewed interest in the study of institutions during the late 1980s, not only from economists such as Oliver Williamson, but also from political scientists such as March and Olsen and Shepsle.[7] One feature that these approaches share is to see through the formal attributes of institutions, be they governments or corporations, to analyse them as sets of rules. These rules may take the form of procedures in a parliament (for example), or they may take a more structural form, such as the organization of administrative machinery or party groupings.[8] Building on this institutional approach has led some to stress that institutions embody traditions of meaning as rules and that by 'shaping meaning, political institutions create an interpretive order within which political behaviour can be understood and be provided continuity'.[9] On such an argument, even an eminently rationalist institutional structure (to use an Oakeshottian term) such as the EC is seen to have an approach to making decisions which is a product of its traditions of behaviour.

Theorizing institutions in this way has two important consequences. The first is that the role of actors such as governmental leaders or policy-makers is related to the institutions through which they operate. Such theorizing seeks 'to explain characteristics of social outcomes on the basis not only of agent preferences and optimizing behaviour, but also on the basis of institutional features'.[10] In practice this will result in a more balanced account of policy-making, one that is less preoccupied with the personal views of governmental leaders. Instead policies are established within a tradition of behaviour, one that is likely to be overturned completely only in the most exceptional circumstances (such as in Eastern Europe).

Such an approach enables a clearer understanding of many EC policies such as agriculture without necessarily engendering empathy for them. Whereas in the policy area of agriculture the institutional structure of the EC, and more specifically the rules through which it is manifested (price support, farmer representation, the special agriculture committee in the Council of Ministers), is very long-standing, rigid and highly formalized, the same is not true of finance. EC institutions (primarily the Directorate General in the Commission which oversees financial matters, DGXV) have been involved in financial regulation for many years, but since 1985 and the internal market programme they have been able to adapt their rule-making role without confronting the sort of constraints facing agricultural policy. As regards finance, market-driven pressures for change to the design of markets are strong and point to competitive deregulation. This has placed government at both the national and EC level in a position where it must react to market-driven change while also seeking to promote broadly similar changes. Governments which have traditionally been innovative and radical, such as the British with reference to financial products like Eurobonds, would provide an example of government being highly proactive in the design of markets. Policy tradition sets limitations. It is because policy-making is carried on through institutions over time that the preferences of governments (of Left or Right) do not fully explain policy out-turns.

The second point follows on from this: that is, that the debate about states and markets is not best thought of as an either/or argument where economic functions are performed by one or the other, as some have argued.[11] This may be true in specific cases, such as state versus market in the distribution of wealth, but in general there are many more cases where state involvement is with the design or operation of the market rather than its replacement. Whether the state involvement comes from a tradition of policy, or is mediated by government agendas (such as party preferences), the state's role is extensive. It has been well analysed (in the United States at least) through the voluminous literature on regulation. What is being stressed here is that such a role extends to the design of the rules which constitute markets, and not just to setting or influencing prices within them. Recent literature has talked of the disengagement of the state through radical breaks, such as privatization, but this is misleading. In areas such as finance, even after any privatization, there remains a permanent role for the state, not simply explicable via the preferences of the party in power, in this area. The resultant policy stems from the institutional structures of government, as found in member states and the political order of the EC. Nevertheless because of constraints on the policy process stemming from the nature of policy-making and the institutions involved, as well as from the factors affecting change in financial markets, the state's role will always be played out in an open-ended situation over which it will have variable and somewhat limited control. The state's control, as we have said, is in the nature of designing markets to achieve more general outcomes through the promotion of competitive advantages over other market designs, not to determine the outcomes of specific transactions.

III From the EEC to the Single Market

The European Economic Community was committed to create a common market for goods, services, capital and labour from its inception in 1958. Although the achievement of a common market was formally announced in 1968, the reality was that many barriers and other market imperfections remained. As regards finance, the commitment has been embodied in three major sets of policies. These policies are, however, discrete and not fully dependent on each other for success. The first and simplest set of policies concerns the creation of a European Financial Area through the removal of all restrictions on the movement of capital. The second set of policies focuses on creating a single market in all financial services. It is embodied in over 30 directives which form part of the Single Market programme, but it is not clear that these directives, even if successfully implemented, will be enough to achieve the policy goal. The third policy set deals with monetary integration and the quest for monetary union with the introduction of a single currency.

Whereas the first of these three sets of policies, the liberalization of capital movements, has been largely achieved, the second, the single market for financial services, despite considerable progress, will require continued policy innovation during much of the 1990s. As to the third, monetary union, it remains a highly open subject, both in the sense of whether or not it will actually be achieved and in terms of whether or not it is necessary for the purposes of creating a single market for financial or industrial products. It is not credible to conceive of a single market in financial services without the ability to move capital freely within the EC, but the existence of separate currencies would not pose an insuperable obstacle to such a market. For example, if an Italian cannot move capital out of his or her country then purchasing investment products based in London or bonds based in Germany is not possible. If he or she can move capital out of Italy (let us assume the capital is lire-denominated) then either of the above transactions can be speedily accomplished with the only additional cost being the transaction of currency conversion. Against this cost, however, has to be weighed the possible benefits of portfolio diversification for the investor, not the least of which may be that currency realignment may bring an extra gain on top of the investment return. As this example shows, the assessment of a possible monetary union must be phrased in terms of costs and benefits. These three policy areas will now be examined in greater detail.

Capital movements
The first set of policies concerns the free movement of capital. Fundamentally this necessitates the movement of capital by individuals and companies without any need to justify that movement in terms of physical transactions. The 'critical factor is that the transfer must be an independent transaction in its own right, and not the corollary of another effected for other purposes'.[12] Considerable progress towards realizing this goal was actually made in the late 1970s and early 1980s when countries such as the UK, Germany and Holland abandoned exchange controls on the movement of capital unilaterally. They did so under the pressure of both the economic forces that were liberalizing international capital markets and the political forces that generated deregulatory policies at a national level. States with strong financial sectors (such as Britain and Luxembourg) and states with robust open economies (such as Germany) removed many restrictions on finance. They acted to maintain the competitive advantage of parts of their domestic financial services industry in international markets and because they believed in the advantages of a more open economy. Other member states, often with weak domestic financial markets buoyed by domestic controls on the way citizens could invest their money, were less keen to change policy.

In response to this partial deregulation a *Capital Movements Directive* (88/361) has been agreed and implemented by the EC. This directive, despite giving derogations to some of the financially less developed states (such as Greece), has nevertheless effectively used public policy to redesign the European market for capital. Although the directive gives member states the right to reintroduce some controls to prevent adverse short-term capital flows (Article 3), it immediately makes these subject to Commission review. The Commission can order the removal of any nationally imposed controls and has the capacity to mitigate the consequences of this action by granting loans to the member state in order to support exchange rate stabilization. It is an example of the way market governance can create new market rules without thereby necessarily controlling the volume of transactions or the prevailing price in the revised market. In this case there is a clear transfer in the powers of governance from nation-states to the EC, though the instruments of policy still remain at the national level, in that the Commission has no direct means of acting in financial markets.

Financial services

The second and most complex set of policies focuses on the right to provide financial services in the same way as any other services, from architecture to accountancy, within the EEC. Initially this right was closely linked to the concept of establishment, whereby companies were given the right to set up in business in other member states and to provide financial services on the same basis as domestic companies. The host state retained considerable powers over the domestic market in these circumstances. With the advent of the Single Market programme this right to provide services has been translated into a more radical agenda in which financial services can be sold across state borders, and in which financial services companies can operate throughout the EC on the basis of mutual recognition of home country authorization by all other national authorities. These benefits would not be restricted to the financial sector. On EC calculations, over 50 per cent of the output of the financial services sector is consumed as intermediate goods by other industries, affecting their costs and performance in turn.[13] This goes some way to explaining the importance of the financial services sector in the European Economy and qualifying the view that financial products are traded completely separately from the supposed 'real economy'.

The redesign of market rules for the single market in financial services has been undertaken so as to allow the development of a European market without prescribing in complete detail what form that market should take. As such the basic approach of policy has been to deregulate, by removing rules and discretion which prevent the offering of particular financial services, and also to enable, by allowing new services such as the cross-border selling of financial products. This approach is to be found in the new rules for the banking, insurance and securities sectors, and in the attempt to anticipate the emergence of financial conglomerates which, to a degree, provide all three. Given the concerns over contagion in the financial sector the redesign of the market has also had to incorporate rules to safeguard the stability of the financial system and of financial institutions within it. As the Commission lacks the staff to implement a policy of this complexity and, in any case, as member states have sought to retain a capability in this regard, the market rules have been designed with these considerations to the fore.

It is possible to distil three core principles in this policy area which underlie the new rules. The first involves a distinction between harmonization and mutual recognition. Rather than seek to design an entirely new Single Market through harmonization of rules in a European-level regime, assuming that to be possible, the approach has been to emphasize mutual recognition of national regimes. On this basis the key directive, the so-called Second Banking Directive (adopted in 1989), allows that a bank which is established and authorized in one EC country (say France) has the right to provide a full range of banking services (as enumerated in the directive) in all other EC countries (*Second Banking Directive*, (89)646). These can be provided via a branch or a subsidiary, or even directly across national frontiers. Given that non-EC based banks can become established within the EC, often in London or Frankfurt, they too can make use of this single passport to provide banking services. Policy agreement to achieve this more open market for financial services has, even so, required some harmonization of rules. This has occurred in a number of technical areas, such as accounting rules, but more importantly it has also occurred in the field of capital adequacy. In support of the openness embodied in the Second Banking Directive there are two highly technical directives, one (*Own Funds Directive*) which defines capital ((89)299), and one (*Solvency Ratio Directive*) which establishes the ratio between the amount of capital required and the riskiness of the commercial business which it is underpinning ((88)647). In adopting directives of this latter kind the EC has engaged in a process of market design. This extends to making rules that rule out competition in some areas (for example the amount or nature of the capital underlying the commercial transaction) in order to facilitate competition on a more transparent set of criteria (such as price and service) in the context of a sound market.

The second core principle deals with the powers of the home and host countries. While the host country, or more specifically the financial sector authorities within that country, has responsibility for overseeing market rules and monetary policy (for the moment at least), primary responsibility for a particular bank or credit institution rests with the home country. The authorization of a French bank is the responsibility of the French authorities and so are its operations in Germany or Spain. This marks a liberalizing change since the First Banking Directive, where host countries could fully control all the operations of foreign banks in their territory and where in consequence national markets with national rules could readily exist. Further, in such a context, non-national banks could be excluded or faced with anti-competitive entry costs of such severity as to forestall market entry. The new approach in the Second Banking Directive makes national markets more open and provides an interconnecting structure of rules which provides the basis for common commercial operations. Interestingly, though, it does not supersede national power, in that the authorization and supervision is still undertaken primarily at the national level, not at some federal EC level.

The third of the core principles used to inform specific rules concerns the question of national treatment and reciprocity. This is focused on the terms of the EC's interactions with the international economy as regards financial services. As globalization has continued this issue moves beyond trade to the right of establishment and local provision – thinking globally but acting locally.[14] As Title III of the Second Banking Directive makes clear, the commitment to liberalization of the international economy is balanced by concerns of openness elsewhere. Article 9 allows, after considerable procedures have been undertaken, for the EC to take limited measures as a corporate actor against countries or trading blocs which do not allow EC banks and credit institutions access to their markets while seeking or enjoying access to the single EC market. This principle of reciprocity is mitigated by the requirement that the EC will only seek national treatment for EC-based banks and credit institutions. That is to say, it will seek the right for EC firms to provide financial services on the same basis as companies based in the country concerned. For example, it would require that EC firms abide by the investment/commercial banking distinction that operates within the United States, even if those companies do not have to operate by it in their domestic or EC market. This power, invested in the Commission by Articles 8 and 9 of the Second Banking Directive, is limited and constrained by procedure. Nevertheless viewed in the context of the EC's trade powers it is evident that the EC is more than an administrative coordination unit and more like a corporate power as regards relations with third countries.

While progress in the areas of insurance and securities has been slower, it has generally been in the same direction. Some areas, such as life insurance, have proved more sensitive to national governments than others, such as large risk non-life insurance, mainly because the latter has a direct impact on fewer voters and is negotiated by 'informed' economic agents. In general, however, there has been a policy success to date with most of the major directives agreed in 1992 for implementation over a relatively short period in most member states. Surveying the entire programme for financial services, the regulatory power to design and implement market rules has not simply passed to a central EC authority, any more than the latter has become a lowest common denominator for nation-state preference. The reality of continuing nation-state power reflects the continued existence of national markets, often identified by culture, language and habit as much as by financial regulation. Furthermore many of these markets are known to be overbanked already, by institutions making strenuous efforts to reduce costs and become more efficient. In this context a unitary market with exactly the same rules is unlikely to emerge quickly, if ever, and the achievement may well be measured in the enforcing of reform on domestic companies and the increased contestability of national markets from non-national firms. The capacity of the state is thus limited by factors which are not specifically political or economic, as well as by factors which are.

Monetary union

The final strand of the commitment to a common market for finance concerns the creation of monetary union. This is a somewhat contentious point because the commitment to complete monetary union is not in Article 3 of the Treaty of Rome as part of the EEC's goals. Furthermore, although a single market for financial services will always be deeply flawed without freedom of capital movement, such a market does not formally require a single currency. The cost-effective management of currency risk and the provision of foreign currency are after all two financial services which could be provided efficiently, even if there is good evidence to suggest the latter is not so provided at the moment.[15] Against this view, however, there is a strong case to be mounted. Monetary union was certainly envisaged as long ago as the Werner Plan in 1970, and has long been regarded as an important part of EC political and economic integration. As a factor in building a common market it would bring a number of substantive benefits, even if it would carry costs for member states as regards their structural adjustment policies.[16]

Some of these benefits are clearly quantifiable, such as the 13 billion ECU gain for consumers through the abolition of foreign exchange transactions within the EC (this means of course that there would be a 13 billion ECU loss of business to the European financial services industry). As with so many aspects of European integration, however, the largest benefits are those which it is most difficult to specify. In particular, as Goodhart has argued, a single currency would provide transparent prices (for financial services, other services and goods).[17] In a single market this would allow customers, retail and corporate, to make better price/quality decisions about the goods and services they would buy. A more competitive and efficient market would be created and there would be gains when measured in static terms (reduction in cost/prices) and in dynamic terms (medium-term macroeconomic growth). A single currency would thus facilitate the optimal allocation of capital, in other words the creation of a single market.

All three of these policies focus on creating a single market for capital, a European Financial Area in the fullest sense of that term. Within the single market for capital, as for goods and services, it is not simply a case of national power being transferred to a new EC level. Even if the question of monetary union is analytically separated from the financial services and capital issues the creation of a single market, the literal transnationalization of finance within the EC, is a massive task. As a leading American economist has noted,

> they are attempting to accomplish in a few years what the United States has yet to complete, that being the freedom of establishment of banking branches and subsidiaries in all member states, with the ability to offer a wide variety of banking and financial securities services.[18]

As the above has indicated, the accomplishment is by no means complete, but the substantive achievements, the speed at which they have been achieved and the innovative approach that has been adopted to attain them all indicate that this has been a successful policy area. National markets are now much more open than before, and the opportunity for cross-border selling of financial products exists. Above all, in so far as some governments have sought to prevent effective markets for the provision of financial services and effectively to ring-fence domestic financial markets, their position has been rendered untenable – indeed, in many regards, illegal. The creation of the EFA has involved the reworking of some national powers and the abolition of others. It has involved the design of new rules for the creation of the EFA. The design of the Single Market prescribes rather less than it facilitates. As such it provided opportunities for the efficient allocation of capital without seeking to second-guess commercial choices. The following section indicates why, despite the design capacity exhibited in the EFA, a second tier of rules has been created to prevent monopoly power in the Single Market.

IV Merger and competition policy

What would constitute a single market for financial services? How much competition is desirable? Is there an optimum number of firms for the market? Can arguments about the essential contestability of markets or the minimum efficient scale of production be applied in this context? While the previous section examined the process of redesigning the market at the EC level for financial services so as to create a single market for finance, this section focuses on attempts to monitor and control the market through competition and mergers policy.

Many of the arguments that underlie the EC Single Market programme for the industrial sector apply with equal force to the financial sector. As the Single Market has gained momentum, more competition has increased from new market entrants in previously closed national markets and from domestic suppliers restructuring to meet this new challenge. As well as large static cost benefits in terms of the reduced price of financial products in more competitive markets, over time there are dynamic effects through increases in the marginal efficiency of capital.[19] These expected gains are considerable (between 0.8 and 2.1 per cent higher gross domestic product (GDP) in the EC over the medium term) and compare favourably with gains associated with the abolition of frontier controls and the opening up of public procurement.[20]

The benefits of this process, one whereby market forces are allowed to operate ever more efficiently within the EFA as a whole, bring with them the danger that the effect of highly efficient markets could well be to undermine the market itself. On the one hand, the EC has a whole range of policies to design more open and competitive markets, within which company-led restructuring and merging can take place. On the other hand, the EC has retained substantive policies to prevent both market collusion and domination (based on Articles 85 and 86 of the Treaty of Rome). Indeed rules to affect market behaviour at the structural level have been specifically developed and reinforced during the Single Market programme, especially through the introduction of a new Mergers Regulation (EC 4064/89). This regulation, along with ancillary Commission notices, also extends to cover such issues as joint ventures and aims to prevent a situation where any financial product markets were dominated by a specific firm or firms to the disadvantage of consumers through higher prices or the disadvantage of competing firms through issues like market entry costs.

In order to facilitate an appropriate division of power between member states and the EC as well as to provide a 'one-stop shop' division of jurisdiction whereby decisions made at the national level are not overturned by the EC Commission, the Regulation contains a series of tests to see how a merger should be dealt with. Although the criteria are well known for manufacturing companies, different criteria are used for credit institutions and other financial institutions (EEC No.4064/89; see especially Article 5). Rather than the 5 billion ECU turnover criterion used for manufacturing companies, a figure of 10 per cent of total assets of the companies involved is used. Above this figure the Commission may become involved; generally below it the decision remains with the member state. The situation is in fact more complex than this because various ratios are also introduced between the amount of business (typically loans) conducted in the EC and the total volume of loans. The aim is to exclude companies that have a relatively small presence in Europe relative to their global operations – neither member states nor the EC would wish to become involved in a proposed merger between two large US banks just because both have subsidiaries based in the EC!

As this specific case shows, design and reform of market rules for competition between financial firms in the EFA is a complex and open-ended affair. Decisions in the implementation of those rules have already had a powerful effect in shaping competition. Unlike some areas where the executive enforcement capacity of the EC is weak, in this area it has clear powers to impose heavy fines (Article 14) and can impose fines of up to 100 000 ECU per day in some cases (Article 15).

In terms of a design capacity, policy-makers are engaged in the sophisticated governance of the market. Merger up to a point is good on grounds of restructuring, but beyond that point it becomes unacceptable on grounds of threats to consumer interests. The degree of concentration and the general operation of the market is not left to market forces or self-regulatory financial organizations to decide. Nor is this problem a marginal one, for, as both De Jong and Jacquemin have noted, periods of increased competitive pressures or major changes in the political–economic environment precipitate enhanced merger activity.[21] As Jacquemin notes, mergers and acquisitions activity is 'stimulated by an increased intensity of competitive pressures, induced by phenomena such as an international opportunity, public deregulation, or recession ... and the welfare results of these operations are usually multidimensional'.[22] In examining mergers, much of the theoretical evidence 'does not yield a general presumption in their favour'.[23] Empirical research by Mueller, cited by Jacquemin, finds relatively little evidence of their success, and De Jong finds that only something between 40 and 45 per cent of mergers can be counted as successes if enhanced profitability is a key criterion.[24] Against this evidence the general point of Majone cited in section 1 above is illustrated in the specific case of mergers. Establishing rules that determine what is and what is not acceptable in a market is necessary to make it work in an efficient way. However, viewed as a policy issue, the institutional framework for governance will not necessarily generate rules for new situations, and knowledge of the policy area may suggest conflicting approaches rather than clear prescription.

In exercising a design capacity to facilitate that part of the Single Market known as the EFA, the various national policy-makers who approved the programme and the EC policy-makers (primarily in the Commission) who are implementing it had in mind the development of cross-border linkages and mergers. In fact, while such mergers have taken place, they represented only 18 per cent of the total within the services sector of the EC in 1988/9 as opposed to 24 per cent in 1984/5. Admittedly the total number of mergers rose during this period from 70 to over 175, but in both years the interesting fact is that about 70 per cent of mergers were between companies within the same member state.[25] In the financial services sector there have been some startling examples of this. In Holland, for example, most of the country's major financial companies have merged, often, as in the case of NMB Postbank and National-Nederlanden, bringing a bank and an insurance company together to build a conglomerate firm capable of offering a comprehensive range of services on the *Allfinanz* model. Such developments make it even more difficult to assess when a dominant position has occurred and whether domination of a national part of the EC market constitutes domination within the EC as a whole. There is a real danger of barriers to entry being created which would make market entry more difficult for non-national firms, possibly by increasing sunk costs.

While the danger of less open national financial markets because of the specific form mergers have taken poses a problem for policy-makers in providing governance for the financial markets of the EC, they are ironically faced with an apparently opposite problem at the same time. At a practical level this problem can be seen in the recently proposed, contested takeover of the Midland Bank in the UK by Lloyds Bank. These are two of the top four UK banks, but a merged bank would still have had less than 10 per cent of the EFA market in banking services. Furthermore merger would have produced a more cost-effective financial institution, through staff cuts, branch rationalization and synergies. Yet despite all these benefits there were grave reservations about such a merger from national and EC-level competition policy-makers. These, along with the opposition of the Midland Bank, prevented it from happening. The effective takeover offer for the Midland by the Hong Kong and Shanghai Bank (HKSB), whose offer had sparked the Lloyds 'possible' bid, was accepted. The HKSB bid did little to create market domination because the Hong Kong bank had a limited presence in Europe; there were, therefore, few grounds on which it could be opposed. So in attempting to create a single market for financial services, the outcome of rules on market domination appears to encourage the development of segmented national markets dominated by a number of domestic firms and the greater possibility of market entry by non-EC financial firms into the EFA market. It does both of these things without appearing to provide correlative support for large integrated EC-level financial firms.

The design capacity of government within financial markets poses uniquely demanding problems. At the same time those designing market rules have to accommodate transnational financial companies extending well beyond the EFA, as well as the possibility of highly restrictive outcomes from competitive forces within certain national sections of the EFA market.

V Financial services companies and the Single Market

The analysis of European financial integration presented so far has indicated that market-based companies are not merely passive entities which have things done to them by governments. Nor can their actions in the market-place be explained solely in terms of the dynamic equilibria models of some economics textbooks. Instead financial markets are subject to evolution, interspersed with occasional radical change. The companies whose products make up those markets regularly change their product profile and pricing to seek market power and profit. However these companies are themselves threatened by market changes which render core business unprofitable and require changes in direction to remain viable.

Although large company corporate lending, for example, or reinsurance will inevitably require reference to prevailing prices for the product at the international level, even if the financial product is delivered through a local company, this does not apply in areas such as retail banking or medium-sized corporate business and investment management. In all of these cases national presence and a network for management and sales are essential. It is in these areas that market access will be enhanced by the Single Market programme. This will create a European Financial Area that goes beyond the free movement of capital to the efficient allocation of capital by a restruc-tured financial services industry. Such a process, which has begun and will continue beyond 1993, will be weakened by the existence of national cham-pions, whether created by national financial elites or from state-led strategies of previous decades. Furthermore these areas are likely to see the fastest growth and highest potential profitability in the coming years. This is be-cause many of the international-level products exist in very competitive and therefore not very profitable markets, being mature and marketable financial services of a largely homogenous nature.

As if this were not a bad enough outcome for EC financial companies seeking to expand beyond national boundaries, these international products are now usually purchased direct by major companies, such as ICI, Siemens, Shell or Plessey, involving a process of disintermediation whereby financial services companies are simply not used. Many of these non-financial compa-nies have better ratings from agencies such as Standard and Poor's than the very financial services companies (usually banks) that supply them, and hence they can borrow money at less risk and therefore more cheaply.

Of the top 100 EC banks only 44 are privately owned, the rest being publicly (that is, state) owned, cooperatives or mutuals.[26] Many of these non-private firms are successful and powerful (such as Crédit Agricole in France), but their strategic choices may well be different from the choices of those privately owned banks that need to make regular profits in order to satisfy institutional shareholders. French banks in particular have expanded strongly without an immediate concern for rate of return on capital – something that the patronage and usually ownership of the French state has allowed them to do.

These issues of market access, disintermediation and state ownership have all produced uncertainty and created a number of markets for financial products which are a long way removed from a simple laissez-faire model. Complex markets exist, differentiated by national and EC rules, and by factors which are not directly attributable to governmental decisions, such as national taste, socioeconomic development and the extent of social welfare provision. It is in this complex market situation that financial firms have to make and change their strategy. Although government can facilitate the transnationalization of finance in Europe, it is the strategic choices of firms that will decide its pace and form.

As the above indicates, strategic decision-making is undertaken in a complex and changing market environment, facing a variety of heterogeneous variables. As Gardener and Molyneux have argued, choices carry major costs, particularly if market conditions change radically.[27] As regards the Single Market, many financial firms developed conglomerate aspirations during the early and mid-1980s, aiming to provide a complete range of products and pricing without regard for risk in order to gain market share and credibility. Failure to make such a 'bar-bell model' of the firm work was brutally highlighted by the stock market crash of 1987 and by subsequent recession.[28] These developments have been exacerbated by the attempts within the EC and internationally (via the Bank for International Settlements) to establish appropriate capital adequacy for all banks and financial conglomerates.

In responding to these appallingly difficult conditions, much strategic thinking has changed towards a less expansionary and more profit-oriented view of the European market. Most firms have scaled down plans for growth and some are actually shedding assets in order to meet capital requirements. Although some major financial firms such as Deutsche Bank, Barclays and Société Générale (France) may approximate to the model of a conglomerate within the European market early in the next century, for most companies this is not an option. Instead firms are looking to a 'cluster strategy' based on a small range of financial products where they have competitive advantage.[29] Recent research has confirmed this analysis as regards retail banking amongst other industries:

> The top managers' views on the dynamics of the European market in the 1990s greatly differ from the estimates of the economists in Brussels ... Brussels insists on cost reductions through economies of scale, whereas top managers think of differentiation strategies, segmentation of markets, and transferring skills. When

managers talk about cost reductions, process (and product) technological innovation appears to be the driving force.[30]

In this market environment the transnationalization of finance will take a complex and changing course, one that may employ greater differentiation of product rather than Europe-wide harmonization. If companies are unable to provide a full range of products themselves, the case for alliance, mergers and cross-border acquisitions becomes much stronger. Indeed in areas such as retail banking or the marketing of insurance products there are competitive advantages to nearly all companies to become involved. Already there have been a number of such deals, including the alliance between Banco Santander of Spain and the Royal Bank of Scotland (1988), which involved a limited share swap in order to formalize the agreement. The companies will distribute each other's products and provide services to the respective clients. More typically there have been a number of cross-border mergers where one party is a major player and the other a relatively small but successful niche player. These have included the Deutsche Bank takeover of the UK investment bank Morgan Grenfell (1989) and Banque Nationale de Paris's purchase of 85 branches from Banco Bilbao Vizcaya (1989), amongst many others. Many alliances lay the foundations for future joint products and possible mergers, while many takeovers are conducted to maintain the autonomy of the company taken over in order to sustain product differentiation. The pace and nature of corporate alliances will no doubt change during the 1990s as companies and their advisers come to have a sharper awareness of what the new market rules (analysed in sections 3 and 4 above) will actually permit.

Much more could be written about the role of companies and the rather different way they perceive markets. The behaviour of companies, in short-term market decisions, in medium-term product innovations and in longer-term strategic choices all affect the market for financial products in Europe. Even where financial firms are state-owned there is growing pressure for them to be run competitively in a deregulated financial environment. If this continues, the major benefit of state ownership will be to prevent control over a major company moving beyond national boundaries – a benefit which may come to be of diminishing significance in an integrated Europe. Financial services companies constitute markets just as much as government rules or market transactions. Their individual decisions, whether short-, medium- or long-term, are self-interested, but their collective outcome provides much of the dynamic of market change and may well lead to different outcomes from those envisaged by the EC.

If the outcomes do not achieve the policy goals envisaged either by EC policy-makers, as regards market design and competition, or by national governments, as regards such matters as growth and the strength of EC financial companies in the wider international marketplace, then further policy innovation is likely during the 1990s. Nevertheless several fundamental issues, including the *intra*-national pattern of mergers in the financial services sector, the continued competition of national states (and their regulatory systems) for market share within both the EC and the international financial arena, the differentiation of markets for different instruments, and the different strategies (such as 'cluster strategies'), indicate that the European Financial Area will be a rather uneven construction, despite the Single Market.

IV Conclusion

The introduction of this chapter stated that its aim was not to provide a general theory of European financial integration, and the argument advanced has shown why that is not a viable goal. Government, at both national and EC level, has developed policy goals for the creation of a single market. At a more specific level, these have turned on the state's capacity to generate and enforce rules for the market which have led to its redesign in the light of agreed policy goals. The result has been a success, both in terms of a more open, competitive, deregulated market for capital in the European Community, and in the corporate changes undertaken to anticipate and respond to such changes. A balanced account, however, has to recognize the role of exogenous shocks (such as the 1987 stock market crash) and the autonomy of financial firms which leads them to different strategic responses. In this light we can see that any discipline-based account from political science as much as economics will be partial, while an interdisciplinary strategy, such as has been adopted here, will have to acknowledge the open-ended nature of market evolution. In consequence the transnationalization of finance in Europe may well involve unpredictable changes and its rate may be uneven. Appreciation of this situation is not an admission of weakness so much as a realistic starting-point from which to continue our enquiries.

At the same time the transnationalization of European finance must be seen in the wider context of American hegemonic decline and the transnationalization of global finance. This, too, has been an uneven process. What is clear is not whether a uniform or homogeneous international financial system is emerging, but rather that previously existing forms of control of financial markets are being replaced by the attempts of states (and the state-like regime which constitutes the EC) to adapt their financial systems to the exigencies of international competition and transnational interpenetration by proactively designing new market structures.

In this context, the EC – especially post-'1992' – does possess a range of existing and potential competitive advantages. For example, it actually now has a more unified single market for many financial services, including banking and insurance, than the United States, with its restrictions on universal banking, its gridlocked regulatory system and its jumble of state regulations. Of course Europe does not have a single currency, and this gives some competitive advantages to the USA in terms of dollar-denominated transactions and the liquidity which that generates. Nevertheless there are also some advantages to not having a single currency, as it gives European national states a wider flexibility in economic and regulatory policy, and market actors a wider range of both speculative and hedging opportunities, than is available within the United States itself. The extension of universal banking within the EFA will continue to strengthen the competitiveness of European financial institutions. Europe will continue to attract new international business to its capital markets, with London still being the most internationalized of all the major world financial centres.

Thus the transnationalization of European finance is symptomatic of the transnationalization of finance in general. It will not create a 'fortress Europe' in the financial field; there is no new European hegemony arising. If anything, it will contribute further to the ongoing process of financial differentiation and cross-cutting linkages across the world, constraining the traditional power of states, especially hegemonic states, and underlining the role of markets in the emerging world order.

Notes

1. Ohmae (1990).
2. O'Brien (1992).
3. Moravcsik (1991).
4. Lindblom (1968).
5. Majone (1989).
6. Ibid., p. 75.
7. Williamson (1985); March and Olsen (1989); Shepsle (1989).
8. Shepsle (1989).
9. March and Olsen (1989, p. 52).
10. Shepsle (1989, p. 135).
11. For example Lane and Ersson (1990).
12. Servais (1988, p. 25).
13. Emerson *et al.* (1988, p. 98).
14. Ohmae (1990).
15. *European Economy*, 1990, **44**.
16. Goodhart (1991).
17. Ibid.
18. Bisignano (1992).
19. Emerson *et al.* (1988).
20. Emerson *et al.* (1988); see tables B1, B2 and B3, pp. 262–3.
21. De Jong (1990); Jacquemin (1990).
22. Jacquemin (1990, pp. 6–7).
23. Ibid.
24. De Jong (1990, pp. 58ff).
25. EC Commission, *Employment in Europe*, 1990.

26. Cited in Bisignano (1992, pp. 170 ff).
27. Gardener and Molyneux (1990).
28. Ibid.
29. Ibid., especially ch. 12.
30. Calori and Lawrence (1992, p. 41).

Bibliography

Bisignano, J. (1992), 'Banking in the European Economic Community: Structure, Competition, and Public Policy', in G.G. Kaufman (ed.), *Banking Structures In Major Countries*, Dordrecht: Kluwer, pp. 155–244.

Calori, R. and P. Lawrence (1992), '1992–Diversity Still Remains – Views of European Managers', *Long Range Planning*, **25**, (2), 33–43.

De Jong, H.W. (1990), 'Mergers and Competition Policy: Some General Remarks', in P. H. Admiraal (ed.), *Mergers and Competition Policy in the European Community*, Oxford: Basil Blackwell, pp. 39–69.

EC Commission (1990), *Employment in Europe*.

Emerson, M. *et al.* (1988), *The Economics of 1992*, Oxford: Oxford University Press (first published in *European Economy*, **35**).

European Community (1988a), *Capital Movements Directive*, (88)361.

European Community (1988b), *Solvency Ratio Directive*, (89)647.

European Community (1989a), *Second Banking Directive*, (89)646.

European Community (1989b), *Own Funds Directive*, (89)299.

European Community (1989c), *Council Regulation on the Control of Concentrations Between Undertakings*, No. 4064/89.

European Economy (1990), **44**, 'One Market One Money'.

Feldstein, M. (1992), 'Europe's Monetary Union: The Case against EMU', *The Economist*, 13–19 June 1992, 23–6.

Gardener, E.P. M. and P. Molyneux (1990), *Changes in Western European Banking*, London: Unwin Hyman.

Goodhart, C. (1991), 'An Assessment of European Monetary Union', *Royal Bank of Scotland Review*, June 1991, 3–25.

Jacquemin, A. (1990), 'Mergers and European Policy', in P. H. Admiraal (ed.), *Mergers and Competition Policy in the European Community*, Oxford: Basil Blackwell, pp. 1–38.

Lane J-E. and Ersson, S. (1990), *Comparative Political Economy*, London: Pinter.

Lindblom, C.E. (1968), *The Policy-making Process*, Englewood Cliffs NJ: Prentice-Hall.

Majone, G. (1989), *Evidence, Argument and Persuasion in the Policy Process*, New Haven, Conn: Yale University Press.

March, J.G. and J.P. Olsen (1989) *Rediscovering Institutions*, New York: Free Press.

Moravcsik, A. (1991), 'Negotiating the Single European Act', in R.O. Keohane and S. Hoffmann (eds), *The New European Community*, Boulder, CO: Westview Press, pp. 41–84.

O'Brien, R. (1992), *Global Financial Integration: The End of Geography*, London: RIIA/Pinter.

Ohmae, K. (1990), *The Borderless World*, London: Fontana.

Servais, D. (1988), *The Single Financial Market*, Luxembourg: Official Publications of the European Communities.

Shepsle, K.A. (1989), 'Studying Institutions: Some Lessons from the Rational Choice Approach', *Journal of Theoretical Politics*, **1**, (2), 131–47.

Williamson, O.E. (1985), *The Economic Institutions of Capitalism*, New York: Free Press.

8 The challenge from the East: Japan's financial rise and the changing global order

Eric Helleiner

For most of the 20th century, the United States has held a hegemonic position in the world of international finance. As the century comes to a close, however, US financial hegemony is rapidly being eroded by two developments. The first is the European Community's decision to move to full economic and monetary union by the late 1990s. The creation of a common European currency and financial space will pose an important threat to a global preeminence of the dollar and American financial markets. A single European central bank, moreover, will be an institution to be reckoned with in global financial politics. Despite the importance of the European challenge, it has been the second development – Japan's financial rise – which has attracted most attention in recent years. Unlike the European challenge, that from Japan has already been felt. Japanese banks and securities houses are increasingly dominant in international financial markets. Japanese money has already played a central role in underwriting American external and budget deficits since the early 1980s. Tokyo's financial markets have already shown their ability produce shock waves through the global financial system.

This chapter addresses two issues associated with Japan's financial rise. The first section seeks to clarify the debate concerning the degree to which Japan has undermined US financial hegemony. By putting Japan's current position in a long historical context, it shows that Japan's financial influence has often been exaggerated. At the same time, however, it argues that there are strong reasons to believe that Japan's financial power will continue to grow in the coming years. In the second section of the chapter, the implications of Japan's financial rise are investigated. It is demonstrated that, after playing a passive role for much of the 1980s, Japan has begun, since the 1987 stock market crash, to take a more assertive stance in global financial affairs. Three important changes to the world of global finance are anticipated over the long run from this change. First, there are strong reasons to think Japan's rise will bring a more equitable, better functioning international financial system than existed in the era of American financial hegemony. Second, Japan will bring a more activist and managerial approach to global financial issues than has existed in recent years. Finally, Japan's rise will accelerate the trend towards financial regionalism in the world economy.

I   Japanese financial power in historical perspective

Despite the more tangible nature of Japan's challenge to American financial dominance, there is today enormous debate over the extent to which Japan's rise has undermined American financial hegemony. While some have argued strongly that Japan is rapidly replacing the USA as the key financial power, others have been equally vehement that Japan's financial power is not only limited but also temporary.[1] At the root of these enormously divergent opinions lies a lack of precision concerning what constitutes financial power in the global political economy.

To try to clarify the concept, it may be helpful to look at the dominant financial powers of the past. Since the origins of the modern world system, three states have achieved a hegemonic position in the global financial system. The first was the Netherlands, whose financial dominance stretched from the mid-17th century to the mid-to-late 18th century.[2] After the Napoleonic wars, the baton passed to Britain, whose leading position in world finance lasted until the early years of the 20th century. The United States then took over Britain's position in a faltering process which was fully consolidated only in the wake of the Second World War.

At a descriptive level, there have been five features which these financial hegemons have had in common. First, they were the leading creditors to the world for much of the period of their financial dominance. Second, they controlled the key public financial institutions of their age. In the Dutch case, the Bank of Amsterdam – operated by the city of Amsterdam – acted as the global central bank of its time. The Bank of England played a similar role in the 19th century, 'conducting the orchestra' of international finance. In the age of American financial dominance, the US Treasury and Federal Reserve System played a key institutional role in global finance both directly and indirectly through the American-controlled international financial institutions of the postwar period, the International Monetary Fund (IMF) and the World Bank. The third common feature of these financial leaders was the dominant role of their private financial institutions in international financial markets of their age. Fourth, the leading private financial markets of each country, those of Amsterdam, the City of London, and New York, were the most important markets of their age. Finally their respective currencies – the Bank of Amsterdam's guilder, sterling and the dollar – acted as the global currency of the world economy of their era.

Japan's creditor status and its limitations

Much of the confusion concerning the degree to which Japan has accumulated financial power since the early 1980s stems from the fact that it has become important in some of these areas and not in others. Most striking has been its emergence as the world's largest creditor since 1985. After spending most of the postwar period as a net borrower of funds from the world, Japan began to accumulate enormous external financial assets after 1981. By 1985 it was the world's largest creditor and by the end of 1990 its external assets were valued at $328 billion.[3] This development has been all the more striking because it has been paralleled by the fall of the USA into a debtor position for the first time since before 1914. It is because the vast bulk of Japan's investment abroad, at least until recently, has been in the form of portfolio investment that observers have come to talk of Japan's new 'financial' power arising from this creditor status.

The causes of Japan's sudden capital outflows have been much discussed. At one level they can be seen simply as the 'flip-side' of Japan's large current account surpluses in the 1980s. Probing more deeply, both the current account surplus and the capital outflows can be seen to have emerged out of an internal imbalance between savings and investment in Japan.[4] When corporate demand for funds dramatically decreased in Japan in the early 1970s with the slowdown in Japanese economic growth, there emerged a large 'excess' of Japanese savings. Initially these savings were absorbed by rapidly growing government deficits. By the late 1970s, however, considerable political resistance to these government deficits had emerged and they were slashed dramatically from 5.5 to 0.8 per cent of GNP between 1978 and 1985.[5] With the savings no longer absorbed at home by either the corporate or the public sector, they went abroad to foreign capital markets to find profitable employment. A final cause of Japan's long-term capital exports in 1980s was its emergence as an international financial intermediary. Like the Netherlands, Britain and the USA at the peak of their financial power, Japan found itself increasingly in the 1980s in the position of borrowing short-term funds from abroad and relending them in the form of long-term capital exports. Tavlas and Ozeki, for example, note that approximately one-third ($205 billion) of the long-term capital exported from Japan during 1983–9 ($620 billion) stemmed from short-term funds borrowed from abroad.[6]

Despite the enormous attention given to it, Japan's creditor status has not in fact brought an enormous degree of power to the Japanese state. There have been two principal limitations on translating its creditor status into power.[7] First, the majority of funds have been lent to a country – the USA – on whom Japan is heavily dependent both militarily and economically. Second, the degree to which the Japanese state exerts control over the private

Japanese financial intermediaries – the life insurance companies, securities houses and banks who have exported the bulk of Japan's financial capital – is questionable. Those who see Japan as having acquired enormous power from its creditor status argue that these intermediaries are strongly influenced in their investment decisions by the Japanese Ministry of Finance (MoF). This financial version of the 'Japan Inc.' thesis has, however, been effectively challenged by others who have shown that the bureaucracy's role is more 'one of mediation and equilibrating the interests of politically powerful interest groups than of formulating policy objectives or controlling policy outcomes'.[8] Moreover several changes in the last decade – the internationalization and deregulation of the Japanese financial system, the growth of government deficits and increased competition between financial institutions – have considerably diminished whatever power the MoF did at one time hold over private financial institutions.

In these two respects, Japan's creditor status is quite different from that of the USA in the 20th century. For the USA, its position as creditor to the world brought with it considerable power. Not only was its vulnerability to its major debtors low, but also the US state exerted a strong degree of control over the capital-exporting process. This was especially apparent in the two decades after 1945, when American funds were sent abroad almost entirely via government channels, but it was also true for most of the 1920s when the State Department required approval of all private loans abroad.[9] Perhaps more similar to the Japanese case was that of the Dutch in the 18th century. Although 'all the states of Europe were queuing up in the offices of Dutch moneylenders'[10] in the 18th century, the Dutch state derived little power from this export of capital. Not only were the loans being made to states much more powerful than it, but also the state exerted little influence over the lending decisions of its private bankers.[11]

It is worth noting that, as Japan has begun to channel an increasing proportion of its surplus through government channels and away from the USA, however, some of the limitations on translating creditor status into power have begun to be overcome. Since 1986, for example, Japan has been rapidly increasing its overseas aid commitments. By 1989 it had become the world's largest aid donor, and for some 25 developing nations Japan is now the largest source of bilateral aid.[12] For many Asian states, where Japanese aid is concentrated, its assistance often makes up as much as twenty per cent of domestic budget spending.[13] Although power is certainly accruing to the Japanese state in many of these cases, there are still limitations. In particular, with just under 1400 officials involved in managing Japan's aid programme (compared with close to 4400 officials involved in America's aid programme), the Japanese government is often forced to rely on the expertise of others, such as the British Crown Agents in Africa, to administer their aid.[14]

An increasing proportion of Japan's surplus is also being funnelled through official international financial institutions. As its contributions increase, its power within these bodies, the second attribute of financial power, should also increase. Once again, however, there have been limitations. Japan's influence has been severely hindered by the absence of Japanese officials in these institutions. There are few Japanese in senior positions in the IMF or World Bank, and only 1.3 per cent of the staff at the World Bank and 2.2 per cent at the Fund are from Japan.[15] Moreover the USA has successfully convinced the Japanese to increase their financial contributions in ways that did not strongly alter the voting structure within these institutions. Despite the fact that Japan's financial contributions to the World Bank have become at least as large as those of the USA, for example, its voting power remains behind that of the USA because of the way in which it has given the money.[16]

There are two final reasons not to put too much emphasis on Japan's creditor status when discussing its rising financial power. First, Japan's capital exports are increasingly taking a non-financial form. Foreign direct investment, in particular, has grown from 8 per cent of Japan's capital exports in 1985 to 40 per cent by late 1990.[17] Second, Japan's creditor status may be rather fleeting. Already in 1990, Japan was surpassed by Germany, albeit temporarily, as the world's largest creditor. In the first half of 1991, there was actually a net inflow of long-term capital into Japan for the first time in 11 years.[18] Some of the factors causing this change are temporary, such as a rapid increase in Japanese interest rates since 1989 and the need for Japanese banks to build up reserves to cover domestic losses and to meet the 1993 deadline in the Bank for International Settlements (BIS) accord on capital adequacy ratios. There are also longer-term trends, however, such as an ageing population and ambitious public infrastructure spending plans, which suggest that Japan will not regain the kind of creditor status it held in the 1980s.[19]

Internationalization and deregulation: a growing source of power
Japan's emergence as a major creditor was not the only development to bring it prominence in the financial sphere in the 1980s. Also important was the internationalization and deregulation of Japan's financial system. Since the 1930s, the Japanese financial system had remained highly regulated domestically and tightly sealed off from international influences under a very rigid set of controls. Beginning in the mid-1970s, however, a cycle of increased competition, deregulation and financial innovation was unleashed by the growth of government deficits, giving a much greater role to markets in allocating financial resources within Japan. These domestic changes have been accompanied by an equally dramatic loosening of external capital

controls since the late 1970s, allowing Japan's financial world to be integrated once again with the global financial system. External liberalization
has been encouraged by an internationalist alliance in Japanese policy circles which saw financial liberalization as a key adjunct to Japan's growing
global economic importance. Japan's emergence as a creditor also eliminated the external balance of payments constraint that had previously provided the major justification for controls.[20]

Japan's financial internationalization and deregulation have had the effect
of giving international prominence to Japanese private financial markets and
institutions – the third and fourth attributes of financial power. To begin
with, as Japan's markets have become incorporated into the global financial
system in the 1980s and as they have grown in size and complexity, it has
become increasingly imperative for financial analysts around the world to
keep a close eye on their movements. Japanese equities markets, for example, before their 1990 collapse, had grown to account for 44 per cent of
world capitalization, up from 15 per cent in 1980. Likewise Tokyo's bond
and foreign exchange markets have come to surpass their New York counterparts in overall turnover figures. Moreover, at an aggregate level, Tokyo's
share of international banking activity increased from 5 per cent in 1980 to
20.6 per cent in 1989, the largest of any financial centre.[21]

The changed position of Japanese private financial institutions was equally
dramatic. Between 1980 and 1988, Japanese banks expanded the number of
their overseas offices, branches and subsidiaries from 299 to 913, while the
rise for securities houses was from 65 to 196.[22] By 1989, Japanese banks had
come to control 40 per cent of all international lending, up from 23 per cent
only four years before.[23] Similarly the four Japanese securities houses, having been small players in the Eurobond sector in the early 1980s, consistently found themselves among the top Eurobond underwriters by the late
1980s. Even more dramatic was the changed position of Japanese financial
institutions in rankings of the overall size of the world's private financial
institutions. In an assessment made at the end of 1988 on the basis of market
capitalization, for example, Japanese financial institutions had come to occupy all top 25 positions.[24]

As was true of financial authorities in past hegemonic states, the Bank of
Japan and the MoF have found themselves in an increasingly central position in the global financial arena as a result of the growing international
importance of their own private financial markets and institutions. Their
regulatory and supervisory initiatives in Tokyo financial markets, for example, increasingly have global effects. The MoF's stemming of the Tokyo
stock crash in October 1987 had the effect of calming the entire world's
markets. In Murphy's words, the crash 'started and stopped' in Tokyo.[25]
Similarly, although it is unclear to what extent the Japanese authorities can

directly control the international lending patterns of Japanese financial institutions, it is true that to the extent that any state can influence their behaviour it will be that of Japan. As Wellons notes with respect to the banking sector: 'the home is the one jurisdiction that can regulate the international operations of banks... Ties at home are so constraining...that the big banks do not switch citizenship'.[26]

There is a second way in which the internationalization and deregulation of Japanese financial markets might have been expected to give power to the Japanese state. In the past, as a set of financial markets has become increasingly central in the world, those markets have come to exert a kind of 'pulling power' over global short-term financial capital. The Dutch, British and American markets, for example, acted as a magnet for global footloose funds at the height of their power. Because of Japan's emergence as an international financial intermediary in the 1980s – importing short-term capital and relending long-term capital – many have concluded that Japanese markets have been increasingly developing this kind of 'pulling power'. This interpretation is, however, inaccurate. Japan's short-term capital inflows came, *not* from foreigners looking to Japanese financial markets as an attractive and safe place to hold money, as was true in the Dutch, British and American cases. Rather, they represented Japanese bank borrowing in London and New York markets where short-term financial instruments were cheaper and more attractive than those in the overregulated Japanese financial system.[27] Instead of showing the increased centrality of Japanese financial markets, this pattern of flows only demonstrated the extent to which Japanese markets, despite their size, still lagged well behind their London and New York counterparts in attractiveness.

In particular Japan still has no domestic financial market to challenge the central role in the global financial system of the US Treasury bill market. The latter's importance was demonstrated, for example, in the way that it was the only market in the world deep enough to absorb the Japanese financial surplus. It was also the market to which Latin American and other capital flight was attracted in the 1980s. As US Treasury Secretary Brady noted: 'The world's mattress is right here in our markets.'[28] The US Treasury market's position has left the USA with an enormous degree of financial influence. The ability of the USA, for example, to borrow enormous sums of money from the world in the 1980s to help finance its growing budget deficits was testimony to the 'pulling power' of this market. In this sense, as Strange has often pointed out, the emergence of the USA as the world's largest debtor has not been a sign of decline but rather one of strength.[29] The continued centrality of US financial markets has also meant that US financial authorities retain an extremely important place in the world of global finance. With the world's major financial institutions wanting to operate in the US financial marketplace, it is inevitable that, as Rosenbluth puts it, 'regulatory changes in the US have far greater bearing on financial regulations in the rest of the world than do regulatory changes elsewhere affect US markets and policies'.[30] In the words of one Daiwa Bank official: 'We have to be in the US. It's the largest and deepest banking market in the world'.[31]

The underdeveloped and over-regulated nature of Japanese financial markets has inhibited Japanese financial power not just in these ways, but also by preventing the yen from becoming a global currency – the fifth and final feature of financial power. Private and official investors, for example, have been dissuaded from holding their assets in yen because the Japanese Treasury bill market is not sufficiently liquid and offers yields that are artificially low. Similarly, without a well-developed market for bankers' acceptances, it has been difficult to acquire trade financing in yen. Although the internationalization and deregulation of Japanese finance could have led to increased use of the yen internationally, these continued barriers have ensured that it has not yet done so to any considerable degree. Only approximately 8 per cent of the world's official reserves were denominated in yen in 1989, in contrast to 19 per cent for the mark and 60 per cent for the dollar. Similarly, in the late 1980s, the yen's share of external bank loans and bond issues in international financial markets was only 5.5 per cent and 8 per cent respectively. Most striking of all is the fact that only 4.3 per cent of world trade was denominated in yen in 1989.[32]

The weak position of the yen within the international monetary and financial system has severely inhibited Japanese financial power. Not only does the USA continue to derive seigniorage benefits of issuing the world's most used currency, but also it greatly benefited in the 1980s from being able to borrow from Japan in its own currency, a situation quite unprecedented between the world's largest debtor and creditor. Moreover, because Japanese financial institutions remain highly dependent on dollar borrowings in order to finance Japanese trade and investments, they remain vulnerable to developments in US financial markets. In the event of a severe financial crisis, they would also be reliant on the US Federal Reserve because of its role as the only official issuer of dollars.

There are thus important limitations imposed on Japan's financial power by the underdeveloped and over-regulated nature of some of its financial markets. Interestingly Japan's continued dependence on America's more highly developed financial markets has parallels in the past. When British traders and bankers, for example, had already become key global financial actors in the 18th century, they continued to use the Amsterdam financial markets to finance their trade because financial operations in and out of London were still overregulated.[33] Similarly, although the USA had become a significant financial power before the First World War – it already held 25 per cent of the world's gold reserves by 1914[34] – the inadequacies of New York financial markets led its merchants and financial operators to continue to use London financial markets as their base until well into the 1920s. Although one state's financial institutions can quickly become dominant globally and creditor status can be rapidly acquired, the process by which one set of financial markets becomes central to the world's financial market-place has been a somewhat longer one.

In sum, although Japan has acquired considerable financial influence, it has clearly not assumed the kind of hegemonic position in global finance once held by the Netherlands, Britain and the USA at the height of their power. Despite this diagnosis, it is also true that Japan's financial power is likely to grow in the coming years. For those who have focused only on its creditor status, this assertion would seem surprising, given that its creditor status is not likely to last. The more important development, however, in contributing to Japan's financial power over the long term will be the internationalization and deregulation process. Unlike Japan's acquisition of creditor status, the momentum behind the internationalization and deregulation process in Japan is accelerating. As this process deepens and is extended in the coming years, not only will the yen become a more attractive global currency, but also Japanese financial markets can be expected to develop an important degree of 'pulling power'. Both of these developments, moreover, will give Japanese financial authorities an increasingly central place in the global financial system. Far from being a flash in the pan, Japan's financial rise in the 1980s should be seen as the first stage in what has been for all previous financial powers a long process of acquiring global financial influence.

II   A changing global financial order?
What will be the impact of Japan's continued rise as a financial power? Believers in the hegemonic stability theory maintain that the erosion of US financial hegemony will lead to an increase in international financial instability and eventually to the collapse of the current open, liberal international financial system. Murphy, for example, argues that 'the alternative to US leadership [in finance] is a series of escalating economic and political crises leading to a breakdown of the liberal economic and political order as we know it'.[35] While the fragility of the international banking system and the stock crashes of 1987 and 1989 might seem to suggest support for this theory, we have argued elsewhere that there are reasons to think that this prediction overstates the danger of financial collapse. Not only does a regime of central bank cooperation exist to promote financial stability, but also three key states – Britain, the USA and Japan – have shown a strong interest in promoting global financial stability despite their non-hegemonic position.[36]

In the absence of a financial collapse, how might Japan's continued financial rise be expected to alter the dynamics and structures of the existing global financial system? In a long historical context, shifts in economic power between states have always had enormous structural effects throughout the global political economy. In French historian Fernand Braudel's words:

> Such shifts...are always significant; they interrupt the calm flow of history and open perspectives that are the more precious for being so rare. When Amsterdam replaced Antwerp, when London took over from Amsterdam or when, in about 1929, New York overtook London, it always meant a massive historical shift of forces, revealing the precariousness of the previous equilibrium and the strengths of the one replacing it. The whole circle of the world economy was affected by such changes and the repercussions were never exclusively economic.[37]

It would be fair to say that, until 1987, Japan's financial rise had done little to 'interrupt the calm flow of history'. To a striking degree, Japan's new-found power was used to support the previous US-centred 'equilibrium' in global finance. We can see this in several ways. To begin with, its enormous capital exports went largely to support America's external current account deficits and its internal fiscal imbalances. Japan thus simply continued to play the role it had along with the Europeans in the 1960s and with the OPEC states in the 1970s.[38] Second, although Japanese banks held a large segment of Latin American debt, the Japanese government deferred to US leadership in the handling of the crisis after 1982 and Japanese banks themselves followed the US strategy for handling the crisis 'even more closely than the US banks themselves'.[39] Third, as already described, Japan initially agreed, as OPEC had in the 1970s, to US demands that its contributions to institutions such as the World Bank be made through mechanisms which would not significantly alter their voting structure. Finally, through high-level bilateral talks initiated as far back as 1978, the USA was able to press Japan into giving large amounts of its growing bilateral aid to countries considered important for US strategic goals, such as Turkey, Pakistan, Sudan and Egypt.[40]

There are several reasons why Japan initially used its financial power in such a passive fashion to support the 'old equilibrium'. First, private Japanese investors, like European and OPEC investors before them, were attracted to the US market because of its 'pulling power' as an attractive, liquid and high-yielding market. At the same time the Japanese government also strongly encouraged this flow of funds through interest rate reductions, tax policies and, arguably, through the use of 'administrative guidance' techniques. Japan's dependence on the USA economically and militarily played a role in encouraging these official policies, as did Nakasone's broad strategy of strengthening US–Japanese relations in the 1980s. The 'reactive' nature of the Japanese state is also often pointed to as a factor which left Japan particularly open to US pressures and precluded any quick, dramatic policy shift.[41] Finally the lack of expertise in global financial affairs among Japanese investors and policy-makers also left them dependent on US initiatives.[42] In the words of one Nomura official: 'We feel worried by the gap between the amount of money we can handle and the knowledge and expertise to do that.'[43]

Interestingly the Japanese experience was not dissimilar to that of Britain and the USA in the early stages of their rise as financial powers. The British, for example, in the late 18th century used their growing financial power initially to support the declining Dutch financial position, partly because of their trade dependence on Dutch markets.[44] Similarly, when American financiers were suddenly propelled into the role of bankers to the world after the First World War, they initially worked closely with British financial institutions and deferred to the Bank of England's greater expertise in rebuilding the international gold standard. Even at the Bretton Woods conference, the British were still boasting that the Americans had 'all the money bags, but we have all the brains'.[45] In general it might be said that there is, as Wallerstein has put it, a kind of 'symbiotic relationship between a formerly hegemonic power and the new rising star' which provides 'graceful retirement income for the one and a crucial push forward against its rivals for the other'.[46]

Towards a more assertive stance

After its initial passive role, Japan began in the late 1980s to take a much more independent, assertive stance in the international financial arena. The first sign of this shift came in mid-1987, when Japanese investment in the USA was reversed for the first time since the early 1980s.[47] The reversal partly reflected the frustration of Japanese private investors as they suffered enormous losses on dollar investments with the dollar's fall after 1985. Some analysts also suggest that the pull-out was an officially led capital 'strike' to force the USA to live up to commitments it had made earlier to correct its fiscal deficits. Even if this case is not accepted, it is certainly true that Japanese officials took an increasingly assertive line towards the USA in this period. In the wake of the October 1987 stock crash, for example, Prime Minister Nakasone publicly refused to meet US officials to discuss the global financial situation until the USA acted to cut its budget deficit. The Minister of Finance also called publicly for the USA to raise taxes in November. Moreover no effort was made by the MoF to encourage Japanese financial intermediaries to support the important early November 1987 auction of US government debt.[48]

There were also calls at this time for the dollar's global role to be reduced. The Bank of Tokyo chairman Kashiwagi, for example, told the European Parliament in September 1987 that the ECU should be strengthened in order to reduce the dollar's dominant global role.[49] In late January 1988 at the Davos Economic Forum, Nakasone – in his first public appearance since his resignation as prime minister – called on the USA to issue foreign currency Treasury bonds similar to those issued by Carter in the 1978/9 dollar crisis.[50] This call was then repeated in May 1988 by Toyoo Gyohten, a senior public financial official, who also argued strongly that the dollar's world role must be reduced.[51] At the September 1988 IMF/World Bank meetings in Berlin, the Japanese representatives, in *Business Week*'s words, 'strongly questioned whether the dollar should remain at the center of the world monetary system', and they declared their support for an increased international role for special drawing rights as well as for the yen.[52]

A more assertive stance was also taken in several other arenas in this period. At the fourth annual April 1988 meeting of the US–Japan Working Group on Financial Markets, for example, Japanese officials demanded for the first time that an equal amount of time be spent discussing Japanese concerns about America's financial markets as was spent discussing American demands for further Japanese financial reforms.[53] Increasingly acrimonious debates also broke out between the USA and Japan in the Asian Development Bank regarding the correct policy mix to be advocated to developing countries by that body.[54] On the debt issue, having silently followed US policy since 1982, the Japanese suddenly in 1988 became quite critical of the US strategy, calling for a more growth-oriented approach. Their alternative 'Miyazawa plan' – which called for international institutions to encourage a securitization of the debt in return for debtors agreeing to structural adjustment programmes – was initially aggressively attacked by US Treasury Secretary Brady at the September IMF/World Bank meetings. Six months later, however, it had become the basis for the new US 'Brady plan'.[55]

Japan's new independence was even more strikingly displayed in late 1989, when the loose monetary policy it had pursued since 1985 in order to support the dollar was dramatically reversed by the new Bank of Japan Governor Mieno. Like the West Germans in the late 1970s, Mieno felt that the costs of supporting the USA financially had become too large. Easy money had encouraged domestic inflationary pressures as well as a 'financial bubble' in which equity and land prices had tripled since 1986. His tight monetary policy was aimed at quelling these inflationary pressures and bursting the financial bubble. Because it also had the effect of drawing Japanese funds back home from the USA, both directly as interest rates rose and indirectly as the collapse of Japanese equity prices forced financial institutions to bring home funds to cover their reserve positions, Mieno's policy was controversial. The MoF, in particular, opposed it, worrying that it would unnecessarily antagonize the USA and destabilize the world economy.[56] Mieno's new assertive stance, however, won the day.

The Japanese also adopted an increasingly independent stance in other areas after 1989. In the discussions leading up to the May 1990 agreement to increase IMF quotas, for example, Japan successfully urged – against initial US resistance – that its voting share be increased to second place in the Fund. The Japanese have also taken a more active role in the Inter-American Development Bank, a shift symbolized by the holding of the IADB's 1991 annual meeting in Japan for the first time. On the debt front, Japanese officials strongly opposed US-sponsored strategic debt 'write-downs' for countries such as Poland and Egypt in April 1991.[57] Finally, also in April 1991, the Japanese government began to carve out a more independent line on aid issues, stressing that it would, in Prime Minister Kaifu's words, 'pay full attention to potential aid recipients' military spending, development and production of mass destruction weapons and their import and export'.[58]

If Japan began in the late 1980s to shake off the passive role it played in the early stages of its rise as a financial power, what kind of role can we expect a more assertive Japan to play in the global financial arena? How might it alter the dynamics and structures of the global financial system? In the summer and autumn of 1991, an array of Japanese financial scandals seemed to cloud any longer-term view of Japan's role in global finance. Indeed, with Japanese financial institutions subject to an unprecedented degree of domestic and international criticism,[59] some analysts suggested that the scandals demonstrate Japan's inability to play any kind of leadership role in global finance. A more accurate view, however, would put the scandals in the context of both the puncturing of Japan's financial bubble and the enormous structural upheavals which have accompanied the liberalization and deregulation of Japan's financial system in the 1980s. Moreover financial manias and scandals were also experienced in the early stage of the rise of other financial powers: from the Dutch tulip mania in 1637–8, to the British South Sea bubble in 1719–20, to the American lending boom and collapse in the 1920s. As was true in these cases, Japan will probably emerge from its recent problems having learned from its mistakes and having developed new institutional structures to prevent their recurrence.

Three changes to expect

Looking beyond the immediate scandals, Japan's rise as a financial power can be expected to have three basic impacts on the global financial order over the longer term. First, although many predict that Japan will be an ineffective financial leader,[60] there are several reasons to think that its rise will lead to a more equitable, well-functioning international financial system than existed in the period of US leadership. It is worth remembering that, by comparison to the Dutch and British, the Americans were not particularly effective financial leaders in the 20th century. In the interwar period, US policy failures played a large role in bringing down the international financial system.[61] In the 1960s and 1970s, US unilateralism in the financial sphere brought the collapse of the Bretton Woods exchange rate system and ushered in an era of volatile exchange rate movements.[62] In the 1980s, by acting as 'borrower of first resort', drawing in capital from the rest of the world to finance its twin deficits, the USA contributed to the severity of the international debt crisis and to the distortion of traditional patterns of trade and capital flows. Even the extension of Marshall aid after the war – usually portrayed as the high point of American financial leadership – has now been shown to have been much less important than previously thought in rebuilding the West European economies.[63]

The USA was prevented by several factors from playing an effective leadership role in global finance. To begin with, in contrast to the Dutch and British, the USA was a continental and largely self-sufficient economic power. With less direct economic interest in global financial stability, the USA was much more tempted to use its central position in the international financial system to, in Calleo's words, 'resolve its domestic difficulties at the expense of the world at large'.[64] The tendency of the USA to abuse its financial position was also compounded by a second factor, the higher priority assigned after 1945 by US policy-makers to global strategic issues. Although security concerns might be seen as having played a positive role in the financial arena in the early postwar years by helping to enlist support for the Marshall aid programme, from the 1960s onwards the USA increasingly used its central position in the global financial system to pay for foreign strategic objectives. The British and the Dutch, by contrast, rarely subordinated their role as financial leaders to such broader strategic objectives. The Dutch, in particular, caught as they were between much more powerful military powers such as France, England and Spain, maintained a neutral foreign policy for most of the 18th century and attempted to make a sharp 'divorce of international finance from diplomatic considerations'.[65] A final factor that compounded the low priority given by the US state to global financial issues was the relative political weakness of the one social group with a strong interest in a well-functioning global financial system: the internationally oriented New York financial community. Their power within the American state, while considerable, never matched that of Amsterdam or London bankers within their respective hegemonic states. Its limitations were especially well demonstrated in the 1920s and during the capital controls programme during 1963–74.[66]

Putting Japan in comparative perspective, it would seem to be more similar to the Dutch and British cases than to that of the USA. First, like the Dutch and British, Japan's trade dependence gives it a strong interest in a well-functioning world economy. Second, Japan does not share the post-1945 American predilection for subordinating its global financial role to strategic considerations. Like the Dutch, it has attempted to divorce international political considerations from its international economic policy.[67] As Stallings puts it, 'the Japanese are willing to deal with governments of virtually any stripe, while the US tends to identify governments as "friends" or "enemies" and treats them accordingly'.[68] Finally the political power of the Tokyo financial community within Japan is more like that of Amsterdam and London bankers within their respective states than that of the New York financial community within the USA.[69]

Given these differences, it seems likely that Japan will use its financial power in a fashion more conducive to a well-functioning international financial system than was true of the USA. The pattern which seems to be emerging is one where Japanese financial leaders are attempting to reorganize and rebuild the postwar American-built international financial system to make it function more equitably and effectively than it has in recent years. On the one hand, an effort is being made to reduce America's asymmetric position in the system by promoting the use of alternative currencies and by attempting to impose greater discipline on American economic policy; on the other hand, depending as it does more than any other developed country on the developing world,[70] Japan has taken a particular interest in improving the mess of financial relations between North and South left by the 1980s. With respect to the debt crisis, Stallings notes that 'the Japanese are prone to take a longer-term view than their US counterparts ... they want to help Latin America resume growth so that the region will be attractive to foreign investment and trade again'.[71] Japan's rapid expansion of aid should also be seen in this light, as Yasutomo observes: 'Japan's contribution to the solution of the North–South issue through aid-giving is becoming a *raison d'être* of Japan as a 21st century international state'.[72]

A second impact that Japan's rising financial power is likely to have on the dynamics of global finance relates to Japan's more interventionist and managerial approach to financial issues. As a recent World Bank Staff Working Paper noted, 'the character of the international financial system is determined to a large extent by the nature of financial system in the dominant countries'.[73] The domestic liberal financial traditions of Britain and the USA, for example, had a large impact on the way in which the global financial system was managed and organized in their respective periods of financial leadership. Given Japan's different financial traditions, its rise as a financial power can be expected to cause a shift away from the liberal traditions favoured by the last two Anglo-Saxon financial leaders.

From the origins of Japan's modern financial system after 1868, Japanese financial authorities have viewed their financial sector as central to the task of modernization and, as such, a sector requiring special attention from the state. Despite Japan's deregulation and liberalization trend in the 1980s, there are two important legacies today of this different, more interventionist domestic tradition. First, Japanese financial officials continue to see the financial system much more as a 'public good' than is true of their American counterparts. This leads them to a more activist, managerial approach to financial issues both domestically and internationally.[74] Second, there are several institutional structures which give the Japanese state the *capacity* to develop a more activist approach to global financial issues. Particularly significant is its control of the Japanese Postal Savings System. Established in 1875 to mobilize rural savings for the purpose of modernization, the system continues to control almost one-third of the nation's savings. These deposits are larger than the deposits of the entire private Japan banking sector and give the Postal Savings System the distinction of being the world's largest bank.[75] This institutional legacy of Japan's 'developmental state' provides a crucial instrument by which the Japanese state can control and direct Japan's savings at the international arena if it so wishes. There have, for example, been detailed proposals from inside and outside Japan concerning ways in which the state might use money from the Postal Savings System to redirect Japan's financial surplus to the developing world.[76] Indeed, in 1987, the system was permitted for the first time to invest in foreign assets, and in March of that year its funds were used to purchase yen-denominated World Bank bonds.[77]

The third and final change to expect from Japan's financial rise is a greater regionalization of the global financial order. Financial regionalism has already been encouraged by the trend towards European monetary integration since the late 1970s and by the 'dollarization' of Latin American economies in the 1980s.[78] In the East Asian case, however, despite all the journalistic references, there has to date been little shift towards a 'yen bloc'. This can be expected to change rapidly in the coming years. The major force driving this change is the growing amount of yen-denominated liabilities being accumulated by East Asian countries. Between 1980 and 1988, the percentage of total external liabilities denominated in yen of Indonesia, South Korea, Malaysia, the Philippines and Thailand, for example, rose from 19.5 to 37.9, while their dollar liabilities fell from 47.3 to 27.[79] These growing yen liabilities have two basic sources. The first is the enormous expansion of Japanese foreign direct investment in East Asia since the yen's rise after 1985. The second is the increasingly dominant aid presence of Japan in the region.[80] Although their official yen holdings are still small, East Asian central bankers are finding that they must begin to accumulate greater holdings of yen in order to hedge against their growing yen debts.[81] With both official and private Japanese capital flows to the region expected to grow dramatically in the near future, these pressures to move towards some kind of a yen bloc will only increase.

Japanese officials have also begun to show a growing interest in promoting a regional financial bloc. The most dramatic symbol of this new interest came in February 1991, when the Bank of Japan organized and hosted a little-noticed meeting of central bankers from Thailand, Malaysia, Indonesia, the Philippines, Singapore, Australia, New Zealand and South Korea. The meeting is apparently intended to become an annual one and, according to Antony Rowley of the *Far Eastern Economic Review*, 'what the Bank of Japan has in mind ultimately is developing something akin to an Asian version of the European-dominated BIS in Basle, Switzerland'.[82] Unlike the other regional economic groupings developing within the East Asian region, this financial grouping excludes the USA.

Since the late 19th century, the competing pressures of being part of both an Asian regional financial system and a Western one have plagued Japanese financial policy. The debate in the late 1800s, for example, surrounding the 1897 decision to leave the Asian silver standard and join the Western gold standard was a very heated one.[83] After suspending gold convertibility during World War I, Japanese financial authorities succeeded in rejoining the gold standard by 1930 with British and American help, but the very next year they turned towards a closed regional yen bloc in the wake of the collapse of the global financial system.[84] After the war the Japanese government followed a two-track policy. At the same time as being readmitted to Western financial institutions such as the Bank for International Settlements,[85] Japan pressed the USA in the 1950s and 1960s to allow it to play a leading financial role in Asia through the creation of some kind of Asian payments union (never agreed to) and the Asian Development Bank (eventually agreed to in 1966).[86] This two-track policy has remained in place in the 1970s and 1980s and can be expected to continue. Rather than retreating into a closed yen bloc, Japan will most likely combine an increasingly dominant financial role in the East Asian region with an active joint leadership role alongside the USA in global financial affairs.

III Conclusion

Developments in both Japan and Europe are rapidly bringing the era of American financial hegemony to an end. Although the challenge from the Japanese side has been exaggerated by many, it can be expected to grow in the coming years, particularly as the deregulation and internationalization process in the Japanese financial system proceeds. The challenge from Europe will be at least as important by the turn of the century as full financial and monetary union is completed. Taken together, these two developments are ushering in a much more multipolar global financial order than has existed for many decades. The importance of this shift should not be underestimated. Just as American financial hegemony deeply influenced the course of world financial history in the 20th century, so too can the new-found influence of Japan and Europe be expected to alter the dynamics and structures of the global financial order in the 1990s and beyond. This chapter has tried to sketch some of the repercussions for the global political economy of Japan's growing financial power. Equally important will be the task of thinking about the implications of Europe's financial rise.

Notes

An earlier version of this chapter appeared in the Spring 1992 issue of the *International Journal* as the recipient of the Marvin Gelber Prize for 1991. The author is very grateful to the editors of the *International Journal* for allowing an extended version to be published in this volume.

1. For examples of the former view, see R. Gilpin, *Political Economy of International Relations*, Princeton: Princeton University Press, 1987, ch. 8; R.T. Murphy, 'Power Without Purpose: The Crisis of Japan's Global Financial Dominance', *Harvard Business Review*, March/April 1989, pp. 71–83. For the latter, see S. Strange, 'Finance, Information and Power', *Review of International Studies*, **16**, 1990, pp. 259–74, and B. Emmott, *The Sun Also Sets: The Limits to Japan's Economic Power*, New York: Times Books, 1989.
2. Although it is the least studied of the three, there are a number of good recent historical works on Dutch financial power: J. Israel, *Dutch Primacy in World Trade 1595–1740*, Oxford; Clarendon, 1989; A. Attman, *Dutch Enterprise in the World Bullion Trade 1550–1800*, translated by Eva and Allen Green, Upsalla: Almquist and Wiksell, 1983; J. Riley, *International Government Finance and the Amsterdam Capital Market 1740–1815*, Cambridge: Cambridge University Press, 1980.
3. *Globe and Mail*, 22 May 1991.
4. See, for example, E. Lincoln, *Japan: Facing Economic Maturity*, Washington: Brookings Institution, 1988. See also K. Sato, 'Saving and Investment' in K. Yamamura and Y. Yasuba (eds), *The Political Economy of Japan: Vol.1 The Domestic Transformation*, Stanford: Stanford University Press, 1987.
5. Lincoln, *Facing Economic Maturity*, pp. 76–7.
6. G. Tavlas and Y. Ozeki, 'The Japanese Yen as an International Currency', January 1991, unpublished manuscript, International Monetary Fund, 2.
7. For a more in-depth discussion, see E. Helleiner, 'Money and Influence: Japanese Power in the International Monetary and Financial System', *Millennium: Journal of International Studies*, **18**, 1989, pp. 343–50.
8. F. Rosenbluth, *Financial Politics in Contemporary Japan*, Ithaca: Cornell University Press, 1989, p. 13.
9. M. Leffler, *The Elusive Quest: America's Pursuit of European Stability and French Security 1919–33*, Chapel Hill: University of North Carolina Press, 1979, p. 62.
10. F. Braudel, *The Perspective of the World*, translated by Sian Reynolds, London: Fontana, 1985, pp. 246–7.
11. Riley, *International Government Finance*, p. 58.

12. D. Yasutomo, 'Why Aid? Japan as an "Aid Great Power"', *Pacific Affairs*, **62**, Winter 1989/90, 490, fn3. According to the OECD's ODA figures released in October 1991, the USA had reassumed its position as the world's largest aid donor but only by including debt forgiveness in official aid figures. Japan strongly challenged this accounting method: S. Wagstyl, 'Japan Challenges US Aid Figures', *Financial Times*, 1 October 1991.

13. R. Orr Jr, 'Japanese Foreign Aid in a New Global Era', *SAIS Review*, **11**, Summer–Fall 1991, p. 146.

14. I. Rodger, 'Crown Agents to Administer Part of Japanese Aid', *Financial Times*, 31 January 1988; S. Wagstyl, 'Japanese Lack Skills for Aid Programmes', *Financial Times*, 10 October 1991.

15. One of the key barriers to increasing the number of Japanese in key jobs in the international financial institutions has been their unwillingness to consider such jobs. Prominent financial officials such as Yasuke Kashiwagi and Toyoo Gyohten, for example, have both declined recent offers of high-level posts at the World Bank: A. Rowley, 'Lots of Money But Few People', *Far Eastern Economic Review*, 20 June 1991, p. 66.

16. Ibid.

17. K. Calder, 'Japan in 1990: Limits to Change', *Asian Survey*, **31**, January 1991, p. 21.

18. *The Economist*, 24 August 1991, p. 68.

19. See, for example, Emmott, *The Sun Also Sets*.

20. For an overview, see for example E. Helleiner, 'Money and Influence', pp. 350–52; J. Horne, *Japan's Financial Markets: Conflict and Consensus in Policymaking*, London: Allen & Unwin, 1985; L. Pauly, *Opening Financial Markets*, Ithaca: Cornell University Press, 1988; F. Rosenbluth, *Financial Politics in Contemporary Japan*, ch.3.

21. For statistical references, see E. Helleiner, 'States and the Future of Global Finance', *Review of International Studies*, **18**, 1992, p. 41; *The Economist*, 16 December 1989.

22. Tavlas and Ozeki, 'The Japanese Yen', p. 15.

23. *The Economist*, 8 December 1990.

24. *Euromoney*, February 1989, p. 95.

25. Murphy, 'Power Without Purpose', p. 42.

26. P. Wellons, 'International Debt: The Behavior of Banks in a Politicized Environment', in M. Kahler (ed.), *Politics of International Debt*, Ithaca: Cornell University Press, 1989, p. 110. See also Helleiner, 'States and the Future', pp. 41–2.

27. Tavlas and Ozeki, 'The Japanese Yen', pp. 22–3.

28. Quoted in A. Murray, 'More than Ever US Relies on Japanese for Financing', *Wall Street Journal*, 19 June 1990. By contrast, Thorn notes that 'Japan is still not regarded as a "safe haven" for "hot money"': R. Thorn, *The Rising Yen: The Impact of Japanese Financial Liberalization on World Capital Markets*, Singapore: Institute for South-East Asian Studies, 1987, p. 73.

29. For example, Strange, 'Finance, Information and Power'.

30. Rosenbluth, *Financial Politics in Contemporary Japan*, p. 223. See also Strange, 'Finance, Information and Power'.

31. Quoted in S. Wagstyl, 'Daiwa Takes on the Japanese Giants', *Financial Times*, 19 September 1989.

32. Statistics from Tavlas and Ozeki, 'The Japanese Yen'; S. Sulkin, 'Currency in Search of a Role', *Financial Times*, 29 April 1991.

33. See, for example, Attman, *Dutch Enterprise*.

34. C.L. Holtfrerich, 'The Evolution of World Trade 1720 to the Present', in C.L. Holtfrerich (ed.), *Interactions in the World Economy*, Hemel Hempstead: Harvester Wheatsheaf, 1989, p. 19.

35. Murphy, 'Power Without Purpose', p. 83.

36. Helleiner, 'States and the Future', pp. 42–8.

37. Braudel, *The Perspective of the World*, p. 32.

38. See especially D. Calleo, *The Imperious Economy*, Cambridge, MA: Harvard University Press, 1982; Gilpin, *Political Economy*.

39. B. Stallings, 'The Reluctant Giant: Japan and the Latin American Debt Crisis', *Journal of Latin American Studies*, **22**, 1990, p. 19.

40. R. Orr Jr., 'Collaboration or Conflict? Foreign Aid and US–Japan Relations', *Pacific Affairs*, **62**, Winter 1989/90, p. 486; J. Inada, 'Japan's Aid Diplomacy: Economic, Political or Strategic', *Millennium: Journal of International Studies*, **18**, Winter 1989, pp. 401–6.
41. K. Calder, 'Japanese Foreign Economic Policy Formation: Explaining the Reactive State', *World Politics*, **40**, 1988, 517–44. This point is made with respect to Japan's debt policy by Stallings, 'The Reluctant Giant', as well as with respect to its aid policy by A. Rix, 'Japan's Foreign Aid Policy: A Capacity for Leadership?', *Pacific Affairs*, **62**, 1989/90, p. 463.
42. See, for example, Stallings, 'The Reluctant Giant', p. 19.
43. Quoted in A. Sampson, *The Midas Touch*, London: Hodder & Stoughton, 1989.
44. C. Kindleberger, *Manias, Panics and Crashes: A History of Financial Crises*, New York: Basic Books, 1978, pp. 183–4.
45. Quoted in R. Gardner, 'Sterling–Dollar Diplomacy in Current Perspective', *International Affairs*, **62**, Winter 1985/6, p. 21.
46. I. Wallerstein, *The Modern World System 2: Mercantilism and the Consolidation of the European World-Economy 1600–1750*, New York: Academic Press, 1980, p. 281.
47. For the politics and economics around this episode, see Helleiner, 'Money and Influence', pp. 347–9.
48. R. Miller, 'Japan Seems Set to End US Domination of World Monetary System', *Financial Times*, 2 November 1988.
49. *Financial Times*, 8 September 1987.
50. *Financial Times*, 29 January 1988.
51. *Financial Times*, 20 May 1988.
52. Quoted in M. Matsuda, 'The Internationalization of Japan's Financial Services Industry', PhD, Claremont Graduate School, 1990, p. 22.
53. *The Economist*, 23 April 1988.
54. 'The Young Pretenders', *The Economist*, 15 October 1988.
55. Stallings, 'The Reluctant Giant', pp. 24–5.
56. D. Hale, 'The Economic Consequences of Global Capital Market Integration', text of the William F. Butler Lecture to the National Association of Business Economists, New York Chapter, 13 September 1990, pp. 13–15.
57. S. Wagstyl, 'Japan Halts $500 loan to Poland', *Financial Times*, 16 April 1991; J. Martin, 'Price of Rapprochement', *Financial Times*, 17 April 1991.
58. Quoted in *South*, June/July 1991, p. 75.
59. In September 1991, the Japanese securities houses, Nikko and Nomura, were even excluded temporarily from underwriting World Bank bonds because of the scandals: S. London, 'World Bank Bans Nomura and Nikko from Bond Issues', *Financial Times*, 13 September 1991.
60. See especially Murphy, 'Power Without Purpose', p. 74: 'Japan lacks the ideology and political commitment necessary to fulfil the obligations that go along with financial power'.
61. C. Kindleberger, *The World in Depression 1929–39*, Berkeley: University of California Press, 1973.
62. For example, D. Calleo, *The Imperious Economy*, Cambridge MA: Harvard University Press, 1982; J. Gowa, *Closing the Gold Window: Domestic Politics and the End of Bretton Woods*, London: Cornell University Press, 1983.
63. A. Milward, *The Reconstruction of Western Europe 1945–51*, London: Methuen, 1984; E. Helleiner, 'Did Hegemony Really Matter? America's Limited Role in the Restoration of European Convertibility 1945–58', mimeo, 1992.
64. D. Calleo, 'The Decline and Rebuilding of an International Economic System: Some General Considerations', in D. Calleo *et al.* (eds), *Money and the Coming World Order*, New York: New York University Press, 1976, pp. 50–1. He continues: 'Abuse seems particularly unavoidable when the hegemon is the most powerful of the world's nation-states, with a domestic economy highly self-sufficient and thus relatively invulnerable to the consequences of the world economic breakdown'.

65. Riley, *International Government Finance*, p. 58.
66. For the former, see for example J. Frieden, 'Sectoral Conflict and US Foreign Economic Policy 1914–40', *International Organization*, **42**, 1988, pp. 59–90. For the latter, see J. Hawley, *Dollars and Borders: US Government Attempts to Restrain Capital Flows 1960–80*, London: M.E. Sharpe, 1987.
67. A prominent former Japanese former diplomat, Hisahiko Okazaki, has recently criticized this aspect of Japan's foreign policy in a book entitled *Seeing Japan in Holland*, on the grounds that the Dutch failure to develop an integrated political–economic 'grand strategy' was a key source of their eventual downfall: *Far Eastern Economic Review*, 21 June 1991, pp. 69–70.
68. Stallings, 'The Reluctant Giant', p. 29.
69. See, for example, A. Spindler, *The Politics of International Credit: Private Finance and Foreign Policy in Germany and Japan*, Washington: Brookings Institution, 1984, p. 116.
70. X. Zhou, 'Japan's ODA Program: Pressure to Expand', *Asian Survey*, **31**, 1991, p. 348.
71. Stallings, 'The Reluctant Giant', p. 79.
72. D. Yasutomo, 'Why Aid?', pp. 499–500.
73. T. Rybczynski, *The Internationalization of the Financial System and the Developing Countries*, Washington: World Banking Staff Working Paper no.788, 1986, p. 41.
74. Toyoo Gyohten made this point in a talk at the London School of Economics, 19 March 1991.
75. For a history and overview of the Postal Savings System, see K. Calder, 'Linking Welfare and the Developmental State: Postal Savings in Japan', *Journal of Japanese Studies*, **16**, 1990, pp. 31–59; T. Ozawa, *Recycling Japan's Surplus For Developing Countries*, Paris: OECD, 1989, pp. 37–8; Rosenbluth, *Financial Politics in Contemporary Japan*, pp. 168–80.
76. See Ozawa, *Recycling*, pp. 19–22.
77. Calder, 'Linking Welfare', p. 43.
78. For the latter, see K. Jameson, 'Dollar Bloc Dependency in Latin America', *International Studies Quarterly*, **34**, 1990, pp. 519–41.
79. Tavlas and Ozeki, 'The Japanese Yen', p. 45.
80. Japan has become the largest single aid donor to all Asian countries except Vietnam, Cambodia, Malaysia, Laos, Pakistan and S. Korea, and its aid has come to account for 63.6 per cent of the aid received by ASEAN countries (excluding Brunei), compared to America's 11 per cent share: Rix, 'Japan's Foreign Aid Policy', M. Tamamoto, 'Japan's Search for a World Role', *World Policy Journal*, **7**, 1990, pp. 493–520.
81. The percentage of reserves held in yen in a group of selected Asian central banks rose from 13.9 per cent to 17.5 per cent: Tavlas and Ozeki, 'The Japanese Yen'.
82. A. Rowley, 'Shy Bloc Builder', *Far Eastern Economic Review*, 14 February 1991, p. 42.
83. K. Sugihara, 'Patterns of Asia's Integration into the World Economy 1880–1913', in W. Fischer, R. McInnis and J. Schneider (eds), *The Emergence of a World Economy 1500–1914*, Wiesbaden: Franz Steiner Verlag, 1986, p. 725.
84. See, for example, M. Barnhardt, *Japan Prepares for Total War: The Search for Economic Security 1919–45*, Ithaca: Cornell University Press, 1987.
85. It is often forgotten that a syndicate of 13 Japanese private banks were among the founding members of the BIS in 1930. Their membership was revoked at the San Francisco Peace Treaty, but the Bank of Japan was readmitted as an observer in 1961 and as a member in 1970: T. Adams and T. Hoshii, *A Financial History of the New Japan*, Tokyo: Kodansha International, 1972.
86. See especially W. Borden, *The Pacific Alliance: US Foreign Economic Policy and Japanese Trade Recovery 1947–55*, Madison: University of Wisconsin Press, 1984.

Index

Acheson, Dean, 33
acquisitions and mergers, 63, 197–200, 203
agriculture, 133, 139–40, 190
aid programmes, 210, 216, 219, 220, 221
airline industry, 58
Aldrich, Winthrop, 31, 32, 33
alliances, corporate, 203
anarchy, 8, 161
Anderson, Benjamin, 32
arbitrage, regulatory, 15, 57, 69–78, 160
Aristotle, 3
arms races, 8
Asian Development Bank, 218, 223
Australia, 20
Austria, 22

Badie, Betrand, 164
Baker, James, 101
balance of payments
  Bretton Woods system and, 26
  financial services trade and, 118, 125–6
  Japan's surplus in, 102, 209
  US deficit in, 102, 125–6, 165–6
balances of power, 9, 161
Bank of England, 34, 208
Bank for International Settlements (BIS), 15, 22, 24, 32, 97, 107, 108–9, 211
banks and banking systems, 15, 212
  capital adequacy of, 175, 176–7
  debt problems and, 103, 216
  disintermediation and securitization and, 62–3
  EC single market and, 194–5
  financial services trade and, 125, 126, 129–30, 134, 137
  gold standard and, 21–2
  mergers and takeovers in, 200, 203
  opposition to Bretton Woods system from, 30–37
  public sector, 201–2

regulation of, 52, 57, 59, 60, 73, 75–6, 77, 109, 117, 137, 159–60, 213
Basle Agreements, 108, 158, 176–7
Bérégovoy, Pierre, 75
Birnbaum, Pierre, 164
Brady, US Treasury Secretary, 213, 218
Braudel, Fernand, 216
Brazil, 131
Bretton Woods system, 7, 20–21, 53, 170, 217
  collapse of, 13, 38–40, 58, 89, 95, 165–6, 171, 173, 220
  historical background to, 21–6
  opposition to, 30–37
  plans for, 26–30, 92–3
Britain see United Kingdom
Brown, Edward, 36
Bryant, R., 20–21
Bundesbank, 60, 97
Burgess, W. Randolph, 33
Buzan, Barry, 162–3

Calleo, David, 97, 220
Canada, 100
  financial services trade and, 129, 139, 141
capital adequacy, 175, 176–7
capital (exchange) controls, 20, 22–30, 39, 93, 192–3
  opposition to, 30–37
Cecco, M. de, 89
Clercq, Willy de, 124
Clinton, Bill, 16
Coalition of Service Industries, US, 126, 139
Cohen, Benjamin J., 166
communist system, collapse of, 103–4
compartmentalization principle, 54, 56–62
competition
  EC policy on, 197–200
  regulation of financial markets and, 57–8